Feminism
and
Addiction

Feminism and Addiction has also been published as *Journal of Feminist Family Therapy*, Volume 3, Numbers 3/4 1991.

The Haworth Press, Inc., 10 Alice Street, Binghamton, NY 13904-1580
EUROSPAN/Haworth, 3 Henrietta Street, London WC2E 8LU England
ASTAM/Haworth, 162-168 Parramatta Road, Stanmore, Sydney, N.S.W. 2048 Australia

Library of Congress Cataloging-in-Publication Data

Feminism and addiction / Claudia Bepko, editor.
    p. cm.
    "Has also been published as Journal of feminist family therapy, volume 3, numbers 3/4 1991"—T.p. verso.
    ISBN 1-56024-220-5 (H : acid-free paper). —ISBN 1-56024-221-3 (S : acid-free paper)
    1. Women—Substance use. 2. Substance abuse—Treatment. 3. Feminist therapy.
4. Family therapy. I. Bepko, Claudia.
RC564.5.W65B47 1991
616.86'0082—dc20
                                      91-38268
                                            CIP

Feminism
and
Addiction

Claudia Bepko
Editor

The Haworth Press, Inc.
New York • London • Sydney

Feminism
and
Addiction

Feminism and Addiction

CONTENTS

ABOUT THE EDITOR

Claudia Bepko, MSW, is a family therapist in private practice in Brunswick, Maine. She has specialized for many years in work with families affected by addiction and has a specific interest in women and gender. She is the senior author, with Jo-Ann Krestan, of *The Responsibility Trap: A Blueprint for Treating the Alcoholic Family*, and co-author with Jo-Ann Krestan of *Too Good for Her Own Good: Breaking Free from the Burden of Female Responsibility*. Ms. Bepko has authored numerous other articles and chapters on gender and addictions and teaches and lectures widely throughout the country. She is a member of the editorial boards of the *Journal of Feminist Family Therapy* and *Family Dynamics of Addiction Quarterly*. She is a consulting editor to the journal *Social Work*.

This project would not have been possible without the patient support and assistance of Jo-Ann Krestan and Lois Braverman.

Introduction

Claudia Bepko

The field of family therapy is currently undergoing a radical revision as feminist clinicians and theorists stimulate and expand our understanding of the ways gender issues impact our work in families. But just as family therapy has been slow in general to integrate useful perspectives on the treatment of addictions, few writers to date extend the feminist critique to issues of addiction in the family.

Feminist analysis examines problems within the context of power: it looks at the ways that inequality of power both historically and currently shapes our internal, interpersonal, and social patterns of relating and our experience of self. If we think of addiction as "a disordered power arrangement embedded in gender" (Bepko, 1989), a process in which individuals make dysfunctional attempts to have control over their own experience within a relational context, then addiction is a microcosmic process that reflects and is perhaps a metaphor for imbalances of power in the larger social arena. A feminist analysis of what is in fact a power-based process is critical to furthering our understanding of effective, gender sensitive intervention.

The field of addiction treatment, like medicine and like family therapy, has recently come under attack for basing much of its thinking about intervention on research focused on men. We know relatively little about the physiological and psychological effects of drugs and alcohol on women, and we know little about differential approaches that might address women's needs more effectively. As family therapists, addiction seems to pose such demanding and complex treatment problems that we often overlook the gender issues that are so deeply embedded at its core.

This collection is an attempt to redress the imbalance of focus in mainstream treatment paradigms by exploring women's issues in detail and by looking at our constructs about addiction at the same time that we challenge our constructs about gender. It represents an effort to struggle with theoretical, social, and clinical issues that are the focus of current debate both among therapists, among feminists, among the addiction treatment

1

community, and among the clients who struggle to integrate their self-help recovery programs with therapy.

The material in this book sits squarely at the intersection of these struggles between men's experience versus women's, therapy versus self-help, and systems therapy versus the more linear approaches of addictions treatment models. A first question posed is whether power is a construct that is clinically relevant to women affected by addiction, and if it is, in what ways. Can women embrace a belief in their powerlessness, as they're taught to in twelve-step programs, and still recover from their female socialization?

What *do* we know about women's addictions—can we integrate research knowledge with treatment? What social forces impact women's drug and alcohol use and what kinds of programmatic changes can make treatment more accessible and effective for women and their families?

One of the most far-reaching developments in the arena of popular psychology and self-help related to addiction has been the evolution of the concept of codependency. Papers in the volume explore this issue at a social level, a clinical level and at the level of speculation and reflection. What does codependency really mean, can family therapists integrate it as a useful concept in their practice, and what do we mean when we talk about male-codependency?

Similarly, it's important to question what we as systems therapists have to offer to clients who are dealing with the wide-ranging problems associated with addiction such as physical and sexual abuse. Do we offer treatment models that can have as compelling an impact as self-help recovery groups? Do we have anything to learn from popular psychology about the treatment of trauma and about the feminist implications of the rampant and continuing realities of violence against women in our culture? Can we integrate cultural difference into our treatment models? Do we understand fully, for instance, the particular difficulties of gay and lesbian clients as they confront problems with addiction?

The volume offers a sampling of some of the most current work being done by family therapists in areas that are of critical importance to women and hence of critical importance to families. The currency of the work is reflected in a major preoccupation of many of the authors—the use of constructivist approaches to understanding and treating women's experience. Constructivist theory may prove to provide the important integrative link between feminism and concepts of systemic neutrality. Constructivism is a philosophical framework for treatment that allows for the interactive recreation and "restorying" of experience in ways that are collaborative, internal, and organic rather than external, hierarchical, and imposed.

Constructivist-based treatment ideally moves clients beyond attribution and blame to a sense of inclusiveness and responsibility. The twelve-step programs have recognized the healing power of story telling for many years. Authors represented in the volume suggest ways that constructivist principles can work effectively in both family therapy training and treatment to address the many difficult dilemmas posed by problems of addiction and abuse.

Feminist analysis of therapeutic theories and technique can be difficult because often what seems politically obvious or correct has no logical counterpart in terms of its practical application in therapy. Very radical feminists suggest that if one fully accepts the premises of feminism, then it is logically inconsistent to ever be in relationship with men. As therapists, and generally as individuals, we do support inclusiveness, however, so we still struggle with these issues on many levels. We speak of women's weight problems and eating disorders as socially constructed, for instance. We understand clearly the patriarchal biases and the processes of medicalization that impact our ideas about women's weight. Yet we still treat women's eating problems and accept as a logical goal that they should eat more or less. We understand the roots of violence and abuse and the ways that they are deeply connected to power imbalances in the larger society. Yet we still work to improve the relationships between men and women in families even though those relationships may have been severely damaged by abuse.

As feminists, addiction places us more directly in the midst of these dilemmas in which our therapeutic job may seem to run counter to our ideological premises. It confronts us with abuses of power and reactions to those abuses at many different systemic levels. The goal of this collection is to grapple with these inconsistencies within the context of addiction treatment. Hopefully the papers in this collection provide some new ideas about positioning ourselves as therapists in some effective, practical role with regard to the issues of power and abuse that are the critical problems of our time.

REFERENCE

Bepko, C. (1989). Disorders of power: Women and addiction in the family. In M. McGoldrick, C. Anderson, & F. Walsh (Eds.), *Women in families*. New York: W.W. Norton.

PART ONE:
THEORY, RESEARCH
AND SOCIAL ISSUES:
EXPLORING ADDICTION
IN CONTEXT

Chapter One

A Descriptive Outline of a Program for Cocaine-Using Mothers and Their Babies

Gillian Walker
Kathleen Eric
Anitra Pivnick
Ernest Drucker

SUMMARY. Crack-using mothers are a population for whom punishment, rather than treatment, has been the norm. The following paper outlines a program for maternal crack users which is based on recent advances in feminist psychology and which defines the moment of childbearing as an opportunity to help women heal those critical relationships which have been fractured by the cycle of drugs and poverty.

The cocaine epidemic has had a particularly devastating effect on women and families. It is estimated that as many as 60% of crack users are women. The majority of these women are mothers of small children and head single parent households. The high percentage of female crack users gives this epidemic a very different profile from earlier drug epidemics where the large majority of users were men, and non-drug-using women held together the families they fathered. For example, New York City reported a 400% increase in maternal drug use in the period 1984-1989

Gillian Walker, MSW, is a family therapist on staff at the Ackerman Institute for Family Therapy in New York. Correspondence may be addressed to her at 149 E. 78th Street, New York, NY 10021. Kathleen Eric, RN, MPH, EdM, Anitra Pivnick, PhD, and Ernest Drucker, PhD, may be reached by contacting Ms. Walker at the same address.

with most of it accounted for by a sharp rise in maternal crack/cocaine use (Kaye, Elkind, Goldberg and Tytun, 1989; Lief, 1985). Between 1982 and 1989, the foster care caseload in New York City went from 10,000 to 50,000 children (New York City Health Department, 1989).

Maternal cocaine use affects whole families. Maternal cocaine use is often associated with inadequate prenatal care, poor nutrition and other adverse prenatal conditions (MacGregor, Keith, Buchina and Chasnoff, 1989; Griffith, Chasnoff and Freier, 1989). Untreated maternal drug use implies substantial risk for fetus and infant (Weston et al., 1989). Mother is placed at high risk for contracting HIV because crack use in women is associated with sexual promiscuity as a means of payment for drugs. If the mother is infected, there is a 30% chance that her baby will contract HIV. Low birth weight and other complications associated with cocaine use during pregnancy (Zuckerman, Frank, Hingson et al., 1989; Chouteau, Namerow and Leppert, 1988; MacGregor, Keith, Buchina and Chasnoff, 1989) appear to place the infant at a developmental disadvantage which is compounded by the emotional instability of the circumstances in which the child is likely to be raised, that is, a revolving door existence between foster care and care by mother and other family members. Neglect and abuse are often the features of this kind of existence. These circumstances may generate a combination of organic developmental handicaps (learning disabilities and the like), psychological traumata, and exposure to drug using behavior which put the child at risk to become a substance user in adolescence.

This multigenerational transmission of substance use has been extensively documented (Harbin and Mazier, 1975; Klagsbrun and Davis, 1977; Madanes, Dukes and Harbins, 1980; Kaufman and Kaufman, 1979; Stanton, 1980). The recursiveness of the drug abuse cycle within such families means that, over time, drug abuse becomes the principle regulator of family behaviors and defines the nature of family relationships, just as family behaviors and relationship patterns maintain drug-abusing behavior (Harbin, 1975; Alexander and Dibbs, 1975; Kaufman and Kaufman, 1979; Stanton, 1980).

Paradoxically, for drug-using women, their children may be their strongest and most loving attachment (Bauman and Dougherty, 1983; Reed, 1985; Deren, 1986), an attachment which is filled with hope for a better future. But few drug treatment programs utilize this powerful and positive motivating factor and, as a result, there are few appropriate drug treatment options available to women who are pregnant and/or who have young children. The majority of New York City programs exclude both pregnant women and crack using women on Medicaid (Chavkin and Kandall, 1990). In-patient detoxification programs and residential drug treatment programs which accept crack using women do not provide for residence with children, or for interim foster care.

The absence of appropriate treatment slots for the crack-using mother creates a Scilla and Charybdis situation where the mother faces losing her children if she seeks treatment but may neglect the children or have them removed from her care if she does not. If she seeks treatment, her children will have to be placed. The majority of siblings will be separated from each other in placement, a terrifying experience for children who, in all likelihood, have already experienced too much trauma. Even brief residential treatment may cost the mother the housing which would permit her to reassemble her family upon release and her children may remain in placement long after she is psychologically able to manage their care. But if she does not seek treatment, and her children remain with her, compulsive drug-taking behavior will impede effective parenting. If she is lucky enough to have family who are willing to take responsibility for her children while she is in treatment, she may find that the additional burden on family members, coupled with the relapsing and chronic aspects of drug use, strains her relationships with her family network.

Relatives feel burdened by additional care demands, and by the emotional problems of children traumatized both by maternal loss and by previous experiences of growing up with a mother who used drugs. Family members are also frustrated that the mother cannot get her act together despite their help. If the drug-using woman is lucky enough to find a treatment slot, the family will frequently find itself viewed by treatment providers as a noxious influence promoting drug use. Since most drug treatment programs do little to reach out to families to provide them with necessary information and support, conflictual interactions between the drug-using woman and her family of origin may become so increasingly frustrating that they may culminate in separation of the drug user and her children from the one system that can give her support.

Furthermore, most drug-treatment programs operate under the philosophy that the client's rehabilitation depends on developing a new set of behaviors independent of the previous context of her life. In order to do this the client must be separated from context in order to be free to work on the self. As a result, treatment programs do not place an emphasis on retaining and working with bonds to family or spouse/partner, at least during the initial phases of treatment. Most inpatient programs do little, if any, family work, even during the critical re-entry phase. If a woman seeks treatment, she may not only be separated from her children but, if her partner uses drugs, she may lose her primary adult relationship. This loss not only costs economic or social support when she returns home, but it may have deep meaning for her. Viewing the partnership only from the perspective of its relationship to drug-taking behavior would lead us to encourage separation as a step away from temptation. But if we believe that drugs are a part, but not *all*, of a person's life, then we may understand that there can be aspects of the relationship which are positive and supportive, the loss of which may be deeply painful to both partners and to the children they may have between them.

THE ORIGINS OF A COLLABORATION

The Program for Maternal Drug Users and their infants was developed by the Division of Community Health and the Women's Center of the Department of Social Medicine, Montefiore Hospital, in collaboration with North Central Bronx Hospital's Ob/Gyn Midwifery Program and Early Family Outreach Project, and the Ackerman Institutes' AIDS and Families Project. The goal was to demonstrate that if the mother's ties to her child could be preserved and social and familial networks strengthened, there would be a reduction in maternal drug use, an improvement in maternal and child health, and a reduction of the number of children placed in foster care.

The groundwork for this project was laid by the Department of Social Medicine's Women's Center, established in 1987, directed by Kathleen Eric, aided by medical anthropologists Anitra Pivnick and Dooley Worth under the supervision of Ernest Drucker (Eric, Drucker, Worth, Chabon, Pivnick and Cochrane, 1989). The goal of the Women's Center and its research is the reduction of destructive patterns of drug use leading to HIV infection, and, for those women already infected, the reduction of transmission to their sexual partners and their children. Peer support in groups, co-counseling and telephone buddy systems have been the main treatment modalities. Family therapy becomes a part of the program after women who join the peer support groups seek help for their partners and children. The program is largely run by volunteers, who include ex-drug using women and their families and friends, and its philosophy is one of consistent peer support and outreach. The group model has evolved from the center's establishment as a place where community women shared their knowledge of their community and its needs with medical anthropologists, to its development as a place where women who are or have been drug users come together to support each other through the ongoing difficulties of their lives in an urban ghetto. These lives inevitably harbor the threat of relapse and the shadow of HIV.

The Women's Center volunteers are expert in obtaining concrete services. The program encourages women to find work or to attend various educational programs. The atmosphere is not one of confrontation but of mutuality, love, trust and respect. Members of the original women's group have become program leaders who provide role models of women who have gotten off drugs, are finding education, have been helped to regain custody of their children, and are working. Two family therapists, a Latina and an African-American, from Ackerman's AIDS and Families Project, who had previous experience working with substance users, joined the Women's Center to work with couples and families. They were flooded with requests for therapy. Women realized that their healing from the experience of substance use required a mending of the tears which drugs had created within the fabric of their families, as well as a the strengthening of bonds to family, partners and children.

The idea for a collaborative grant between Ackerman and the Montefiore Department of Social Medicine to work with cocaine-using mothers and their addicted babies came out of the work of the Women's Center, an Early Family Outreach Program at North Central Bronx Hospital, and two projects of the Ackerman Institute, the AIDS Project and The Women and Violence project. The Early Family Outreach Program has successfully used outreach workers to aggressively pursue families in order to improve pediatric follow-up on children born at North Central Bronx Hospital. The Ackerman AIDS and Families Project began to treat increasing numbers of inner-city women who had been, or were, active drug users and who were HIV infected. This work included other family members who had become substitute caretakers for their children. Work with HIV-infected women who were currently using drugs or who had recently become drug-free created a dual awareness: there is a lack of adequate drug treatment services designed to meet the needs of women and their families, and most drug treatment programs operate on theoretical models designed for men.

The work of Ackerman's Women and Violence Project, in which four clinicians — Virginia Goldner, Marcia Sheinberg, Peggy Penn and Gillian Walker — explored spouse abuse through the lens of new developments in feminist thought, provided a conceptual framework for understanding women's psychosocial development, relative to their families, that could be applied to the particular needs of drug-using women (Goldner, Penn, Sheinberg, and Walker, 1990). For example, Gilligan's work on care versus justice perspectives in moral development (Gilligan et al., 1988) provides the framework for explaining why many women have felt alienated by the confrontational and punitive nature of the therapeutic community. Therapeutic communities operate primarily from a justice perspective. Programs use levels of achievement as indicators of cure. Fears that substance users will use "care" as "manipulation" — that is, as a way of "getting over" or avoiding responsibility — are countered by the emphasis on the importance of adhering to rules, rules which are often immutable — even when ordinary compassion might dictate otherwise.

By contrast, women find that the Women's Center programs, based on a therapeutic approach which emphasizes a care perspective, provide a more positive and sympathetic environment. These programs promote bonding to positive female role models, attend to the repair of connections to family and children damaged by the cycle of drug use, encourage positive empathic exploration of the feelings leading to the decision to use drugs, and provide concrete family-building services.

The Montefiore/Ackerman grant for maternal drug users has been funded by the National Institute of Drug Abuse, and will test the efficacy of a feminist-oriented family case management approach. The grant considers the moment when a woman gives birth to a cocaine-addicted baby as a crisis for the mother. This crisis often results in further alienation from the non-drug-using culture along with the creation of a cycle of foster care placement for the baby, which all too often leads to the replication of the mother's drug-use patterns in the next generation. Alternatively, it can be an opportunity to reach the mother, and to offer her and her family the kinds of services that Ackerman and the Women's Center have been able to provide for other populations.

In this program, family case management is provided for women bearing an infant who is identified as cocaine toxicology positive, and every effort is made to engage the family in a constructive relationship with the drug-using woman. The family is encouraged to take responsibility for the child, or children, while we work with the mother in peer groups, or she enters detoxification or other drug treatment. During our work with the mother we address parenting issues to strengthen her bond with her child or children. We hope to enable her to see herself as a potentially effective mother. Our belief is that her bond with her children is a critical factor not only in recovery, but also in future reproductive decision making (Pivnick, Jacobsen, Eric, Hsu, Drucker, 1990).

THE PROGRAM OF FAMILY CASE MANAGEMENT

The Family Case Management program is directed by two senior family therapists from the Ackerman Institute who provide ongoing training and supervision of the team(s). The Family Case Management team consists of a family therapist with a background in treating substance abuse, a social worker who acts as family case manager, and an outreach worker associated with the Woman's Center.

Recruitment and Initial Phase

Following initial contact with a prospective mother, intensive work in a crisis intervention model is done with the mother and her family during the post-partum period to develop a treatment plan addressing the best interests of the child and mother. The focus of the initial family work is fourfold: to help the family support the mother in obtaining drug treatment, to insure appropriate care for the children, to establish an ongoing collaborative relationship between family members and the Family Case Management team, and to assess family factors such as violence, sexual abuse, intimidation of the woman and her children by a male partner, which may support substance use (Worth, Drucker, Eric and Pivnick, 1990).

Both the mother and other family members are actively involved in drawing up the treatment plan. The plan includes care provision for the child and drug treatment plans for the mother. The plan is presented to the Child Welfare Association by the Family Case Management Team and the birth mother. Child Welfare's mandate is care disposition of all babies born addicted. This engagement of mother and family in a collaborative relationship with the treatment team, starting with the initial phase of treatment establishes a context where family and team will be actively engaged in collaborative problem solving. A psycho-educational model of intervention is introduced to help the family understand drug use as a chronic disease, reduce family hostility towards the drug using person, and help family members anticipate future crises. One or more home visits during this initial phase are used to assess family living conditions and interactions.

The mother designates family members who will work with the team as they provide a support system for the mother and her baby. If the baby is discharged to the mother, a family member is designated to provide emergency care for the baby and other children at home during detoxification, relapses or periods of in-patient drug treatment. Whenever possible, the father and father's family of origin are included in the initial process.

Initial Family Case Conference

The family case conference may take place in two sessions. The first session focuses on negotiation with CWA for the placement of the child and, if other children are in placement, a second case conference includes representatives of their foster care agencies. During these case conferences, a coordinated treatment plan is developed in collaboration with the birth mother and participating family members, and with the agencies engaged in working with the family to reduce fragmentation of care. The

Family Case Management Team continues to disseminate information and coordinate care during the treatment phase. The goal, insofar as it's possible, is to reunite family, and to improve family functioning so that it can successfully and safely assume the care of its children.

Treatment Phase

Family progress is monitored by the Family Case Management team with the assistance of the designated family members who are trained to become "family problem solvers." Therapy is posited on a non-pathologizing model which assumes that families have the resources to heal themselves and that the role of the Family Case Management team will evolve over time from active intervention to family consultant.

The team supplies family intervention as needed in a variety of settings including home visits, office meetings with one or more family members, meetings with the family in agencies (e.g., foster care), and schools or drug treatment programs. Problem-focused feminist informed therapy provides a theoretical basis for sessions held within the family case management process. Family requests for concrete services, help with parenting, help with educational problems, or assistance with drug usage provide a context for helping the family restructure its organization and modify dysfunctional patterns. Multiple family therapy will be used to provide families with a network of other supports, to disseminate information both about drug use and HIV risk, and to empower family members in order to utilize their abilities to help others. The birth mother's bonds to non-drug-using nurturing family and friendship figures are enhanced and developed through family network meetings and the Women's Center women's peer support groups. Peer groups are used as a means of helping women empower each other since powerlessness seems implicated in drug use in women. Similarly, couple therapy is used to address issues contributing to drug use in women, most particularly sexual and physical abuse (Worth, Drucker, Eric and Pivnick 1990). Couple sessions will also address safer sex issues, because crack-using women are highly vulnerable to contracting HIV from sexual partners.

Pediatric Outcomes

Pediatric health is assessed at regular health care maintenance visits of index newborn subjects (2 weeks; 2, 4, 6, 9, 12, 15, 18, 24 months) in the primary care clinics at NCBH. Outcomes include both measures of health and of health care utilization: kept appointments; non-appointed visits to the clinic, emergency room, or other health care facilities; growth parameters; immunizations; and anemia or iron sufficiency.

At 6, 12, 18, and 24 months pediatric visits, a standardized assessment of behavior and development is administrated. The Health Professional Inventory organizes observations of both adaptive and maladaptive features of the child's social behavior and relationships. Scores characterize the child in terms of both assets and number of indicators of concern in the areas of feelings and affect, relationships, and parental care. The Denver Developmental Screening Inventory-Revised provides a standardized context for estimating cognitive maturity, language level and motor functioning.

The child's custody status (with mother, other family, or extra-familial care) is determined at discharge and at 6-month intervals throughout the study. Additionally, health, developmental, and custody information will be obtained on the natural siblings of the index child.

Maternal-Infant Interaction Outcomes

Early parent-child interactions have been associated with later childhood development and cognitive function. Assessment of early interaction may also act as an intervention by helping to develop adaptive behavior between the caregiver and child. The clinician may give the caregiver information and support which may increase caregiver sensitivity and promote growth-fostering efforts.

CONCLUSION

If cocaine is appealing to women precisely because it gives an illusion of power in circumstances where a woman's experience of powerlessness may be absolute, then it would follow that drug treatment programs for women must empower the disempowered. Drug treatment for women must empower them by utilizing women's gifts for creating and recreating communities of their own rather than requiring women to be the subjects of male-dominated hierarchies. Both the Women's Center Program and the program for crack-using mothers and their babies utilize women's experience to create the programs which serve them. While the Women's Center includes men in its community, the context of their inclusion is one of an essentially non-hierarchical "family."

Effective drug treatment must help women find their authoritative and authentic voices and help them reauthor their lives so that they are supported by webs of meaningful, non-oppressive relationships. The Women's Center Program and the program for crack-using mothers and their babies are two programs whose emphasis is on linking drug treatment to the strengthening of women's ties, both to their families and to other women, as well as offering women the opportunities for education and meaningful work hitherto denied them.

REFERENCES

Alexander, B. K. and Dibbs G.S. (1975) Opiate addicts and their parents. *Family Process*, 14, 499-514.

Bauman, P. S. and Dougherty F.E. (1983). Drug-addicted mothers' parenting and their children's development. *International Journal of Addiction*, 18, 291-302.

Chavkin, W. and Kandall S.R. (1990). Between a 'rock' and a hard place: Perinatal drug abuse. *Pediatrics*, 85, 223-225.

Chouteau M., Namerow P.B.and Leppert P. (1988). The effect of cocaine abuse on birth weight and gestational age. *Obstetrics and Gynecology*, 72, 351-354.

Deren, S. (1986). Children of substance abusers: A review of the literature. *Journal of Substance Abuse and Treatment*, 3, 77-94.

Eric, K., Drucker, E., Worth, D., Chabon, B., Pivnick A. and Cochrane K. (1989). The women's center: A model peer support program for high risk IV drug and crack using women in the Bronx. V International Conference on AIDS, Montreal Canada, June 4-10.

Gilligan C. et al., (Eds.) (1988).*Mapping the moral domain: A contribution of women's thinking to psychological theory and education*. Cambridge: Harvard Press.

Goldner, V., Penn, P., Sheinberg, M., Walker, G. (1990). Love and violence: gender paradoxes in violent relationships. *Family Process*, 29, 343-364.

Griffith, D. R., Chasnoff, I.J., and Freier, M.C. (1989). Effects of maternal psychopathology on the neurobehavioral development of cocaine exposed infants. *Pediatric Resident*. 25, 13A.

Harbin, H. T., and Mazier H.M. (1975). The families of drug abusers: A review, *Family Process*, 14, 411-431.

Kaufman, E. and Kaufman P., (Eds.) (1979). *Family therapy of drug and alcohol abuse*. New York: Gardner Press.

Kaye, K., Elkind, L., Goldberg, D., and Tytun, A. (1989). Birth outcomes for infants of drug abusing mothers. *New York State Journal of Medicine*, 89, 256-261.

Klagsbrun, M. and Davis, D.I. (1977). Substance abuse and family interaction. *Family Process*, 16, 149-173.

Lief, N. R. (1985). The drug user as parent. *International Journal of Addictions*, 20, 63-97.

MacGregor, S. N., Keith, L.G., Buchina, J.A., and Chasnoff, I.J. (1989). Cocaine abuse during pregnancy: Correlation between prenatal care and perinatal outcome. *Obstetrics and Gynecology*, 74, 889-894.

Madanes, C., Dukes, J., and Harbin, H. (1980). Family ties of heroin addicts *Archives of General Psychiatry*, 1980; 37, 889-894.

New York City Health Department. (1989). Maternal drug abuse—New York City: In 10 years, a 20-fold increase. *City Health Information*, 8, 1-4.

Pivnick, A., Jacobsen, A., Eric, K., Hsu, M., Drucker, E. (1990). Reproductive decision making among HIV Positive IVDU women. New York Public Health Association's 118th Annual meeting. New York: September 30—October 4.

Reed, B. G. (1985). Drug misuse and dependency in women: The meaning and implications of being considered a special population or minority group. *International Journal of Addictions*, 20, 13-61.

Stanton, M. D. (1980). Some overlooked aspects of the family and drug abuse. In B. G. Ellis' (Ed.) *Drug Abuse From the Family Perspective* (National U. S. Government Institute on Drug Abuse; DHHS Pub. No. [ADM] 80-910). Washington, DC: U. S. Government Printing Office.

Weston, D. R., Ivins, B., Zuckerman, B., Jones, C., and Lopez, R. (1989). Drug exposed babies: Research and clinical issues. *Zero to Three*, 9:1-7.

Worth, D., Drucker E., Eric K. and Pivnick A. (1990). Sexual and physical abuse as factors in continuous risk behavior of women IV drug users in a South Bronx methadone clinic. VI International Conference on AIDS, San Francisco, CA, June, 20-24.

Zuckerman B., Frank, D.A., Hingson, R. et al. (1989). Effects of maternal marijuana and cocaine use on fetal growth. *New England Journal of Medicine,* 320, 762-768.

Chapter Two

Sugar and Spice and Everything Nice: Gender Socialization and Women's Addiction — A Literature Review

Jahn L. Forth-Finegan

SUMMARY. Gender socialization is overlooked as a primary factor in the development of alcoholism, addiction, and other compulsive behaviors among women. This paper reviews the literature regarding women and alcoholism/addiction, suggesting a feminist critique. The paper also offers some alternative interpretations of gender-role conflict and gender socialization as critical factors in the development of addiction among women. Treatment issues are discussed.

What are little girls made of?
Sugar and spice and everything nice,
that's what little girls are made of.

What are little boys made of?
Frogs and snails and puppydogs' tails,
That's what little boys are made of.

(Nursery Rhyme)

This cultural message describing gender beliefs about ideal femininity and masculinity has been sung to small children for a very long time.

Jahn L. Forth-Finegan, PhD, NCC, CAC, is a feminist psychotherapist in private practice in Rochester, New York. Correspondence may be addressed to her at 149 North Greece Road, Hilton, NY 14468.

19

Human children however, tend not to fit ideals. They are born with opinions and desires and natural characteristics. They get dirty and hungry and cranky, and do things that horrify their parents. If the child is a little boy, the behavior is explained away by the cultural message, boys will be boys. If the child is a little girl, it is likely to be a different story.

While the American public reports itself to be supportive of the goals of the women's movement, it also favors traditional gender-role behavior among women (Fleming, 1988). In a society which reveres traditional gender norms, the little girl who does not fit the "sugar and spice" ideal will be pressured and shaped until she does, or looks like she does. The little boy who would rather be playing the piano than football will also be forced into gender-appropriate molds. The question is, at what cost?

It may be, then, that individuals who become alcoholic or chemically addicted or engage in compulsive behavior are mirrors of this conflict in today's western culture, and that addictions are a logical response to the suppression of the identity and self-concept. Rigid gender socialization injures and hampers the fullness of life experience for everyone. The female who grows in this milieu is denied access to her powerful self, while the male who grows in this milieu is denied access to his nurturant and expressive self. An important difference however, is that females in this male-defined culture belong to the subordinate group.

There have been many attempts to connect the issue of gender-role conflict with drinking behavior, however, "to this date, no clear or conclusive statement about the way in which these factors relate to alcoholism is available" (Bepko and Krestan, 1985). Why? While it is a particularly thorny problem to try to identify the "alcoholic woman," or any "women's issues," there do seem to be some important points to examine in answer to this.

UNDERSTANDING RESEARCH ON WOMEN ALCOHOLICS IN THE CONTEXT OF THE FEMINIST CRITIQUE OF SCIENCE

Science is not a neutral force, and as it is historically presented, it is socially and culturally constructed. Kuhn (1962) argued that science is subject to the influence of special interests, and that it is produced in response to the social and historical forces currently at work in any given setting. The cultural setting which has articulated modern science has been one which framed nature as being feminine and a force that requires subduing, that being the point of scientific research.

The objectivist stance is a particular outcome of traditional research

(Keller, 1982; 1985), and the outcome of this demand for objectivity may miss important information. Women's biology and psychology has been misinterpreted, controlled, and misunderstood within this paradigm, leading to perpetuation of norms which have kept women from participating in culture fully (Bleier, 1984). In spite of the advances made by the women's movement, the cultural messages continue to play subtle but very powerful roles in the disempowerment of women.

The androcentric view of science, based in the cultural norms which perpetuate male dominance and hierarchy is noticeable in the fields of mental health and medicine. The women's health movement has made many salient points, particularly that mainstream medicine has constructed scientific knowledge around a male-centered cultural view of the proper place of women (Zimmerman, 1987). The implicit cultural assumptions surrounding gender: ". . . probably exert as much social control over the sexes as do societal prescriptions and appropriate gender-role behavior" (Hare-Mustin, 1990, p. 131).

The fields of mental health and medicine have recently generated a growing body of research investigating alcoholism among women, often creating and perpetuating myths about the woman alcoholic, generating stereotypes and misinformation (Annis, 1980), such as the often-stated myth that women are sicker or harder to treat than male alcoholics (Vannicelli, 1984; Karn, 1990), and often demonstrating sexist attitudes in all aspects of treatment (Henderson & Anderson, 1982; Babcock & Connor, 1981). This occurs through the use of male-oriented questionnaires and surveys, sexist interpretation of findings (e.g., the frequently stated description of the female alcoholic personality as narcissistic), and male-dominated research that is generalized to treatment programs that include women.

In 1957, Lisansky (later Gomberg) studied the existing literature and found it full of stereotypes and ambiguities about women alcoholics, including for example, the supposition that sexual promiscuity and female alcoholism were somehow linked. She noted that the linkage probably had less to do with sexual behavior than with public intoxication and the way it is viewed by the culture.

A feminist immediately notices that women's alcoholism issues are frequently listed under such titles as *Alcohol and Substance Abuse in Special Populations* (Lawson & Lawson, 1989), or Women's Issues: A Class in Special Problems in Addictions (taught but not titled by the researcher at a local treatment facility, in cooperation with an area college 1989, 1990). The federal publication *Alcohol and Health* (1990) lists women's issues under "Population Subgroups." A 1990 publication on AIDS and substance abuse published for physicians and health care professionals by the state of New York, under the listing of "Women's Issues," spoke only of child care and pregnancy.

Titles of this sort did not appear with any frequency in publications on alcoholism before the 1970s. These titles reveal a subtle but pervasive acceptance of the "woman as a problem" stereotype which is perpetuated by language, psychology, and medicine and mental health (Hare-Mustin, 1990). This subtle perception exists throughout the treatment world. Hare-Mustin (1987), and Goldner (1988) have initiated a challenge to the field of family therapy to examine the subtle sexism which perpetuates cultural gender norms, such as power imbalances and idealization of the traditional family.

The fact that the issue of women's alcoholism was overlooked and incorporated in the work of men's alcoholism until the late seventies is an example of this gendered view. While the theme of "woman as a problem" often prevails, a paradoxical view that women's problems are of little interest or consequence also exists.

In 1980, a group of researchers called the study of women and alcoholism a "non-field" (Kalant, 1980), with no experts and no specialized literature. Marianne Sandmaier (1980) uncovered only 28 English-language articles on alcoholic women. During the eighties, there has been more interest in the development of the literature, but that interest needs to be expanded. This review examined over 1,000 references which were either directly or peripherally related to women and alcoholism or addiction. Some articles are now being written from a feminist orientation, but this, again, is a relatively new development.

ALCOHOLISM PATTERNS AMONG WOMEN: AN OVERVIEW OF THE LITERATURE

Demographics

Of the 17.6 million Americans experiencing significant consequences associated with drinking, approximately 5.7 million are women. Of these, 3.3 million are alcoholic and 2.4 million are alcohol abusers. NIAAA projects that by 1995 the numbers of U.S. women who are alcohol abusers and alcoholics will increase to a total of nearly 6 million (Williams et al., 1987).

Age cohorts and the sociodemographic differences offer a way to examine the incidence, because there is no single, typical, alcoholic woman.

The age group, 18-34, shows higher rates of drinking-related problems than women in the 35-49 age group. The 34-49 age group show higher rates of chronic problems or acute alcoholism (Hilton, 1987; Williams et al., 1987; Wilsnack, 1990). Women who have attained higher educational levels report higher rates of use, but Wilsnack (1990) reports that there are no consistent socioeconomic patterns to rates of chronic dependence in this group. Among the 50-64 age group, drinking has increased in the last 20 years, but not necessarily heavy drinking (Hilton, 1988).

Epidemiological surveys reveal that younger women (under 35) and older women (over 35) exhibit very different patterns of substance use, with a high incidence of eating disorders, childhood antisocial behavior, and abuse by boyfriends and spouses occurring for younger women (e.g., Clark & Midanik, 1982; Rohsenow, Corbett & Devine, 1988; Wilsnack et al., 1986). A cultural shift in the 1970s relating to the advent of widely-available illicit drugs, and the use of which was defined as normative, probably was the significant factor in these patterns of use for younger women. Changes in attitudes influenced by the women's movement are also a possible factor.

Native American women have higher rates of fetal alcohol syndrome according to Bertolucci et al. (1985) and Leland (1984), and also higher incidence of cirrhosis and other alcohol-related deaths. Hispanic women tend to abstain more than non-Hispanic women (Wilsnack et al., 1984). Little research is available on these groups of women, and that is also true for Black women. Gary and Gary (1985) found that Black women tended to abstain more than other populations, but that when they drank, they reported heavier drinking.

While it is risky to speak of women who are lesbian as if they are a specific subgroup of women, Finnegan and McNally (1987) citing several sources, speak of alcoholism in the lesbian women's population to be reported at somewhere between 28%-32%. They also cite the findings of McNally's 1987 work that found that often women who are lesbian drank in order to cope with the associated problems encountered in a homophobic culture, and also to participate in the bar scene which may be a part of the lesbian lifestyle (Beckman, 1978; McKirnan & Peterson, 1989).

The idea of women's drinking converging with the rate of men's drinking has received attention, although evidence does not support convergence. Wilsnack (1984) suggests that the data is probably explained by a delayed social reaction to increases in women's drinking patterns after World War II, as well as increased awareness.

While there do not appear to be major changes in women's drinking in general, there are changes within specific groups such as increased heavy drinking in the 21-34 age group. Women drinkers are more visible for several reasons, including the social changes related to women's roles. For instance, it is more acceptable for women to drink in public, especially for this age group. In general, women also are seeking treatment more readily and demanding attention to their special needs (Wilsnack et al., 1986).

The targeting of women by the media as passive economic subjects, the exploitation of the connection between power, attractiveness, desirability, and the use of alcohol and cigarettes (Ettore, 1986) has resulted in a criticism of liberal feminism which has been accused of inducing women to demand rights equal to men in all aspects of life, including areas which create more problems for them, such as drinking (Morrissey, 1986).

Physiological Factors in Women's Alcoholism

Studies of women alcoholics show that significant physiological differences exist between women and men related to absorption and metabolism of alcohol, with less quantity creating more damage. The physical damage due to ingestion is especially dramatic in the liver (e.g., Frezza et al., 1990; Gallant, 1990; Kumpfer, 1987; Saunders et al., 1981; Schenker & Speeg, 1990; Sherlock, 1988). Women do not drink as long before becoming alcoholic, a condition known as telescoping of alcoholism (Piazza, 1989). There are also negative consequences of alcoholism to the nervous system known as PAWS or protracted acute withdrawal syndrome which can go on for years (Hoffman, 1986).

Sexual problems of all types exist for alcoholic women, some preceding the alcoholism and some as an outcome. Reproductive, sexual, and menstrual problems are reported consistently among alcoholic women, with alcohol and drug use having significant repercussions on hormone production and the reproductive system (Gavaler, 1990; Gomberg & Lisansky, 1987; Wilsnack et al., 1984).

Alcohol, as a disinhibitor, and the use of drugs are central to one of the most critical and growing problems in the field of healthcare today, that of the transmission and incidence of HIV infection and AIDS (Karan, 1989; Kumpfer et al., 1990). Women's awareness of vulnerability to HIV is an important issue due to the increasing numbers of those infected. For example, in July, 1990, the Center for Disease Control announced that 1 in 10 women in the 15-44 age group, in New York state, dies of AIDS. Transmission is related to sexual contact, which frequently occurs in the context of alcohol or drug use. Seventy-one percent of all women who have AIDS are either Hispanic or Black (Hopkins, 1987). Drug and alcohol treatment programs are just beginning to prepare for this problem. In addition there is the related concern of the child born to the HIV mother.

Concern about infants created a response in medical literature regarding damage due to fetal alcohol or drug syndrome. This has raised public awareness and created a large body of research (see Little & Ervin, 1984; Weiner & Morse, 1990), as well as controversy. With the damage clearly occurring in the gestational period, charges of maternal neglect or abuse of the fetus by use of alcohol or drugs have been brought to public and judicial attention.

Because of cultural factors (i.e., it is more acceptable to be a crazy woman or depressed than to be a drunk woman), alcoholic women are more often prescribed, and become cross-addicted to, prescription drugs than men (Bissell, & Skorina, 1987; Cafferata, 1983; Curlee, 1970; Leone, 1981; Mulford, 1977; Ogur, 1986; Peluso & Peluso, 1988; Snell et al., 1987) and use of illicit drugs is growing among women, especially in the youngest age groups and among the urban poor (Celentano & McQueen, 1984; Reed, 1985).

Genetic predisposition tends to be less clear in women than in men, and even for men the findings are equivocal. This question has been studied more among men than among samples of women. In at least one study, alcoholism in mothers was found to be linked to alcoholism in daughters (Bohman et al. 1981). McKenna and Pickens (1981) discovered that 41% of female alcoholics have alcoholic fathers, and 8% have alcoholic mothers, and Clark and Midanik (1982) found strong evidence for familial factors among the women surveyed. It is clear that genetic and environmental factors need to be considered in the transmission of alcoholism, and research continues in this area.

Psychosocial Factors in Women's Alcoholism

Family factors have a fundamental role in the development of alcoholism. Difficult and physically abusive childhood experiences are reported to be frequent (Kramer, 1990), and the incidence of sexual abuse among women alcoholics has been shown to be very high, often as high as 75% of women in treatment (e.g. Beckman, 1984; Bennett, 1975; Benwald & Denson-Gerber, 1975; Kramer, 1990; Lindberg & Distad, 1985; Rohsenow et al., 1988; Sandmaier, 1977; Wilsnack et al., 1986; Winfield et al., 1990). At least one study identified sexual problems among 98% of chemically dependent women in treatment (Wasnick, Schaffer & Bencivengo, 1980). Sexual abuse frequently results in post-traumatic stress syndrome which can be a significant factor in relapse occurrence (Root, 1989; Winfield et al., 1990).

Women alcoholics have more alcoholic relatives (Kumpfer et al., 1990; Silvia et al., 1988), are often the daughter of an alcoholic (Ackerman, 1989; Gomberg & Lisansky, 1984), and tend to come from dysfunctional families (Bepko, 1987; Bepko & Krestan, 1985; Kaufmann & Kaufmann, 1979; Stanton & Todd, 1982; Steinglass et al., 1987) where they experienced disruption such as divorce or early death of a parent (Gomberg, 1980b).

Daughters of alcoholics were found to suffer from depression more frequently, and were more friendless in childhood (Goodwin et al., 1977). Seeing alcohol use modeled by parents and family members is also reported to be a significant factor in the development of alcohol problems later in life (Gomberg, 1984).

Women alcoholics also have a high occurrence of associated depression and other mental illness (e.g., Gomberg, 1984; Turnbull, 1988; Wilsnack & Beckman, 1984) and consistently low self-esteem (e.g., Beckman, 1978, 1978a, 1980 1984; Braiker, 1984; Turnbull & Gomberg, 1988). Younger women who are alcoholic and also have mental health problems are being found among the homeless who are reaching the streets at younger ages (Harrison & Belille, 1987).

Several alcoholism studies have also found women alcoholics to have dependent personality characteristics (Hoar, 1983), and report feelings of deprivation and lack of approval from their parents. This is especially apparent among women in the under 35 age group (Corrigan, 1980; Gomberg, 1988; Quadrio, 1984). A history of being overresponsible in the family is frequently reported (Bepko, 1987; Bepko & Krestan, 1985, 1990; Ackerman, 1989) often creating significant boundary issues for the woman alcoholic (Bepko, 1989).

Women alcoholics struggle with very powerful shame issues related to their alcoholism (Gomberg, 1988), and to messages received while growing up in a dysfunctional family (Fossum & Mason, 1986). Lifelong sexual shame is a major factor in recovery also (Evans, 1987). Sexual dysfunction, non-traditional gender-role orientation and non-traditional sexual behavior, and sexually abusive adult relationships often are reported to be factors which are mediated by alcohol for some women (Beckman & Amaro, 1984, 1986; Bersak, 1988; Gomberg, 1984; Covington, 1982, 1984, 1986; Murphy et al., 1980; Wilsnack et al., 1986; Wilsnack, 1990). Women alcoholics speak of self-medicating for sexual problems and often report having to drink in order to feel comfortable enough to engage in sexual activity (Romand, 1988).

High degrees of psychological stress and suicide attempts were reported to be more frequent among women alcoholics (Trice & Beyer, 1979;

Wilsnack et. al., 1984/85). Earlier thinking that the stress of role overload caused alcohol problems has changed. Research has shown that, to the contrary, it is the lack of roles or role loss which cause stress leading to alcohol abuse, not role overload (Wilsnack and Cheloha, 1987). Additional stressors include grief and loss; women alcoholics have a high need for grief and loss or a total lack of a spiritual connection which often results in hopelessness and adds to the stress of loss (MacAndrew, 1986). As early as 1957, Lisansky identified the recent loss of a loved one, as well as other major trauma, as precipitating the onset of heavy drinking. This is congruent with the findings of Stanton and Todd (1982), who have identified unresolved grieving as a critical factor for families who develop chemical abuse problems.

A high incidence of concurrent compulsive behaviors among women alcoholics has been identified, including negative body images and associated eating disorders (Beary et al., 1986; Blume, 1990; Bulik, 1987; Silva, 1988; Weathers & Billingsley, 1982). Kasl (1989) indicates that alcoholic women often turn to other addictive behaviors in recovery, including sexual and food addictions, caffeine, nicotine, sugar, and shopping, among others.

Kumpfer (1987) investigated the question of why one woman in a family will become alcoholic and her sister will not and concluded that there are probably biological factors which influence a woman's ability to cope with life stressors. Others report that the sisters may have very different relationships in the family (Gomberg, 1988). Kasl (1989) believes that the nonconforming female child is always scapegoated in the dysfunctional family. Bepko and Krestan (1985) state, along with others, that the alcoholic or dysfunctional family tends to be very rigid in gender-role expectations and performance, and the lack of adaptation of this child may increase the pressure on her to conform, resulting in more disapproval and perceived distance from other compulsive behaviors such as eating-disordered behavior, rather than substance abuse.

Marital status and conditions surrounding it are frequently viewed as a measure of female success in this culture (Laws & Schwartz, 1977; Schur, 1984). Several at-risk factors related to marital status make some women more vulnerable to problem drinking or substance abuse, including recent divorce or separation. Never having married has been found to create vulnerability for some women also, and cohabitation, especially cohabitation with a partner who uses substances abusively, may create significant problems (Room, 1989; Wilsnack et al., 1984). Women alcoholics have a higher incidence of spouses with drinking problems, and assortative mating is suggested as a possible explanation (Corrigan, 1980; Dahlgren, 1979; Rimmer & Winokur, 1972). Women alcoholics also have a substantially higher rate of divorce (Furman & Selbyg, 1982), and Valentich (1982) found that their husbands are seen as blameless victims while they are seen stereotypically as weak willed.

Role loss and major changes appear to be connected to problem drinking for some women. "Empty nest" mothers have been shown to be vulnerable, probably due to role loss (Gomberg, 1976), and those who are unemployed, seeking work, part-time employed, or recently widowed may develop problems with alcohol (Alcohol & Health, 1990; Blankfield, 1989; Wilsnack et al., 1984; 1986; Wilsnack and Beckman, 1987).

The pressures and inequalities of the workplace may also increase pressures and opportunities to drink (Sandmaier, 1977), and Shore (1985) indicated that there is a possible connection between drinking among women and moving up and into the ranks of managerial and professional positions. Women have few norms for guidance about appropriate behavior in such a setting, and few norms regarding power in the workplace.

The extensive work of the Wilsnacks and associates, based in a nationwide survey, also notes that women with lowest economic and educational status tend to drink less than women from higher income and educational brackets, but when they drink, they may drink more heavily. Women who are moving up in business may drink more, and also have fewer norms by which to regulate their drinking behavior (Shore, 1985). However, problem drinking seems to be unrelated to socioeconomic level (Wilsnack, 1990).

Stigma remains a very serious issue for women who are alcoholic or addicted in this society. Regardless of social changes in the past 20 years, women still are measured by subtle and pervasive gender norms. Schur (1984) notes the pervasiveness of sexual objectification of women in the culture suggesting that the condition is omnipresent. Related to this cultural phenomenon is the stigma and shame of the woman alcoholic which is proposed to be related to social presumptions of sexual promiscuity, and availability, whether or not that is a fact. Social response to women who become intoxicated, or frequent bars appears to emerge from a cultural double standard.

Intoxication and drinking behavior is seen as a male rite-of-passage, and symbolic of masculine behavior (Lemle & Mishkind, 1989; Landrine et al., 1988), and as unattractive, delinquent or overtly promiscuous behavior for a female (George et al., 1988; Lupton, 1979; Miller et al., 1989). Other authors identify shame as a critical issue for the woman alcoholic, and the shame is reported to be connected to a perception of having failed at the gender expectations of being female (Conrad & Schneider, 1980; Gomberg, 1989; Leone, 1981; Rosenbaum, 1981).

Chodorow (1978) defines the importance of motherhood in this culture when she says, "Women's mothering is a central and defining feature of the social organization of gender" (p. 9). Laws (1979) argues that the role of motherhood subsumes within it a total suppression of a woman's needs in favor of the needs of the child. Schur (1984) argues that the role of mother is the only acceptable role for women in this culture, and joins with others who have explored nonmotherhood and the experience of perceived deviance associated with such a decision (Bernard, 1975; Laws, 1979). These norms inform the guilt and sense of failure at childcare and quality of parenting reported by the women in the studies conducted by Black and Mayer (1980), Corrigan, (1980) and Sandmaier (1980).

Women who are alcoholic and addicted are found to have difficulty in accessing treatment, because of lack of child care as well as the fear of the threat of neglect accusations, and custody implications. Third party payments, availability of treatment, and sexist attitudes within the treatment experience are also problematic for women seeking treatment (Beckman & Amaro, 1984; Blume, 1986). Women also experience relationship difficulties, and lack of social support including higher incidence of divorce, and are often supported more by their parents and children than husbands (Schilit & Gomberg, 1987; Johnson et al., 1990).

The U.S. Department of Labor points out that in 60% of families with children, both spouses work, and divorced mothers are more likely to be working or looking for work than mothers of any other marital status (1981). Married working women reported drinking problems twice as often as single working women, and high levels of drinking problems were reported among women seeking work (Johnson, Armor, Polisch & Stanbul, 1977).

Areas of lack of consensus include the study of gender-role conflict and alcoholism, as well as a clearly-spelled-out etiology of alcoholism among women. The above review points out that etiology is a multifactorial problem, intertwining physiological, psychological and social characteristics. The woman alcoholic is a microcosm of the social macrocosm. She experiences all of the problems which women face in this society in general, but sometimes she may feel as if she alone has them all. The portrait of the alcoholic woman is a portrait of the powerlessness of women.

Gender Research in Alcohol Studies

The clinical alcoholism literature has made many attempts to connect the issue of gender-role socialization and gender with drinking behavior (e.g., Beckman, 1978; Greenblatt & Schuckit, 1976; Landrine et al.,

1988; Lisansky, 1957; Lundy, 1987; McLachlan, Walderman, Birch-more, & Marsden, 1979; Parker, 1971; Scida & Vannicelli, 1979; Wilsnack, 1973, 1976; Wilsnack & Wilsnack, 1978). Gender-role conflict and incongruence between perceived role requirements and self-perception continue to be enticing questions to researchers because of an apparent link with alcoholic drinking patterns, but the explanatory power of the androcentric epistemology may fall short in analysis.

The discussion of gender-role conflict leads to a discussion of the changes in the social climate influenced by the women's movement. The intricate relationship between the women's movement and the changes in women's roles is described by Gomberg (1982), who concludes that these forces are complex, and while it may be more acceptable for a woman to drink in public, drinking heavily and being intoxicated is not. Gomberg's (1982) conclusion that there is still less acceptance for a woman alcoholic than for a man alcoholic is supported by the findings of Hunter (1990).

Further, this norm implies that women who act out-of-(traditional) role are, as a result of feminism, drinking more heavily and are poorly-socialized females. The formulations which suggest that the loss of traditional female roles are causative of the development of drinking problems and alcoholism also seem to suggest that the treatment and solution would be to help alcoholic women accept traditional female gender roles (Morrissey, 1986; Valentich, 1982). Greater social stigma leading to low self-esteem and shame occurs for the woman alcoholic because out-of-control behavior is more narrowly defined for women than for men in this society (Sandmaier, 1980).

Wilsnack (1973;1976) explored the question of sex-role identity in alcoholic women, reporting a general consensus in the literature that there must be some disturbance of feminine identification, including inadequate adjustment to female roles, or masculine identification. She concluded that there was support for the disturbed feminine identification hypothesis, but that it derived from identification with the "masculine behavior" of their mothers, not the "unmasculine behavior" of their fathers.

These women were identified as having "incomplete feminine identification" and described as having conscious attitudes and values which were typically feminine, but they did not fit cultural norms behaviorally, which Wilsnack concluded may have aroused insecurity about their adequacy as women. Wilsnack notes:

> If this formulation is correct, the alcoholic woman does not necessarily have an unconscious wish to be a man. In fact she may have a basic wish to be a more adequate woman. . . . Disturbances of sex-role identity may be one of the psychological preconditions for the development of alcoholism. (pp. 259-60)

The idea of defective or incongruent femininity was also noted by Parker (1971), who concluded that women alcoholics suffered from a conflict between self and social role, and ended his treatise by quoting another team of researchers with whom he agreed: "Alcoholism represents the ransom woman pays for her emancipation" (p. 656).

Beckman (1978) studied sex-role conflict among alcoholic women, and she concluded that the alcoholic woman in treatment was not significantly different from other women who were being treated for other mental problems in terms of sex-role conflict. She mentions that emotional disorder among all women may have a connection to gender-role identification, and that gender-role conflict may be related to disturbed or pathological behaviors on a wider scale.

Beckman found alcoholic women to have a pattern of conscious femininity, unconscious masculinity, and lower self-esteem, which she saw as either a determinant or consequence of alcoholism. In addition, Beckman concluded that the ability to integrate all aspects of self, including those behaviors labelled masculine or feminine by society may be an indicator of healthy behavior, and also that gender-role conflict did not appear to be causative in alcoholism among women. She also noted that the women's movement appeared to be associated with women's alcoholism due to changes in behaviors and norms.

Women, Depression and Alcoholism

Landrine et al. (1988) suggest that under stressful life conditions, men tend to drink more, and women tend to demonstrate depression more, and that stereotypical masculinity may be a necessary predisposition for alcoholism in either sex, and is a component of gender roles and expectations. This is congruent with the findings of a special panel on women and depression, commissioned by the American Psychological Association. The 1990 report to the APA by the leaders of the panel, Dr. Ellen McGrath and Dr. Bonnie Strickland (McGrath, Kieta, Strickland, & Russo, 1990) reported a clear connection between depression and being female in the contemporary world. They reported that women's rates of depression were more that twice than of men.

The literature is replete with references to female alcoholic differentness and weakness, yet recent investigations have begun to show that roles and expectations may be the culprit. Braun (1989) found that female alcoholics were less optimistic than male alcoholics when sober, and that they have different needs during sobriety. Corrigan (1980) reports a high incidence of depression among women entering treatment for alcoholism.

Turnbull and Gomberg (1990) have shown that the structure of alcohol-induced depression does not differ from the structure of depression of nonalcoholic control women. Farid-Basem et al. (1989) showed there was a strong relationship between severity of alcoholism and dissatisfaction with the role of housewife. Change of occupation, including the occupation of housewife, resulted in improvement in alcoholism for one group of women (Herr & Pettinati, 1984).

Ferrence (1984) noted that there are significant social components of women's alcoholism, including women's employment and earning patterns, and major responsibility for childcare, among others. Braiker comments on the relationship of anger, frustration and helplessness as a precipitating circumstance for excessive drinking (1984), and Sanford and Donovan (1984) point out the cultural sanctions against anger for women. They argue that women have no role models for the appropriate expression of anger, and that the culture allows and encourages men to be angry, often inappropriately, adding to a fear of anger for women.

Older women are forced to cope with many negative stereotypes in our society, as well as loss, divorce, loneliness and social isolation which may exacerbate alcoholism or prescription drug usage (Porcino, 1985). Blume (1980), Ferrence (1984), and Youcha (1978) report social isolation as a factor for women alcoholics in general, especially when overwhelmed by difficult family situations.

Beckman and Amaro (1984) reported stereotypical thinking in alcoholism treatment programs. The findings of Vannicelli (1984) did not confirm the idea that women alcoholics were harder to treat than their male counterparts. They also refer to the double standard of mental health for women in this society, citing several studies including Broverman et al. (1970). An important issue emerging from this work by Beckman and Amaro is that treatment stays may be unduly lengthened, not only because of gender-role stereotypes about women being sicker and more dependent, but also because of male therapists' sexual curiosity about female patients, as found by Abramowitz et al. (1976) (cited in Beckman and Amaro, 1984). Braiker (1984) also discusses and debunks the mythologizing of the woman alcoholic as harder to treat.

Other Gender Factors

Family, Power and Gender

Bepko and Krestan (1985) point out that there are significant blocks to the access of power within the traditional family for women, including the power of choice, economic decision making and freedom to choose roles. Bepko and Krestan (1985), and Bepko (1989) also report that the abuse of power in alcoholic relationships is often extreme. Power in relationships is essentially a political issue about who gains self, or gives it up, at whose expense. Power in relationships tends to be defined by the norms of the larger society, and by the larger family system, and alcohol is often used to ameliorate the perceived imbalances within a relationship (Bepko and Krestan, 1985).

This finding is supported by the recent critique of family therapy as a supposed gender-neutral change agent (Goldner, 1988; Hare-Mustin, 1987). Family therapy often works to restore the family to its original patriarchal structure, including old roles, boundaries and hierarchical arrangement, as well as continuing the damaging mother-blaming which is inherent in the field of mental health (Caplan, 1989; Chodorow & Contratto 1982; Walters et al. 1988).

Beckman and Amaro (1984) identify that alcoholic women are more likely to report drinking or feeling like drinking than are men when they feel powerless or inadequate. Bepko (1989) proposes that the core of the addictive process is based in a set of beliefs, and that beliefs are colored by gender socialization. This reflects the earlier work of Bateson (1972), who argued that addiction was rooted in a fundamentally erroneous belief system.

Kasl reports that heterosexual women are often drawn to lesbian women because they are attracted by their apparent power (1989). She also notes that the strong-willed female child often becomes the center of scapegoating in abusive families and relates this to strong unconscious fears of powerful females in this society.

Addiction serves to mediate the dilemmas of the female experience in many ways, blunting the conflicts between dependence and independence internally, interactionally and at the social level, the dilemma between personal power and powerlessness (Bepko, 1989). She also states that it is clear that gender role socialization both shapes and is challenged by addictive behavior. Women in general are more likely to be socialized to be overfunctioning caretakers of all family members, and may drink to relieve the strain of this overresponsibility.

Yet, passivity, victimization and caretaking behavior are built into the code for the appropriate female gender behavior. The cost of appropriate female gender-role behavior may well be addiction, which helps to numb the pain of powerlessness and lack of freedom and choice. The conflict is only incidentally intrapersonal; instead, it is a conflict between the natural expression of sexual identity, and the socially-imposed expectations of the good girl.

TREATMENT

Power and shame become significant issues when developing treatment approaches. They are embedded in the fundamental structure of the medical model, and in the cultural structure of gender-role expectations, as we have seen in the previous discussion, and must be addressed in order for women to be able to claim any healing which is effective. Certain aspects of current treatment approaches may serve to reinforce the negative experiences of power and shame (Kirkpatrick, 1977, 1986; Kasl, 1989).

A recent feminist critique of Twelve-Step programs (Lerner, 1990; Kasl, 1990; Unterberger, 1991) has identified the androcentric bias in the steps, which are the framework of many of the treatment approaches, and the framework of most of the self-help groups suggested to support recovery. The present structure of treatment for addictions is adamant about participation, and usually incorporates these steps into the core of the treatment process, often combining with some form of family therapy (Steinglass, 1987).

Family Therapy

The recommendation for family treatment is congruent with the findings of Bowen (1976), who contended that the dysfunction of the alcoholic can only exist with the support of the family system. Steinglass et al. (1987) describe family life as a process of regulation interacting with family growth and development. They describe alcoholism as a chronic psychopathological condition around which the family organizes and regulates itself.

Vannicelli (1984) discusses effective treatment approaches for women alcoholics and notes the findings of Meeks and Kelly (1970), who suggest that family therapy is a necessary component of treatment for the woman alcoholic because of the disruption of family relationships which occurs for her. However, unless the family therapy addresses the power imbalances mentioned by Bepko and Krestan (1985), and Bepko (1989), it is destined to fail for the reasons raised by the feminist critique of family therapy.

Goldner (1988), argues that "gender is a fundamental organizing principle of all family systems" (Goldner, 1988, p. 17). In this view, women are expected ". . . to be sexual objects for men and to facilitate environments for everybody" (Goldner, 1988, p. 17). The critique admonishes that not only are women made to disappear within family therapy theory, but that the theories essentially reinforce the universality of the hierarchical traditional family. Power becomes neutralized as an issue, and arrangements of gender inequality "may be structurally essential to family relations" (p. 22). Hare-Mustin notes that the privacy of American family life has isolated women, and hidden the real domination of women from public scrutiny.

Treatment models have been criticized for developing programs based exclusively on research with alcoholic men (e.g., Braiker, 1984; Murray, 1989), and research is now beginning to recommend differences in treatment approaches for women alcoholics (e.g., Braiker, 1984; Turnbull, 1989; Vannicelli, 1984; Zankowski, 1987). Rolls (1989) lists the factors which are necessary for women to successfully utilize treatment, including family therapy, but not family therapy which focuses on returning the woman to her traditional roles. It also notes that women tend to readily participate in husbands' treatments, but husbands often do not see any reason to be involved in their wives.' Changes in the drinking patterns of these women, which occurs with the choice of sobriety, destabilizes the family unit, and often the need for total sobriety on the part of the woman, is sabotaged.

The issue of family violence must be treated in the alcoholism program according to the findings of Covington (1986). This suggests that staffing for programs must consider attitudes of staff members toward women, and that victimization must be dealt with very directly.

Shame and Guilt, and Other Issues

Gomberg and Lisansky (1987) note the importance of including treatment of shame and guilt for women alcoholics, and of other coexisting problems such as the dual diagnosis of a mental disorder, or eating disorder (Bulik, 1987; Curlee, 1970), or sexual abuse problems (Kovach, 1986; Pinhas, 1987; Wasnick et al., 1980). Wasnick et al., (1980) discovered that although 98% of women alcoholics report sexual problems, 86% report never being asked about, or helped with these concerns. Sexual harassment by treatment staff was also reported by 39% of the women in this study, and corroborated by the findings of Cuskey, Richardson and Berger (1979), and Soler, Psner and Abod (1974).

Cultural considerations need to be taken into account (Comas-Diaz, 1986; Gade, 1985; Smith, 1981), as well as the lack of support systems for women. Childcare arrangements are necessary for successful women's programing (Beckman & Amaro, 1984). Beckman and Amaro summarize the barriers to treatment for women very comprehensively, and all issues will not be reported here.

Feminist therapy has been shown to raise self-esteem, and change gender-role perceptions (Alyn & Becker, 1984), and attention to the specific needs of women are required for effective programming (Babcock & Connors, 1981; Lemay, 1980). The APA report on depression and women by McGrath et al. (1990), specifically recommended feminist therapy and cognitive-behavioral therapy as the most effective in assisting women to recover from depression. Programs such as Women Reaching Women (Kravetz & Jones, 1988), and Women for Sobriety, founded by Jean Kirkpatrick (1977), offer alternatives to traditional Twelve-Step programs.

For treatment to be effective, women alcoholics must be taught to care about themselves, and to become empowered. Empowerment is taught by giving choices, and images to hold on to, to help define a self (Bepko, 1989). Women alcoholics tend to be very self-critical and full of shame. The shame often is a result of having failed at achieving the idealized gender image expected by the family and the culture (Woodman, 1982).

This image of perfection cannot be attained by a human being, and failure to do so results in destruction. Woodman suggests that addiction is healed by giving permission to the self to express and to own the full range of feminine energy, the energy of the wet, moist, earthy, strong, expressive and intuitive; by taking one's power, and developing the power from within. It is not a question of suppressed masculinity or suppressed femininity, but of full freedom to express the power of being female.

CONCLUSION

The alcoholic/addicted woman is a complex creature, the social product of a history full of domination and subjugation. She has a variety of physical and psychological problems and stresses which lead her to choose to use mood-altering chemicals or to engage in compulsive behaviors. When these problems are explored, it is apparent they are connected to specific stresses related to the gender-roles which women are assigned or adopt within this society.

Glenn (1987) states that women are so central to thinking about the family, that they are virtually equated with and fused with the concept of family, and it becomes difficult to find the individual. Her work suggests that women's place in the family is really a debate about women's place in society, and that in a gendered construct such as the family and family experience, it is necessary to speak of the breakdown of the ideal of women's constant service and presence in the family.

In addition, the lack of archetypal images for women in this society has deprived all females of the necessary metaphors and ideals for the full acceptance of self, and for the acceptance of a range of differences and similarities among individuals. Woodman (1990) says: "An addiction re-enacts a traumatized relationship to the body" (p. 38).

Marriage is good for men, (Bernard, 1972), but may not be so good for women. It perpetuates the family as the center of the gender system (Chodorow, 1978), and continues to be seen as an ideal goal for all women. In the center of the family sits a woman, and because of the continuation of traditional viewpoints and power imbalances, she sits there often feeling powerless, and sometimes eventually turning to mood altering substances, or compulsive behaviors, to ease the pain.

According to some, the healing of addictions can take place only when women accept their full identities and create a self. The old images and gender identities do not work for many women, and they are seeking to re-create a picture which allows for the fullest range of what it means to be human. Woodman comments on this eloquently:

> . . . we children of the patriarchy have to learn to love the body — the goddess in her mother aspect. . . . We have to learn to connect with the primal wisdom that assures us that we are loved, that life is our birthright, that we need not prove ourselves or justify our existence. (1990, p. 32)

REFERENCES

Abramowitz, S.I., Abramowitz, C.V., Roback, H.B., Corney, R., & McKee, E. (1976). Sex-role related countertransference in psychotherapy. *Archives of General Psychiatry, 33,* 71-73.

Ackerman, R. (1989). *Perfect daughters: Daughters of alcoholics.* Deerfield Beach, FL: Health Communications Press.

Alcohol and Health, From the Secretary of Health and Human Services, (January, 1990). Seventh special report to the U.S. Congress. U.S. Department of Health and Human Services. Public Health Service. Alcohol, Drug Abuse, and Mental Health Administration, National Institute on Alcohol Abuse and Alcoholism, 5600 Fishers Lane, Rockville, Maryland 20857.

Alyn, J.H., Becker, L.A. (1984). Feminist therapy with chronically and profoundly disturbed women. *Journal of Counseling Psychology, 31,* 202-208.

Annis, H.M. (1980). Treatment of alcoholic women. In G. Edwards, & M. Grant (Eds.), *Alcoholism treatment in transition,* London, England: Croom Helm.

Babcock, M.L., Connor, B. (1981). Sexism and treatment of the female alcoholic: A review. *Social Work, 26*(3), 233-238.

Bateson, G. (1972). *Steps to an ecology of mind.* New York: Chandler Publishing Company.

Beary, M.D., Lacey, J.H., Merry, J. (1986). Alcoholism and eating disorders in women of fertile age. *British Journal Of Addiction, 81*(5), 685-689.

Beckman, L., & Amaro, H. (1984). Patterns of women's use of alcohol treatment agencies. In L.J. Beckman, & S.C. Wilsnack (Eds.)., *Alcohol problems in women*. New York: Guilford Press. pp. 319-348.

Beckman, L. & Amaro, H. (1986). Personal and social difficulties faced by women and men entering treatment. *Journal of Studies on Alcohol, 46,* 135-45.

Beckman, L. (1978). Sex role conflict in alcoholic women: Myth or reality? *Journal of Abnormal Psychology, 87,* 408-417.

Beckman, L. (1978a). Self-esteem of woman alcoholics. *Journal of Studies on Alcohol, 39,* 491-498.

Beckman, L. (1980). Perceived antecendants and effects of alcohol consumption in women. *Journal of Studies on Alcohol, 41,* 518-530.

Beckman, L.J. (1984). Treatment needs of women alcoholics. *Alcoholism Treatment Quarterly, 1,* 101-114.

Bennett, L.J. (1975). Women alcoholics, A review of social and psychological studies. *Journal of Studies on Alcohol, 35.*

Benwald, J., & Denson-Gerber, J. (1975). Incest as a causative factor in antisocial behavior: An exploratory study. New York: Odyssey Institute.

Bepko, C., & Krestan, K. (1985). *The responsibility trap.* New York: Free Press.

Bepko, C. (1989). Disorders of power, women and addiction in families. In M. McGoldrick, C. Anderson, & F. Walsh, (Eds.), *Women in families, A framework for family therapy.* New York: Norton. pp. 406-426.

Bepko, C. (1987). Female legacies: Intergenerational themes and their treatment for women in alcoholic families. In L. Braverman (Ed.) *Women, feminism and family therapy.* New York: The Haworth Press, Inc.

Bepko, C. & Krestan, J. (1990). *Too good for her own good.* New York: Harper & Row.

Bernard, J. (1972). *The future of marriage.* (1982 edition) New Haven: Yale University Press.

Bernard, J. (1975). *The future of motherhood.* New York: Penguin Books.

Bersak, C. (1988). The feminine self-concept of alcoholic women. *Affilia: Journal Of Women And Social Work, 3,* 17-26.

Bertolucci, D., Noble, J. and Dufour, M. (1985). Alcohol-associated premature mortality—United States, 1980. *Morbidity and Mortality Weekly Report, 34,* 493-494.

Bissell, L. & Skorina, J.K. (1987). One hundred alcoholic women in medicine: An interview study. *Journal Of The American Medical Association, 257,* 2939-2944.

Black, R., & Mayer, J. (1980). Parents with special problems: Alcoholism and opiate addiction. *Child Abuse and Neglect, 4,* 45-54.

Blankfield, A. (1989). Grief, alcohol dependence and women. *Drug And Alcohol Dependence 24*(1), 45-49.

Bleier, R. (1984). *Science & gender: A critique of biology & its theories on women.* New York: Pergamon Press.

Blume, S. (1980). Clinical Research: Casefinding, diagnosis, treatment and rehabilitation. *Alcoholism and Alcohol Abuse Among Women: Research Issues* (DHEW publication No. ADM-80-835). Washington, DC: U.S. Government Printing Office.

Blume, S. (1986). Women and alcohol: A review. *Journal of the American Medical Association. 256,* 1467-1470.

Blume, S.B. (1986). Women and alcohol: Public policy issues. In *Women And Alcohol: Health-Related Issues.* (Research Monograph No. 16). Washington, DC: U.S. Government Printing Office.

Blume, S.B. (1990). Alcohol and drug problems in women: Old attitudes, new knowledge. In: H.B. Milkman and L.I. Sederer (Eds.), *Treatment choices for alcoholism and substance abuse.* Lexington, MA: Lexington Books.

Bohman, M., Sigvardsson, S., & Cloninger, C.R. (1981). Maternal inheritance of alcohol abuse: Cross-fostering analysis of adopted women. *Archives of General Psychiatry. 38,* 965-969.

Bowen, M. (1976). *Family therapy in clinical practice.* New York: Jason-Aronson.

Braiker, H. (1984). Therapeutic issues in the treatment of alcoholic women. In Beckman, L. & Wilsnack S., (Eds.) 1987 edition. *Alcohol problems in women.* New York: Guilford.

Braun, J.L. (1989). Variations in scores of sex-role identity measures before hospital detoxification and after hospital rehabilitation in diagnosed alcoholics. *Dissertation Abstracts International, 49,* 5015-B.

Broverman, I.K., Broverman, D.M., Clarkson, F.E., Rosenkrantz, P.S., & Vogel, S.R. (1970). Sex-role stereotyping and clinical judgments of mental health. *Journal of Consulting and Clinical Psychology, 34,* 1-7.

Bulik, C.M. (1987). Alcohol use and depression in women with bulimia. *American Journal of Drug & Alcohol Abuse, 13*(3), 343-355.

Bulik, C.M. (1987). Drug & alcohol abuse by bulimic women and their families. *American Journal of Psychiatry, 144,* 1604-1606.

Cafferata, G.L., Kasper, J., & Bernstein, A. (1983). Family roles, structure, and stressors in relation to sex differences in obtaining psychotropic drugs. *Journal Of Health & Social Behavior, 24*(2), 132-143.

Caplan, P.J. (1989). *Don't blame mother: Mending the mother-daughter relationship.* New York: Harper & Row.

Celentano, D.D., & McQueen, D.V. (1984). Multiple substance abuse among women with alcohol-related problems. In S. Wilsnack, & L. Beckman (eds.) 1987 edition, *Alcohol Problems in Women.* New York: Guilford.

Center For Disease Control. Atlanta, GA. (Radio Announcement), July 1990. Women and AIDS.

Chodorow, N. (1978). *The reproduction of mothering.* Berkeley: University of California Press.

Chodorow, N., & Contratto, S. (1982). The fantasy of the perfect mother. In B. Thorne, and M. Yalom, (Eds.) *Rethinking the Family.* New York: Longman Press. pp. 54-75.

Clark, W.B., & Midanik, L. (1982). Alcohol use and alcohol problems among

U.S. adults: Results of the 1979 national survey. *Alcohol Consumption and Related Problems.* (NIAAA Alcohol and Health Monograph No. 1, DHHS Publ. No. [ADM] 82-1190). Washington, DC: U.S. Government Printing Office.

Comas-Diaz, L. (1986). Puerto Rican alcoholic women: Treatment considerations. *Alcoholism Treatment Quarterly, 3,* 4757.

Conrad, P., & Schneider, J. (1980). *Deviance and medicalization: From badness to illness.* Columbus, OH.: Merrill.

Corrigan, E.M. (1980). *Alcoholic women in treatment.* New York: Oxford U. Press.

Covington, C.C. (1982). Sexual experience, dysfunction and abuse: A comparative study of alcoholic and non-alcoholic women. Doctoral Dissertation. Union Graduate School.

Covington, S., & Kohen, J. (1984). *Women, alcohol and sexuality: Social and sociological aspects of alcoholism and substance abuse.* New York: Hawthorne.

Covington, S. (1986, April). *Alcohol and family violence.* Paper presented at the Annual conference of the National Council on Alcoholism, San Francisco, CA.

Curlee, J. (1970). A comparison of male and female alcoholics at a treatment center. *Journal of Psychiatry, 74,* 239-247.

Cuskey, W.R., Richardson, A.H., & Berger, L.H. (1979). Specialized therapeutic community program for female addicts. Department of Health and Human Services Publication No. (ADM) 79-800. Washington, DC: U.S. Government Printing Office.

Dahlgren, L. (1979). Female alcoholics. IV. Marital situations and husbands. *Acta Psychiatrica Scandinavaca, 59,* 59-69.

Ettorre, B. (1986). Women and drunken sociology: Developing a feminist analysis. *Women's Studies International Forum, 9,* 515-520.

Evans, S. (1987). Shame, boundaries and dissociation in chemically dependent, abusive and incestuous families. *Alcoholism Treatment Quarterly, 4*(2), 157-179.

Farid-Basem, B., Elsherbini, M., Ogden, M., Lucas, G., Williams, R. (1989). Alcoholic housewives and role satisfaction. *Alcohol and Alcoholism, 24,* 331-337.

Ferrence, R.G. (1984). Prevention of alcohol problems in women. In L.J. Beckman, & S.C. Wilsnack (eds.) 1987 edition, *Alcohol problems in women.* New York: Guilford Press. pp. 413-442.

Finnegan, D.G. & McNally, E.B. (1987). *Dual identities: Counseling chemically dependent gay men and lesbians.* Center City, MN.: Hazelden.

Fleming, H. (1988). Public opinion on change in women's rights and roles. In Dornbusch & Strober (Eds.), *Feminism, children, and the new families* (pp. 46-66). New York: Guilford.

Fossum, M., & Mason, M. (1986). *Facing Shame: Families in Recovery.* New York: Norton.

Frezza, M., DiPadova, C., Pozzato, G., Terpin, M., Baraona, E., & Lieber, C.S. (1990). High blood-alcohol levels in women: The role of decreased gastric alcohol dehydrogenase activity and first-pass metabolism. *New England Journal Of Medicine, 322,* 95-99.

Furman, L.E., & Selbyg, A. (1982). Rural alcoholic women: Study and treatment. *Human Services in the Rural Environment, 7,* 15-23.

Gade, E., Hurlburt, G. (1985). Personality characteristics of female American Indian alcoholics: Implications for counseling. *Journal of Multicultural Counseling and Development, 13*(4), 170-175.

Gallant, D.M. (1990). Female alcohol abusers: Vulnerability to multiple organ damage. *Alcohol: Clinical And Experimental Research, 14*(2), 260.

Gary, L.E., & Gary, R.B. (1985). Treatment needs of Black alcoholic women. In F.L. Brisbane, & M. Womble (eds.) *Treatment of black alcoholics.* New York: The Haworth Press, Inc.

Gavaler, J. (1990). Alcohol and hormones: reproductive and postmenopausal years. In R. Engs, (Ed.), *Women: Alcohol and other drugs,* a monograph of Alcohol and Drug Problems Association. Dubuque, Iowa: Kensington Hill Press.

George, W.H., Gournic, S.J., McAfee, M.P. (1988). Perceptions of postdrinking female sexuality: Effects of gender, beverage choice, and drink payment. *Journal Of Applied Social Psychology, 18*(15, PT 1), 1295-1317.

Glenn, E. (1987). Gender and the family. In B. Hess & M. Marx-Feree (eds.), *Analyzing Gender: A Handbook of Social Science Research.* Newbury Park: Sage.

Goldner, V. (1988). Generation and Gender. *Family Process, 27,* 17-31.

Gomberg, E., & Lisansky, J. (1984). Antecedents of alcohol problems in women. In S. Wilsnack & L. Beckman (Eds.), *Alcohol problems in women* (2nd. ed.). New York: Guilford.

Gomberg, E., & Lisansky, J. (1987). Shame & guilt issues among women alcoholics. *Alcoholism Treatment Quarterly, 4*(2), 139-155.

Gomberg, E. (1976). The female alcoholic. In Tarter & Sugarman (Eds.). *Alcoholism: Interdisciplinary Approaches to an Enduring Problem.* Reading, MA.: Addison-Wesley.

Gomberg, E.S. (1980b). Risk factors related to alcohol problems among women: Proneness and vulnerability. In *Alcoholism and Alcohol Abuse Among Women: Research Issues.* National Institute of Alcoholism and Alcohol Abuse Research monograph #1, Department of Health, Education and Welfare Publication No. (ADM), 80-835, Washington, D.C., U.S. Government Printing Office.

Gomberg, E.S. (1982). Historical and political perspective: Women and drug use. *Journal Of Social Issues, 38,* 9-23.

Gomberg, E.S. (1988). Alcoholic women in treatment: The question of stigma and age. *Alcohol and Alcoholism, 23,* 507-14.

Gomberg, E.S. (1989). *Alcohol and women.* New Jersey: Alcohol Research Documentation.

Goodwin, D.W., Schulsinger, F., Knop, J., Mednick, S. and Guzi, S.B. (1977). Psychopathology in adopted and nonadopted daughters of alcoholics. *Archives of General Psychiatry. 34,* 1005-1009.

Greenblatt, M., & Schuckit, M.A. (Eds.) (1976). *Alcoholism problems in women and children.* New York: Grune & Stratton.

Hare-Mustin, R. (1987). The problem of gender in family therapy today. *Family Process, 26,* 15-27.

Hare-Mustin. R. (1990). *Making a difference: Psychology and the construction of gender.* New Haven: Yale University Press.

Harrison, P.A., & Belille, C.A. (1987). Women in treatment: Beyond the stereotype. *Journal Of Studies On Alcohol, 48,* 574-578.

Henderson, D.C., & Anderson, S.C. (1982). Treatment of alcoholic women. *Focus on Women: Journal Of Addictions And Health, 3,* 34-48.

Herr, B.M., & Pettinati (1984). Long-term outcome in working and homemaking alcoholic women. *Alcoholism (NY), 8,* 576-579.

Hilton, M.E. (1987). Drinking patterns and drinking problems in 1984: Results from a general population survey. *Alcoholism: Clinical and Experimental Research, 11,* 165-175.

Hilton, M.E. (1988). Trends in U.S. drinking patterns: Further evidence from the past 20 years. *British Journal of Addiction, 83,* 269-278.

Hoar, C.H. (1983). Women alcoholics—are they different from other women? *International Journal Of The Addictions, 18*(2), 251-270.

Hoffman, A.L. (1986). Relationship between severity of alcohol dependence and protracted alcohol withdrawal symptoms. In A. Carmi & S. Schneider (Eds.), *Drugs and Alcohol.* New York: Springer-Verlag.

Hopkins, D.R. (November-December, 1987). AIDS in minority populations in the United States. *Public Health Report, 102*(6), 677-681.

Hunter, G.T. (1990). Survey of the social context of drinking among college women. *Journal Of Alcohol And Drug Education, 35,* 73-80.

Johnson, D., Armor, J., Polisch, P., & Stanbul, C. (1977). Sex differences, women's roles and alcohol abuse. *Journal of Social Issues, 38,* 93-116.

Johnson, N.P., Robbins, K.H., Hornung, C.A., & Gallman, H.S. (1990). Characteristics of women alcoholics. *Substance Abuse, 11,* 23-29.

Kalant, O.J. (1980) (ed.). *Research advances in alcohol and drug problems. (Vol. 5: Alcohol and drug problems in women).* New York: Plenum.

Karan, L.D. (1989). AIDS prevention and chemical dependence treatment needs of women and their children. *Journal of Psychoactive Drugs, 21,* 395-399.

Karn, E.R. (1990). Comparison of male and female alcoholics' response to treatment process in an outpatient alcoholism treatment center. *Dissertation Abstracts International, 50*(10), 3156-A.

Kasl, C.D. (1989). *Women, sex, and addiction: A search for love and power.* New York: Ticknor Fields.

Kasl, C.D. (1990). *Paths of recovery.* Monograph, Minneapolis: Castle Publishing.

Kaufman, E., & Kaufman, P. (1979). *Family therapy of drug and alcohol abuse.* New York: Gardner Press.

Keller, E.F. (1982). Feminism and science. *Signs, 7,* 589-602.

Keller, E.F. (1985). *Reflections on gender and science.* New Haven: Yale University Press.

Kirkpatrick, J. (1977) (3rd ed.). *Turnabout: New help for the woman alcoholic.* Seattle: Madrona Press.

Kirkpatrick, J. (1986). *Goodbye hangovers, hello life: Self-help for women.* New York: Atheneum Press.

Kovach, J.A. (1986). Incest as a treatment issue for alcoholic women. *Alcoholism Treatment Quarterly, 3,* 116.

Kramer, R. (1990). Alcohol and victimization factors in the histories of abused women who came to court: A retrospective case-control study. *Dissertation Abstracts International, 50,* 3372-A.

Kravetz, D., & Jones, L.E. (1988). Women reaching women: A project on alcohol and other drug abuse. *Administration In Social Work, 12*(2), 45-58.

Kuhn, T. (1962). *The structure of scientific revolution.* Chicago: University of Chicago Press.

Kumpfer, K. (1987). Special problems: Etiology and prevention of vulnerability to chemical dependency in children of substance abusers. In B.S. Brown, and A.R. Mills (Eds.) *Youth at risk for substance abuse,* Rockville, MD.: National Institute of Drug Abuse.

Kumpfer, K., Prazza, A.H., & Whiteside, H.O. (1990). Etiology of alcohol and other drug problems: Nature vs. nurture. In R. Engs (Ed.), *Women: Alcohol and other drugs,* a monograph by ADPA, Dubuque, Iowa: Kendall Hunt Publishers. Pp. 31-41.

Landrine, H., Bardwell, S., Dean, T. (1988). Gender expectations for alcohol use: A study of the significance of the masculine role. *Sex Roles, 19,* 703-712.

Laws, J.L., & Schwartz, P. (1977). *Sexual scripts: The social construction of female sexuality.* Hinsdale, IL: The Dryden Press.

Laws, J. L. (1979). *The second X: Sex role and social role.* New York: Elsevier Press.

Lawson, G., Lawson, A., & Peterson, J. (1983). *Alcoholism and the family: A guide to treatment and prevention.* Rockville, MD: Aspen Publication.

Lawson, G., Lawson, A. (1989). *Alcoholism and substance abuse in special populations.* Rockville, MD.: Aspen.

Leland, J. (1984). Alcohol abuse in ethnic minority women. In S. Wilsnack and L. Beckman (Eds.) *Alcohol Problems in Women.* New York: Guilford Press.

Lemay, D. (1980). The need for an awareness of specialized issues in counseling alcoholic women. *Personnel and Guidance Journal, 59,* 103-106.

Lemle, R., Mishkind, M.E. (1989). Alcohol and masculinity. *Journal of Substance Abuse Treatment, 6,* 213-222.

Leone, R. (1981). Stigmatized woman. In P. Russianoff, (Ed.), *Women in crisis.* New York: Human Sciences Press, pp. 44-48.

Lerner, H.G. (1991). 12-stepping it: Women's roads to recovery. A psychologist tells why. *Lilith,* Spring 1990, pp. 15-16.

Lindberg, F.H., Distad, L.J. (1985). Post-traumatic stress disorder in women who experience childhood incest. *Child Abuse and Neglect, 9,* 329-334.

Lisansky, E.S. (1957). Alcoholism in women: Social and psychological concomitants. *Quarterly Journal Of Studies On Alcohol, 18,* 588-623.

Little, R.E., Ervin, C.H. (1984). Alcohol use and reproduction. In L.J. Beckman, and S.C. Wilsnack (Eds.) *Alcohol problems in women.* New York: Guilford.

Lundy, C. (1987). Sex-role conflict in female alcoholics: A critical review of the literature. *Alcoholism Treatment Quarterly, 4*(1), 69-78.

Lupton, M.J. (1979). Ladies' entrance: Women and bars. *Feminist Studies, 5*(3), 571-588.

MacAndrew, C. (1986). Similarities in self-depictions of female alcoholics and psychiatric outpatients. *Journal of Studies on Alcohol, 47*(6), 487-484.

Mandel, L.L., & North, S. (1982). Sex roles, sexuality and the recovering woman alcoholic: Program issues. *Journal Of Psychoactive Drugs, 14*(1-2), 163-166.

McGrath, E., Kieta, G.P., Strickland, B., Russo, N.F. (1990). *Women and depression: Risk factors and treatment issues.* Washington, D.C.: American Psychological Association.

McKenna, T., & Pickens, R. (1981). Alcoholic children of alcoholics. *Journal of Studies on Alcohol. 42,* 1021-1029.

McKirnan, D.J., & Peterson, P.L. (1989). Alcohol and drug use among homosexual men and women: Epidemiology and population characteristics. *Addictive Behaviors, 14*(5), 545-553.

McLachlan, J.F.C., Walderman, R.L., Birchmore, D.F., & Marsden, L.R. (1979). Self-evaluation, role satisfaction, and anxiety in the woman alcoholic. *International Journal of the Addictions, 14,* 809-832.

Meeks, D., & Kelly, C. (1970). Family therapy with the families of recovering alcoholics. *Quarterly Journal of Studies on Alcoholism 31,* 399-413.

Miller, B.A., Downs, W.R., Gondoli, D.M. (1989). Delinquency, childhood violence, and the development of alcoholism in women. *Crime and Delinquency, 35,* 94-108.

Morrissey, E.R. (1986). Contradictions inherent in liberal feminist ideology: Promotion and control of women's drinking. *Contemporary Drug Problems, 13*(1), 65-88.

Mulford, H.A. (1977). Women and men problem drinkers: Sex differences in patients served by Iowa's community alcoholism centers. *Journal of Studies on Alcoholism. 38,* 1624-1639.

Murphy, W.D., Coleman, E., Hoon, E. & Scott, C. (1980). Sexual dysfunction and treatment in alcoholic women. *Sexuality and Disability,3,* 240-255.

Murray, J.B. (1989). Psychologists & alcoholic women. *Psychological Reports, 64,* 627-644.

National Center for Health Statistics (1988). *Vital Statistics for the United States,*

1985, Vol. 2: Mortality, Part A. DHHS Pub. No. (PHS)88-1101. Washington DC: U.S. Govt. Printing Office.

National Institute on Alcohol Abuse (1986). *Women and Alcohol: Health Related Issues.* Research Monograph No. 16. DHHS Pub. No. (ADM) 86-1139. Washington, DC: U.S. Govt. Printing Office.

Ogur, B. (1986). Long day's journey into night: Women and prescription drug abuse. *Women and Health, 11,* 99-115.

Parker, F.B. (1971). Sex-role adjustment in women alcoholics. *Quarterly Journal Of Studies On Alcoholism, 33,* 647-657.

Peluso, E. & Peluso, L. (1988). *Women & drugs: Getting hooked and getting clean.* Minneapolis: CompCare Publishers.

Piazza, N.J. (1989). Telescoping of alcoholism in women alcoholics. *International Journal Of The Addictions, 24,* 19-28.

Pinhas, V. (1987). Sexual dysfunction in women alcoholics. *Medical Aspects of Human Sexuality, 21,* 97-101.

Porcino, J. (1985). Psychological aspects of aging in women. *Women-Health, 10*(2-3), 115-122.

Quadrio, C. (1984). Families of agoraphobic women. *Australian and New Zealand Journal of Psychiatry, 18,* 164-170.

Reed, B.G. (1985). Drug misuse and dependency in women: the meaning and implications of being considered a special population or minority group. *International Journal of The Addictions, 20,* 13-62.

Rimmer, J., & Winokur, G. (1972). The spouses of alcoholics: An example of assortative mating. *Diseases of the Nervous System. 33,* 509-511.

Rohsenow, D.J., Corbett, R. & Devine, D. (1988). Molested as children: A hidden contribution to substance abuse? *Journal of Substance Abuse Treatment, 5,* 13-18.

Rolls, J.A. (1989). *The recovering female alcoholic: A family affair.* Paper presented at the annual meeting of the Speech Communication Association, San Francisco, CA.

Romand, P.A. (1988). Biological features of women's alcohol use: A review. *Public Health Reports, 103*(6), 628-637.

Room, R. (1989). U.S. general population's experiences of responding to alcohol problems. *British Journal Of Addiction, 84*(11), 1291-1304.

Root, M.P. (1989). Treatment failures: The role of sexual victimization in women's addictive behavior. *American Journal of Orthopsychiatry, 59,* 542-549.

Rosenbaum, M. (1981). *Women on heroin.* New Brunswick, NJ: Rutgers University Press.

Russo, N.F. (1990). Overview: Forging research priorities for women's mental health. *American Psychologist. 45*(3), 368-373.

Sandmaier, M. (1977). *Alcohol programs for women: Issues, strategies, and resources.* Washington, D.C.: National Clearinghouse for Alcohol Information.

Sandmaier, M. (1980). *The invisible alcoholics.* New York: McGraw Hill.

Sanford, L.T., & Donovan, M.E. (1984). *Women & self-esteem: Understanding and improving the way we think and feel about ourselves.* New York: Penguin.

Saunders, J.B., Davis, M. and Williams, R. (1981). Do women develop liver disease more readily than men? *British Journal of Medicine, 282,* 1140-1143.

Schenker, S. & Speeg, K.V. (1990). The risk of alcohol intake in men and women: All may not be equal. *New England Journal of Medicine, 322,* 127-129.

Schilit, R. & Gomberg, E.L. (1987). Social support structures for women in treatment for alcoholism. *Health-Society-Work, 12,* 187-95.

Schur, E. (1984). *Labeling women deviant: Gender, stigma and social control.* New York: Random House.

Scida, J., & Vannicelli, M. (1979). Sex-role conflict and women's drinking. *Journal of Studies on Alcohol. 40,* 28-44.

Sherlock, S. (1988). Liver disease in women: Alcohol, autoimmunity, and gallstones. *Western Journal of Medicine, 149,* 683-686.

Shore, E.R. (1985). Alcohol consumption rates among managers and professionals. *Journal of Studies on Alcohol, 46,* 153-156.

Shore, E.R. (1985). Norms regarding drinking behavior in the business environment. *Journal of Social Psychology, 125,* 735-741.

Silva, L.Y., Sorell, G.T., & Busch-Rossnagel, N.A. (1988). Biopsychosocial discriminators of alcoholic and non alcoholic women. *Journal Of Substance Abuse, 1,* 55-65.

Smith, E.H. (1981). Mental health and service delivery systems for black women. *Journal of Black Studies 12,* 126-141.

Smith, J.W. (1986). *Mother goose: A careful and full selection of the rhymes.* New York: Derrydale Books.

Snell, W.E., Belk, S.S., & Hawkins, R.C. (1987). Alcohol and drug use in stressful times: The influence of the masculine role and sex-related personality attributes. *Sex Roles, 16*(7-8), 359-373.

Soler, E., Psner, L., & Abod, J. (1974). The ABC's of drug treatment for women. Paper presented at the North American Congress on Alcoholism and Drug Abuse. San Francisco, CA.

Stanton, M.D., & Todd, T. (1982). *The family therapy of drug abuse and addiction.* New York: Guilford Press.

Steinglass, P., Bennett, L., Wolin, S. and Reiss, D. (1987). *The alcoholic family.* New York: Basic Books.

Trice, H.M., & Beyer, J.M. (1979). Women employees and job-based alcoholism programs. *Journal of Drug Issues, 9*(3), 385.

Turnbull, J.E. (1989). Treatment issues for alcoholic women. *Social Casework: The Journal of Contemporary Social Work, 70,* 364-369.

Turnbull, J.E., & Gomberg, E.S.L. (1988). Impact of depressive symptomatology on alcohol problems in women. *Alcoholism: Clinical And Experimental Research, 12,* 374-381.

Turnbull, J.E., & Gomberg, E.S.L. (1990). Structure of depression in alcoholic women. *Journal of Studies On Alcohol, 51,* 148-155.

Unterberger, G. (1991). A feminist tells how. *Lilith.* (Spring, 1991), pp. 16-17.

Valentich, M. (1982). Women and drug dependence. *Journal Of Alcohol & Drug Education, 28,* 12-17.

Vannicelli, M. (1984). Treatment outcome of alcoholic women: The state of the art in relation to sex bias and expectancy effects. In L.J. Beckman, & S.C. Wilsnack (Eds.), *Alcohol Problems in Women,* (2nd. ed.). New York: Guilford Press.

Vannicelli, M. (1984). Barriers to treatment of alcoholic women. *Substance And Alcohol Actions/Misuse, 5,* 29-37.

Vannicelli, M., & Hamilton, G. (1984). Sex-role values and bias in alcohol treatment personnel. *Advances In Alcohol And Substance Abuse, 4,* 57-68.

Walters, M., Carter, B., Papp, P., & Silverstein, O. (1988). *The invisible web: Gender patterns in family relationships.* New York: Guilford.

Wasnick, C., Shaffer, B., & Bencivegno, M. (1980). The sex histories of fifty female drug clients. Paper presented at the National Alcohol and Drug Coalition Conference. Washington, DC.

Weathers, C., & Billingsley, D. (1982). Body image and sex role stereotype as features of addiction in women. *International Journal of The Addictions, 17,* 343-347.

Weiner, L. & Morse, B. (1990). Alcohol, pregnancy, and fetal development. In R. Engs (Ed), *Women: Alcohol and Other Drugs.* An ADPA monograph. Dubuque, Iowa: Kendall-Hall. 61-71.

Williams, G.D., Stinson, F.S., Parker, D.A., Harford, T.C., and Noble, J. (1987). Epidemiological Bulletin No. 15: Demographic trends, alcohol abuse and alcoholism 1985-1995. *Alcohol Health and Research World, 11,* 80-83.

Wilsnack, R., & Thompson, K. (1984). Drinking and drinking problems among female adolescents: Patterns and influences. In L.J. Beckman, & S.C. Wilsnack (Eds.) *Alcohol Problems in Women* (2nd ed.). New York: Guilford Press.

Wilsnack, R.W., & Wilsnack, S.C. (1978). Sex roles and drinking among adolescent girls. *Journal of Studies on Alcohol. 39,* 1855-1874.

Wilsnack, R.W., Wilsnack, S.C., & Klassen, A.D. (1984). Women's drinking and drinking problems: Patterns from a 1981 national survey. *American Journal Of Public Health, 74,* 1231-1238.

Wilsnack, R.W., Wilsnack, S.C., & Klassen, A.D. (1986). Antecedents and consequences of drinking problems in women: Patterns from a U.S. national survey. *Nebraska Symposium On Motivation,* 86-147.

Wilsnack, R.W., & Cheloha, R. (1987). Women's roles and problem drinking across the lifespan. *Social Problems. 34,* 231-248.

Wilsnack, S. (1973). Sex-role identity in female alcoholism. *Journal of Abnormal Psychology, 82,* 253-261.

Wilsnack, S. (1976). The impact of sex-roles in women's alcohol use and abuse. In Greenblatt & Schuckit (eds.), *Alcoholism problems in women and children.* (p. 178) New York: Grune & Stratton.

Wilsnack, S. (1990). Alcohol abuse and alcoholism: Extent of the problem. In R.

Engs (Ed.) *Women: Alcohol and other Drugs* an ADPA monograph, (pp. 17-31), Dubuque, Iowa: Kendall Hall.

Wilsnack, S. & Beckman, L. (1987). *Alcohol problems in women* (2nd ed.). New York: Guilford.

Wilsnack, S.C., & Wilsnack, R.W., and Klassen, A.D. (1984/85). Sex differences and alcoholism in primary affective illness. *British Journal of Psychiatry, 113,* 972-979.

Winfield, I., George, L.K., Swartz, M., & Blazer, D.G. (1990). Sexual assault and psychiatric disorders among a community sample of women. *American Journal Of Psychiatry, 147,* 335-341.

Woodman, M. (1982). *Addiction to perfection.* Toronto: Inner City Books.

Woodman, M. (1990). *The ravaged bridegroom.* Toronto: Inner City Books.

Youcha, G. (1978) (2nd. ed.). *Women and alcohol.* New York: Crown Publishers.

Zankowski, G.L. (1987). Responsive Programming: Meeting the needs of chemically dependent women. *Alcoholism Treatment Quarterly, 4,* 5366.

Zimmerman, M.K. (1987). The women's health movement: A critique of medical enterprise and the position of women. In B. Hess, & M. Marx Feree (Eds.). *Analyzing gender: A handbook of social science research.* Newbury Park, CA: Sage.

Chapter Three

Codependency:
The Social Reconstruction
of Female Experience

Jo-Ann Krestan
Claudia Bepko

SUMMARY. The familiar language of codependency, while it represents an effort to name and articulate pain, has become a mythology in which the leading characters are defined as victims and as sick. This paper describes the historical evolution of the concept of codependency and discusses the dysfunctional dynamics in families that are seen as the origins of codependent behavior. An alternate language for describing such families is offered.

Very few of us can be in clinical practice today without being challenged not only to treat alcoholism, but to treat clients whose frame of reference for seeking treatment is to define themselves as codependent. The alternate terminology we hear is "I'm an Adult Child of an Alcoholic, or an Adult Child of a dysfunctional family." The terms are, or have become, synonymous. They reflect the client's awareness that he or she has been affected by the addiction of a parent or other significant member of a family or intimate relationship. Increasingly the terms suggest that the client has been negatively affected by almost any non-nurturing behavior that can occur in a family. For women more specifically,

Jo-Ann Krestan, MA, LSAC and Claudia Bepko, MSW are family therapists with a clinical and consulting practice in Brunswick, ME. Correspondence may be addressed to them at 1081 A Hillside Road, Brunswick, ME 04011.

This paper is adapted from an invitational lecture given at the Smith College School for Social Work in July, 1989. It was originally published in the *Smith College Studies in Social Work*, June 1990, Volume 60, No. 3 and is reprinted by permission.

49

codependency suggests the process of "losing" one's identity to an over focus on another person or relationship.

As clients come to us armed with a definition of their problem, they have also usually acquired a large self-help armamentarium of materials that point to the solutions to that problem. The self-help movements as typified by such groups as Alcoholics Anonymous, Al-Anon and their other counterparts have been unquestionably significant in relieving the pain associated with addiction. They have become more successful than most forms of professional treatment in promoting healing and change (Withorn, 1986). But when embraced as a response to so-called "codependent" behavior, the self-help paradigm and its extension, the "recovery" paradigm, has its unproductive elements. The uniqueness of the client's individual set of life experiences tends to become blurred within the framework of an over-defined and over-generalized identity. One might argue that the addicted person does need for a time to adopt the new and structured identity that the recovery programs provide (Bepko and Krestan, 1985). But loss of identity is precisely at the core of the dominant definitions of codependency. Immersion in an external structure that rigidly defines self in terms of deficits and disease only seems to perpetuate rather than address the so-called problem.

Beyond providing a frame for our clients' sense of their treatment needs, the adoption of the language of co-dependency has become a social phenomenon that seems to reflect a more global search to name and articulate pain. In part what we are witnessing in the codependency movement is the emergence of a mythology for our time. It's a mythology that tells a story about our hope for redemption from our common human woundedness. Unfortunately however, the myth is one that defines its characters as victims rather than participants in a complex relational drama. The mythical codependents have become very subtly the new social bearers of pathology. They are increasingly viewed as sick and diseased. We see a proliferation of hospital and privately-based treatment programs springing up to treat them. What is less clear is the precise nature and definition of the "disease" that's being treated.

The phenomenon that has become the codependency movement forces us to explore the power of language and story to shape our views of reality and our definitions of ourselves. It challenges us to look again at the political and economic forces that often underlie concepts of mental health and sickness. It forces renewed awareness of the concerns of the minority that most often inherits labels of pathology, that is, women.

As a part of this exploration, this paper will describe the historical evolution of the concept of codependency, and discuss the dysfunctional dynamics in families that are viewed as the origins of codependent behavior. Finally, we will suggest an alternate language that can more effectively direct how we treat the problem in its redefined form.

THE PROBLEMS OF DEFINITION

Codependency has had an interesting evolution as a concept. It has developed from being a term of description to assuming the status of a diagnosis. That fact relates, in some ways, to its association with the disease concept of alcoholism.

When we examine the origins of the term co-dependency, we should remind ourselves that the movement originally began with the very powerful and important observation that children who grew up with alcoholic parents were affected in predictable and traumatic ways and that they had specialized needs for treatment that were going unrecognized. The traumatic nature of their experiences with parental alcoholism was viewed as connected to their relational problems as adults. This growing awareness of the factors affecting family members who lived with alcoholism had its roots in two other important historical developments in our understanding of addiction. The first was the more widespread acceptance that addiction or more specifically, alcoholism, was a medically diagnosable and treatable disease.

In the 1930's and 1940's, alcoholic behavior moved from being defined as a moral evil to being "medicalized" and subsumed under a disease umbrella of professional diagnosis and treatment (Conrad and Schneider, 1980). While it's important to note that this trend had very positive consequences for our over-all approach to treating and researching problems of addictive behavior, it also raised still-unresolved controversy in the mental health field about the validity of calling addiction a disease. But nevertheless, the prevailing view that alcoholism was a physiological process that rendered the victim out of control was accepted and promoted by both the medical profession and the new self-help movements that were developing during this period.

The second related development was the growth of family systems thinking. As newer ideas about alcoholism finally began to define abusive drinking as a phenomenon that might be something other than an intractable moral failure, family systems thinkers began to view the drinker in a relational context (Steinglass, 1979). The family was acknowledged as affecting and being affected by the problems of its individual members.

In 1977, Claudia Black (1981) pioneered in promoting wider acceptance and understanding dysfunctional patterns that children in alcoholic homes grow up with. But slowly, it became commonplace to call those who lived with alcoholism, both children and particularly spouses, code-pendents. The idea was that while the alcoholic was addicted to the drug, other family members were also out of control in terms of the compulsive behaviors they developed in response to the alcoholic's drinking. It was not a difficult leap to decide that if the alcoholic had a disease, then so must the other people in the family. Gradually came the shift from de-scribing a problem to ascribing pathology. Surely, part of the basis for this shift was purely economic. If one is dealing with a disease, there is justifi-cation for establishing high-cost programs to treat it.

Just as alcoholic behavior had become "medicalized," the increasing tendency to refer to codependent behavior in the context of disease speaks to a general social tendency to render behavior that is problematic or con-fusing a legitimate focus of medical treatment and control. Since codepen-dents are primarily women, it's not surprising that this aspect of their experience, along with many others (Reissman, 1983), should be brought under the aegis of the professional expert. That expert, then, supposedly has the power to cure a "disease" which some would argue has been created by diagnostic labels that reflect primarily to the self-serving and self-reinforcing standards of the treating profession itself.

Another part of the "leap" to ascribing pathology to the entire family may have been even more broadly political, however. Since many fam-ilies in treatment were affected by the behavior of the male alcoholic, describing the female spouse and children as also sick helped to detour responsibility away from the male alcoholic. Since defining the alcoholic husband as sick implies that the wife is somehow stronger or "better" or more healthy, threatens the balance of power in traditional families, the notion of "codependency" became a useful way of applying so-called family systems principles in the interests of maintaining a cultural status-quo. Women are ascribed more pathology in this culture than men, so in any situation where the male clearly has the impairment, it *must* be the case that the woman as well as her children are sick too. The codepen-dency label, on a political level, becomes simply another tool in the op-pression of women fostering denial of male accountability.

An even brief review of the history of the developing definitions of codependency quickly establishes the struggle to legitimize and maintain the lexicon of sickness. These definitions also point to the increasing glob-alization of the problem.

"Codependency is a primary disease and a disease within every member of an alcoholic family" (Wegscheider-Cruse, 1984).

"Codependency is a pattern of learned behaviors, feelings and beliefs that make life painful" (Sondra Smalley as quoted in Schaef, 1986).

"Codependency is an emotional, psychological, and behavioral pattern of coping that is born of the rules of a family and not as a result of alcoholism" (Subby, 1984).

"Codependence affects not only individuals, but families, communities, businesses and other institutions, states, countries" (Whitfield, 1984).

"A codependent is anyone who lives in close association over a prolonged period of time with anyone who has a neurotic personality" (Larsen, 1983).

"A codependent person is one who has let another person's behavior affect him or her, and who is obsessed with controlling that person's behavior" (Beattie, 1987).

"Codependence is a toxic brain syndrome" (Cruse, 1989).

"Codependence is immaturity" (Mellody, 1989).

These definitions are irresponsible and so vague as to be meaningless. If we view all behavior as adaptive, they demonstrate how adaptive responses to stressful and traumatic situations can be pathologized in ways that are of little benefit to those needing relief from them. They are definitions that suggest that one is "bad" for having a problem with the difficult dilemma of being in relationship with an addicted person. More recently, some students of alcoholism (Cruse, 1989) have attempted to "disease" this adaptive behavior in the same way that alcoholism was finally defined as a disease—by suggesting a physiological basis for the problem.

The basic message of codependency implied in these definitions is a relational one—it reflects on the common struggle that we all face to maintain the integrity of our separateness in the face of our need for relatedness. Most of the descriptions of codependent behavior are a commentary on that struggle. The question is, how does one avoid ever being affected by the behavior of another person? The culture's current obsession with codependency may be, on a metaphorical level, another version of the quest for painless relatedness. Since being affected by another is viewed as sick, a corollary assumption would be that a healthy relationship is one in which individual needs are always gratified but the self remains invulnerable from the effects of another's behavior. Relational "health" would be represented by a curious cross between total autonomy and perfect need gratification. Recovered from codependency, one could magically achieve the paradoxical feat of being perfectly fulfilled in relationship without ever focusing on the other person.

FAMILIES AS THE SOURCE
OF CODEPENDENT BEHAVIOR

Clearly, the definitions outlined above could apply to almost anyone whether or not they grew up with or were in any way involved with alcoholism. Another widely accepted definition of a codependent is anyone who grew up in a "dysfunctional family." The dysfunctional family is viewed as the source of codependent behavior. Subby (1987), a family therapist who lectures widely on codependency, defines the phenomenon as a "dysfunctional pattern of living and problem solving which is nurtured by a set of rules in the family system." He says that codependency is a condition that can emerge "from any family system where certain unwritten, even unspoken rules exist."

What kind of family is dysfunctional? Conversely, what kind of family is normal? By whose standard is any family dysfunctional? For whom is it dysfunctional? These questions tend to cloud the issue further and to add an even greater level of complexity to any efforts to clarify the nature of the problem. To speak of "dysfunctional family" without a context for defining the term tends to be as globalizing and pathologizing a process as creating a condition called "codependency."

Black (1981) summarized the three unspoken rules that she felt organized behavior in an alcoholic family. They were, DON'T TALK, DON'T TRUST, AND DON'T FEEL. These rules reflect the intense forms of denial, repression, distortion, and emotional constriction that are the hallmark of a family affected by alcoholism or addiction.

But if these characteristics suggest dysfunction in a family, what is the corollary set of characteristics of a functional family? Most of us tend to share some common assumptions about health and normalcy. Culture-bound as we are, they are assumptions that reflect the dominantly white, middle or upper-class values.

Family therapists tend to define the functional family as one that establishes clear boundaries, clear rules and roles, and correct hierarchies of power. In the functional family, children are not expected to be adults before their time, and the parents do not act like children. In a functional family, marital partners do not detour their problems through the children. There is an absence of addiction and of any kind of internal or interactional abuse. Members of the family can talk with one another, and feelings are expressed and accepted. The family operates without denial, without secrets, without the need for shame and isolation. It is flexible enough to meet the challenges posed by the different tasks required at different developmental life stages, and it is flexible enough to reorganize and change, when, for example, a new baby is born, a grandparent dies, or a child reaches adolescence. Almost everything written in the past ten years about addictive or dysfunctional families suggests that they do not function in these ways.

But descriptions or theories about the dynamics of functional families are often far different from the forms family life actually assumes in a rapidly changing culture. These definitions of "functional" presume a family form and structure that is largely mythical and they presume a family power arrangement that, it could be argued, was never functional. In other words, the assumptions we share about functional families are assumptions about rules, roles, and communication that exist within a larger context of gross power imbalance between men and women. That power imbalance itself is dysfunctional.

Ideas about the causes of codependency presume that there *is* such a thing as a functional family not influenced by gender inequality and that if we could re-achieve this seemingly functional structure, codependency could become a diagnosis of the past. But think for a moment about the typical vision of a normal family. Is it still 2.5 children, daddy working, mother working part-time, an Irish Setter and a station wagon? Is it two lesbians raising the children of one from a former partnership? Is it a remarried family? Is it a single adoptive father?

Many of our theories about the functional family structure assume the traditional, normative white middle-class family balanced around a more overtly powerful working father who has access to economic resources and many options for self-definition complemented by a mother who is fully responsible for children and the family emotional environment. Such theories deny the enormous changes in family form and structure that have taken place in the last two decades. The impact of the divorce rate alone means that as many as four children in ten born in the 1970's are expected to spend part of their childhood in a one parent household (Leupnitz, 1988).

However, fantasy is notoriously resistant to fact. Despite these changes in the American family, changes that may be necessary as part of an evolutionary process, we still often subconsciously hold in our heads a kind of mythic idealized version of the family that rarely exists today. It could be argued that it is in fact our *mythology* about what constitutes a normal family that gives rise to our notions that not living in one causes codependency. Looked at more closely, it becomes evident that the mythical "normal" family was never functional, not for women, not for children, and not really for men, although it looked like it worked for a time for white males. We could not have avoided codependency if we had normal families. It was our so-called "normal" family structures that in fact set the stage for dysfunction to begin with.

IMAGES OF NORMAL FAMILIES

Often we find compelling commentaries on current social conditions in movies. The film, *The Great Santini* depicts a family that by all standards would be considered both normal and normative. Santini is an Air Force Captain, successful, powerful, all-man. He drinks heavily to prove it. Lillian, his wife is the picture of both Southern and female gentility. During one scene in the film, Santini's oldest son Ben beats him at a game of basketball as Lillian and the rest of the family cheer Ben on from the sidelines. Santini tries to rob Ben of the victory and Lillian accuses Santini of cheating. In reaction, Santini becomes abusive. He threatens to "kick" Lillian, and bounces the basketball off of Ben's head, taunting him by calling him "my sweetest little girl." Ben and Lillian talk about it later and she tells Ben that his father's abuse is really his way of saying "I love you."

How does this scene represent the normative American family? Surely the Santinis are an alcoholic family, a dysfunctional family. But if we look at what IS normative about it in the context of power relations we see how this normative structure can generate codependent behavior.

Lillian in her submissiveness and willingness to tolerate Santini's abuse can be considered codependent; Ben would probably also be defined as codependent. The structure in which that codependency evolves is one in which the woman and children all sit around watching the men, the important ones, while the men compete. Mother has a covert coalition with her son, which becomes overt when she accuses father of cheating and openly roots for the son. But when she roots for the son in a way that challenges Santini's power, he ups the ante. "Who the hell asked you anything?" He expresses his rage at the boy: "Mama's boy. . . . let's see you cry." Then he abuses Ben by bouncing a basketball off his head: "my sweetest little girl . . . ," the worst insult a man can give another man and a reinforcement of the myth of masculinity.

In an environment such as this where any challenge to the accepted power structure creates the potential for abuse, the roles played by Lillian and Ben are adaptive and understandable. Adult children of alcoholics and of dysfunctional families, those whom we now call codependent, learn to scan their environments constantly, and to adjust their behavior in an effort to keep the emotional climate safe. They come to believe that they are powerful enough to control the environment if they only figure it out right, that it is their job to control it. In the process they lose the sense of their own identities.

Lillian has lost so much sense of herself as a person that she does not even recognize abuse. And if Ben learns to deny his anger as she instructs, his "codependency" too, will be assured. It's clear that Lillian has had years of practice in being hypervigilant in her focus on others. But to call her behavior codependency is to blame the victim.

Like most women, Lillian has been socialized to be emotionally central in the family, codependent, and responsible for relationships. She caretakes the relationship between Ben and his father, reframes her husband's intentions in a way that the most elegant of strategic/systemic therapists might do: "what happened today won't matter in five years . . . he does what he does because he loves you and wants you to be the best . . . he's out there practicing in the rain because he's admitting that he's getting older . . . it's the only way he knows how to say I'm sorry."

The Santini's are the normative white American family. The men are socialized to be competitive, dualistic, impulsive, "TOP GUNS." The women are socialized to be other-focused and responsible for sustaining all family relationships.

The film *On Golden Pond* tells a similar story about a "normal" family. As Jane Fonda talks about the hostile and distant relationship she had with her father, Katherine Hepburn, as her mother, explains her father's behavior to her daughter. The mother, in effect makes apologies, interprets his behavior for him. Without the extreme exaggerations created by the alcoholism in the Santini story, the scene is almost identical.

In both cases, the women never question their centrality in family life, their expertise on relationships. They automatically take the emotional responsibility for explaining and interpreting the men to the children, thus maintaining the men's immobility to deal with emotional relationships.

This same scene is played out on a very small scale in many of our lives in the following vignette: we call home and when our father answers the phone, he immediately, without really talking with us says, "just a minute, . . . I'll get your mother."

What is going on in these three family scenes and how does it relate to codependency? What is going on is business as usual. It is, in general, a woman's prescribed role to tend to relationships, to focus on relationships, to make sure all relationships work, to put the needs and feelings of the other ahead of their own. And a woman inevitably loses her relationship with herself in the over-responsible focus on the other. Women are programmed this way in the "normal" version of family life and if they grow up in an overtly dysfunctional family they are taught to do more of the same. In the process men have been crippled in their capacity for emotional relatedness. Why call this socialized behavior codependency? Why use the language of sickness for behavior that has been celebrated as normal all along? As we recognize that family form and structure are changing, we need to acknowledge that the "normative" family of time-honored tradition was perhaps never functional. If it were, it wouldn't need to change.

CLINICAL ALTERNATIVES
TO THE LANGUAGE OF CODEPENDENCY

Our clinical model for intervention with codependency developed in response to our work with families affected by addiction (Bepko and Krestan, 1985). We assume that the key dynamic to interrupt in the alcohol-affected family is the reciprocal one that evolves when one person is over-responsible and the other under-responsible. Briefly, we view the problem as one of a complementary imbalance. If one person does too much either functionally or emotionally for another, that first person becomes increasingly under-responsible for his own well-being and inevitably maintains and perpetuates under-responsibility in the other. The two play reciprocal roles.

Alcoholics, by the very nature of the addictive process, exaggerate the over-responsible/under-responsible dichotomy. Over-responsible behavior has come to be called codependency. But to talk in terms of extremes of over or under-responsibility is, we feel, a much more effective and less blaming language. It points to the need for behavioral change rather than suggesting the need for recovery from a "disease."

Since over-responsible behavior is the natural growth of women's socialization in this society, living in an addiction-affected system naturally exacerbates it. Hypervigilance about emotional climates, if not carried to an extreme, is considered necessary and appropriate behavior for women. We call what has been termed either enabling and codependent behavior over-responsible behavior.

The over-responsibility that women are trained to assume is not confined to the emotional arena of life. They are also taught to perform almost all of the other services that maintain family life but in a way that makes it appear that they remain in some way dependent on men.

In men, codependency may refer to female qualities that have been learned in response to a particular role in a given family. For example, many men who grew up in addiction-affected families learned to be nurturing, but in an inappropriate way. Focusing on the needs of others became a survival role and many men learned it only because of the absence of a female sibling in the system. The man who learns to be emotionally over-responsible is behaving in a stereotypically female way. Codependency is still a term thought to be more applicable to female behavior. Men may *do* codependent things, but women *are* codependent.

REBALANCING POWER AND RESPONSIBILITY

Clinically, as we move to restore what we consider to be an appropriate distribution of responsibility within the family system, both functionally and emotionally, we are inevitably challenging old normative structures. In working with alcohol-affected systems it is traditional to assess and change those patterns that enable the drinking to continue. It is understood that if the wife of an alcoholic is told not to make excuses for her husband with his employer, she's being asked to stop enabling his alcoholic behavior. But if one intervenes further and asks her not to pick up his dirty towel from the bathroom floor or not to referee the relationship between him and his children, one may be inciting social revolution. Calling his employer, and picking up the dirty towel, and refereeing the relationship with the children are, in fact, the same behaviors within different contexts. They are all over-responsible behaviors. If she keeps calling the employer with excuses, we know the alcoholic won't get sober. But are we willing to look at what might happen if she stopped picking up the dirty towel, buying the Mother's Day card for his mother, and managing his relationship with his children? Quite simply, the old normative structure would break down.

In one example Nancy, the wife, has been asked to stop haranguing her husband Mike, who is 28 days sober, about filing the income tax that has gone unfiled for three years. Nancy works for the government. Her anxiety is understandable. But the more she prods Mike, the more he resists. Nancy has great difficulty understanding why she needs therapy and why her prodding and "nagging" of Mike results in such reactivity on his part.

Is Nancy codependent? Is she controlling? Is she helpful? Mike feels controlled. But Nancy feels so focused on what Mike is and isn't doing that she feels her only reason for needing therapy is to understand why Mike behaves the way he does.

Since she's so focused on Mike and so affected by his behavior, Nancy could be defined as codependent. But it is perhaps more clinically useful to call her over-responsible and to see her over-responsibility and his under-responsibility as co-created and maintained in a context in which the rule is that she *should function as over-responsible for him but in a way that lets him save face.* If she took over filing the taxes for him rather than telling him how to do it she would be even more over-responsible but Mike would be less upset. Over-responsibility for a woman is sanctioned, but only if acted out in a way that maintains the myth that Mike is not accountable for his under-responsibility. But when Nancy nags and controls, pointing attention to his under-functioning, in the current lexicon of disease, she is called codependent.

In response to Nancy's over-responsibility, Mike behaves in a reciprocally under-responsible way that leaves him feeling incompetent. The alcoholism masks the incompetence. But these imbalances in responsibility, exaggerated by alcoholism, are reinforced by a socialization that trains men and women to assume one set of behaviors while displaying another. So Nancy is socialized to actually manage many, if not most, of the details of her life with Mike, but she is also to show dependence. And Mike is socialized to rely on Nancy for his total emotional life, but to display autonomy. Mike appears to be very passive, but in fact, he has spent years doing what he's been taught to do as a man — deny his feelings. Nancy and Mike are trapped in their reciprocal roles by their mutual family socialization and by the larger societal rules that define gender-appropriate behavior and that maintain gender inequality.

To upset this inequality of responsibility clinically, we first ask that couples make lists of all the functional and emotional responsibilities it takes to run their life together. The lists are typically very similar to this sample one from one couple in treatment. One partner's responsibilities were as follows:

> child care, house repairs, cleaning, laundry, decorating, dry cleaners, paying bills, problems with tenants with our rental properties, problems with local real estate, dental appointments, doctors visits, chauffeuring, buying presents, buying cards, hiring repair people, school contacts, income tax preparation, car repairs, shopping, food preparation, cleaning of all types, reminding . . . for example, insurance, car inspections, taking care of dogs and cats. Emotional responsibilities were listed as: getting in the middle between spouse

and children, buffering bad feelings between family, reminding each family member of each other's needs, attempts to get spouse to talk about what's going on with spouse, attempts to smooth over tension, make sure no one feels bad or sad.

The other partner's list was: financial, children's physical needs provided for with money, driving the car, shielding problems from spouse, avoiding conflict and confrontation.

It would be a correct assumption to guess that the longer list is the wife's and the second list, with financial concerns being foremost, is her husband's. Responsibilities in couples don't always break down this way, particularly when the woman is alcoholic, but these represent the typical female and male lists.

Extremes of over- and under-responsibility also develop in gay and lesbian couples when addiction is involved. But since these relationships tend to be more egalitarian (Blumstein and Schwartz, 1983), the implications are somewhat different.

The point clinically is that the normative family structure in heterosexual relationships is a codependent structure. If one works toward a redistribution of the codependent structure through equalizing the distribution of responsibilities a blow is struck at the heart of that codependent structure, but another is struck at what is considered normal for the white, middle-class American family.

When we work toward this redistribution of responsibility within the family we assume that women and men must both give up inappropriate responsibility for others and take appropriate responsibility for self. For a women, relinquishing over-responsible behavior may create a crisis of "emptiness" for a time because her entire sense of self has been, in many cases, predicated on being *for* others (Miller, 1976; Gilligan, 1982). Men are typically asked to give up over-responsibility for work in some way. As an example, a psychiatrist recently sought consultation because of concern with his relationship with his mother. She was flying in from the west coast for a family therapy session and although he was seeking help because of issues in his relationship with her and had initiated the idea of the therapy session, he insisted he could not take time off from work to pick her up at the airport. He had assumed that his wife would have to do that. The intervention, of course, was to insist that he rearrange his schedule to pick her up himself. On his drive to the airport, and as he sat waiting for her delayed flight, he encountered a good deal of anxiety and depression that his busy schedule usually shielded him from.

In intervening to redistribute responsibility, it is critical that we not ask women to give up over-responsibility for their relationships in ways that shame them for being nurturing or that rob them of all responsibility. Equally, it's important not to ask men to rebalance their work lives in ways that shame them for trying to be good men.

FOSTERING RELATIONAL RESPONSIBILITY

As we better equalize responsibility within the family and replace an over focus on others in women with a healthy focus on self, it is also crucial to maintain a concept of relational responsibility. Treatment must have as its goal the fostering of appropriate responsibility for self at the same time that it maintains a focus on concepts of relational responsibility and emotional responsiveness to others. If for women, recovery from "codependency" means recovering from female socialization enough to care about oneself as much as one cares about relationship, that is a needed correction. But if recovery for men points in the direction of being even more self-focused and of further devaluing the need for mutual caring and connectedness, that may represent an over-correction.

One of the greatest dangers of the codependency movement is that in its attempt to restore appropriate responsibility to the individual, it espouses in some instances a very linear and blaming view of relationships that does not assume the mutual responsibility of both partners for the successes and failures of relatedness. Concepts that have to do with focusing on self rather than the other are often misapplied so that people stop being over-responsible, but they also stop taking appropriate responsibility for their part in relationships. They forget that the antidote to over-responsibility is responsiveness, not a failure to be responsible at all (Bepko and Krestan, 1990). If the movement perpetuates an illusion of perfectibility by suggesting that if one recovers perfectly then one has painless relationships, it simply maintains the errors and illusions of a patriarchal culture that promotes a false belief in the value of total independence and autonomy and fails to recognize the need for healthy interdependence.

EXPECTATIONS OF CHANGE

The following brief story illustrates the potential for misapplication of the ideas of codependency, a misapplication that ignores a process view of change.

A man involved in a long term relationship with a woman began to experience serious conflicts with her. He had not been in the habit of asking directly for her time or attention, he had simply made assumptions that she would focus on his priorities and agendas. Over time, she tended to withdraw her focus on him and his needs, and he learned that he needed to be more direct in asking for what he wanted from her. When he did, she often said no and got angry as well. He went to his codependency group and asked why, when he asked for his needs to be met, he was ignored and abandoned. He was told that it was because he picked people who were not capable of giving.

In focusing on the inability or the refusal of his partner to give, both he and his group were ignoring a process view of change. By asking for something directly, this man was changing the rules of his relational system, and the first thing any participant in a relational system does when confronted with change is to directly or indirectly insist that things change back to the way they were. If this man listens to his group and cuts off emotionally from his partner without understanding the ways in which he has changed his own part in the system, the system itself is not going to change. It may not anyway, but he needs to act with the understanding that change is a process, and that a first negative response does not make her a villain or him a "sick codependent" who chooses the wrong kind of people.

There is a dangerous underlying assumption in the message that the group gave to this man, which is the myth that simply having a need entitles one to get it met. The recovery movement, Adult Children of Alcoholics, and its sister programs espouse the need to recover childhood. But here the movement poses further difficult questions regarding responsibility. How can one be an "adult child". . . . what kind of responsibility is then appropriate? Can one really have unmet childhood needs met as an adult? Too often "recovery" from codependency in this sense can seem like an abandonment of responsibility and an exercise in blaming or in being victim.

Clinically then, in an attempt to create more functional families, we need to challenge the distribution of responsibility and power that exists in the normative American family. A "functional" family needs to meet the needs of women, of children, and of men. Codependency needs to be redefined as over-responsibility and over-responsibility needs to be understood as a positive impulse gone awry. Relational responsibility needs to coexist with responsibility to self, and the feminine emphasis on feeling needs to be acknowledged and celebrated while the feminine focus on relationship needs some redirection without its being pathologized. The codependency movement possesses the potential to direct our attention to a redressing of the gendered imbalances between the male and female sensibilities within us. Hopefully that redressing can occur in a way that doesn't overcorrect for the female tendency to focus on relationship. If that overcorrection occurs, our social mores will simply return us to the old narcissistic position, I HAVE TO GET MY NEEDS MET and it's codependent to care about your needs.

CONCLUSION

This discussion has focused on the codependency movement as representing the creation in language of a syndrome that is difficult to treat because it is so global and vague in definition. It's a movement that tends to perpetuate society's tendency to pathologize behavior that is typically defined as female, as women's work.

The codependency movement is probably best viewed as a fascinating and compelling example of the evolution of a social phenomenon. It speaks to the power of our descriptions of reality to invent reality and to invent disease for economic and political gain whereby certain segments of society profit from treating others whose experience is controlled by being defined as sick. It speaks to our tendency to over-identify with negative and pathologizing views of ourselves. And it speaks to our tendency to think in generalized extremes that fail to acknowledge contradiction, complexity, distinction.

There is unquestionably some pattern of behavior and feeling that characterizes the experience of many people who have felt the negative power of an addictive process somewhere in their lives. An understanding of these patterns can only inform and enhance our clinical work. But our understanding so far remains at a fairly elementary, unresearched level. The codependency movement can be credited with bringing these patterns to our attention and awareness, but it has also created another set of problems.

The language of codependency blames people, women in particular, for assuming a social role that has previously been viewed as normative and functional. It takes what was once considered healthy, defining it as sick. In the process it fails to acknowledge that change needs to occur at the level of social belief, attitude and expectation. The patterns of behavior that we see today as "codependent" are symptoms of the damage done by adhering to constricting and patriarchal definitions of normative family structure. But the language of codependency personalizes the problem and locates it in individuals instead of acknowledging that the problem or "sickness" is in the larger structure itself.

"Codependency" proposes a change in individual behavior that doesn't take the process of relationship into account. It overdefines as sick some qualities that are necessary to the maintenance of relationship. It ignores the concept of relational responsibility.

Finally, the myth of codependency may need some revision. We need to create a new story about mutual responsibility and about relational responsibility. We need a story in which the characters are no longer constricted by rigid parameters of maleness and femaleness. We need a story in which power is balanced, and we need a story in which victims are replaced by wounded but responsible heros and heroines. In the new story, those heroes and heroines view themselves not as sick reactors, but as courageous actors on the ever demanding, complex stage of life.

NOTES

Beattie, M. (1987). *Co-dependent no more.* New York: Harper/Hazelden.

Bepko, C. & Krestan, J. (1990). *Too good for her own good: Breaking free from the burden of female responsibility.* New York: Harper and Row.

Bepko, C. & Krestan, J. (1985). *The responsibility trap: A blueprint for treating the alcoholic family.* New York: Free Press.

Black, C. (1981). *It will never happen to me.* Denver, Colorado: M.A.C.

Blumstein, P. & Schwartz, P. (1983). *American couples.* New York: Morrow.

Conrad, P. & Schneider, J. (1980). *Deviance and medicalization: From badness to sickness.* St. Louis: C.V. Mosby Company.

Cruse, J. (1989). *Painful affairs: Looking for love through addiction and co-dependency.* Deerfield Beach, Florida: Health Communications.

Gilligan, C. (1982). *In a different voice.* Cambridge, MA: Harvard University Press.

Larsen, E. (1983). *Basics of co-dependency.* Brooklyn Park, MN: E. Larsen Enterprises.

Leupnitz, D. (1988). *The family interpreted: Feminist theory in clinical practice.* New York: Basic Books, 1988.

Mellody, P. (1989). *The roots of codependency.* Audio tape produced by Listen To Learn Tape Library, Phoenix, AZ.

Miller, J. B. (1976). *Toward a new psychology of women.* Boston, Beacon Press.

Reissman, C.K. (1983). "Women and medicalization." *Social Policy, 14, 1.*

Smalley, S. (1986). Quoted in Anne Wilson Schaef, *Co-dependence: Misunderstood, mistreated.* San Francisco: Harper and Row.

Subby, R. (1984). Inside the chemically dependent marriage: Denial and manipulation, in *Co-dependency: An emerging issue.* Pompano Beach, FL: Health Communications.

Subby, R. (1987). *Lost in the shuffle: The co-dependent reality.* Pompano Beach, FL: Health Communications.

Steinglass, P. (1979). Family therapy with alcoholics: A review. In Kaufmann and Kaufmann, (Eds.) *Family therapy of drug and alcohol abuse.* New York: Gardner Press.

Wegscheider-Cruse, S. (1984). Co-dependency: The therapeutic void, in *Co-dependency: An emerging issue.* Pompano Beach, FL: Health Communications.

Whitfield, C. (1984). Co-Dependency: An emerging problem among professionals. In *Co-dependency: An emerging issue.* Pompano Beach, FL: Health Communications.

Withorn, A. (1986). Helping Ourselves. In Conrad and Kern, (Eds.) *Sociology of health and illness,* second edition. New York: St. Martin's Press.

Chapter Four

Powerlessness — Liberating or Enslaving? Responding to the Feminist Critique of the Twelve Steps

David Berenson

SUMMARY. Alcoholics Anonymous has gained acceptance as an important if not potentially necessary adjunct to therapeutic work with substance-abusing clients. Yet feminists take issue with the core belief of the Twelve Steps: I am powerless over alcohol. Powerlessness is viewed as the source of women's oppression within a patriarchal society. This paper explores alternative views of the concept of powerlessness and sets a context for a new understanding and translation of the Twelve Steps that may provide an alternative for more feminist-informed use of them in treatment.

Alcoholics Anonymous was initially a program run by men for men. In fact one of the titles considered for the AA Big Book, *Alcoholics Anonymous*, was *One Hundred Men*. At first women were denied admission to AA because "nice" women didn't become drunks, and it took four years until Marty Mann became AA's first woman member. Since then the percentage of women has grown until it is now estimated that women comprise more than a third of the American membership of Alcoholics Anonymous and approximately half in some parts of the country (Robertson 1988). More striking, however, is the high percentage of women in the

David Berenson, MD, is Director of the Family Institute of San Francisco. Correspondence may be addressed to him at 215 Main Street, #207, Sausalito, CA 94965.

Twelve Step offshoots of AA like Al-Anon, Adult Children of Alcoholics, Codependents Anonymous, and Overeaters Anonymous. Not only are many women attending Twelve Step meetings, but they also constitute the majority of customers for the burgeoning industry of workshops and self-help books based directly or indirectly upon the Twelve Steps.

Some feminist thinkers and therapists have viewed the upsurge of the recovery movement with some alarm. They are particularly concerned about the Twelve Steps' emphasis upon powerlessness as liberating. In contrasting the codependent/ACA/recovery movement with the women's movement, Marianne Walters (1990) points out that "one movement encourages individuals to surrender to a spiritual higher power, while the other encourages people to join together to challenge and restructure power arrangements in the larger society. . . . One is based on a deficit model of human personality; the other, on a model of competency. . . . I suggest that the codependent movement and the self-help literature, while clearly intended to empower, in fact pathologize behaviors and personal characteristics that are associated with the feminine" (p. 55).

In a critique of the Twelve Steps, Charlotte Davis Kasl (1990) states: "Women who question 'the program,' as it's often called, have been shamed, called resistant and threatened with abandonment. They have been trained to believe that male models of nearly anything are better than whatever they might create for themselves. . . . The steps were formulated by a white, middle-class male in the 1930's; not surprisingly, they work to break down an overinflated ego, and put reliance on an all-powerful male God. But most women suffer from the *lack* of a healthy, aware ego, and need to strengthen their sense of self by affirming their own inner wisdom." She further suggests "many women abuse chemicals or stay in harmful relationships *because* they feel powerless in their lives. Thus, many women prefer to affirm that they have the power to *choose* not to use chemicals or have dependent relationships" (p. 30).

Sonia Johnson (1989) puts it more emphatically: "Alcoholics Anonymous is simply another male institution, different in neither quality nor kind from the churches or schools or political parties or from any other group dedicated to maintaining men's oppressive and destructive value structure and hierarchy. There are no new values there, nothing that is recognizable as nonparadigmatic to patriarchy. . . . Recovery groups— particularly when they center around the Twelve Steps steps of AA—often have the same self-abasing, powerless, external focus, an ultimate rejection of responsibility inherent in male religion and politics" (p. 131). As an alternative to Alcoholics Anonymous and its Twelve Steps, she offers

Women for Sobriety and its Thirteen Steps which she sees as "present-time oriented, positive, self-affirming and self-directed, guilt-free" and as having "some metaphysical sophistication" (p. 139). The difference between the first step of each program is certainly striking: AA's, "We admitted that we were powerless over alcohol—that our lives had become unmanageable," contrasted with WFS's, "I have a drinking problem that once had me."

APPROACHES TO THE FEMININE
AND THE MASCULINE

Before more closely examining the central issue of powerlessness and the practices associated with the Twelve Steps, it may be useful to consider the different meanings that have been attached to the words feminine and masculine. They are used in at least three different ways, and in sorting them out we may be able to differentiate contexts where the experience of powerlessness is liberating and where it is enslaving.

The first two ways in which the labels feminine and masculine are used refer to biological gender and to social role. (With regard to gender the terms female and male may be more appropriate.) A simplistic, non-feminist view, would hold that social roles and behaviors that are seen as female and male are strictly determined by biology. Women are supposedly programmed to act instinctively in a "feminine" way and men in a "masculine" way. Deborah Luepnitz (1988) points out that feminists see gender as "socially constituted, not biologically given" (p. 14). What society has labeled as feminine and masculine have more to do with historical, cultural, economic, political, and family role factors than with biology.

Luepnitz further distinguishes within feminism between what she calls the cultural school and the sex-role school: "To simplify tremendously, cultural school feminists emphasize the differences between the sexes, and sex-role feminists emphasize the samenesses." Adherents of the cultural school see essential differences between what it is to be female and what it is to be male in our society and "have made us reconsider the social contempt for connection, nurturance, dependency, and care—things that have been associated with women and women's work" (p. 15).

Sex-role feminists worry that focusing on the differences between men and women will reinforce "the separate-spheres doctrine, according to which men belong to one world and women another (and always lesser) world." They are concerned that, if women are preoccupied with being caring and cooperative, "they will never take their place in the public

sphere, competing for office, demanding pay equity. . . . Sex-role feminists often argue the desirability of androgyny—an ideal human condition
in which gender differences would be submerged in individual differences" (p. 15).

With the polarities of biological gender and socialized sex-role it is
possible to fall into the traps of either overemphasizing gender differences
or of denying them, what Rachel Hare-Mustin (1987) has termed respec-
tively alpha and beta prejudices. To possibly resolve this dichotomy and
then to address the issue of powerlessness, it is useful to look at a third
way that the words masculine and feminine are used: as principles or
qualities (French 1985), ways of knowing (Belenky et al. 1986), archetypes (Wehr 1987), or types of energy. Whether called feminine and masculine, Eros and Logos,[1] or Yin and Yang, these various descriptions all
point to complementary, interactive principles that are also ways of being
or modes of consciousness.

Upon hearing words like Yin and Yang or listening to people speak of
"energy," there is frequently a tendency to dismiss what is being spoken
of as muddled West Coast thinking or Eastern mysticism, depending upon
one's frame of reference. Indeed many people who use words like these
do lack a certain amount of intellectual rigor. It is also possible, however,
that the automatic dismissal of these terms as fanciful and unscientific
may reflect the overvaluation that our culture has placed upon a masculine, instrumental, analytic mode of thinking.

In discussing the cultural school of feminism, Luepnitz points out that it
emphasizes women's greater tendency to *continuity* and men's greater tendency to *discontinuity* in relationships. Her use of the words continuity
and discontinuity has at least a surface resonance with Buckminster
Fuller's (1975: 1979) description of the structuring principles of the universe: continuous tension and discontinuous compression. He describes
tension, or the force of pulling, as comprehensive, encompassing, cohe-
sive, integrative, associative, and *im*plosive and compression, or the force
of pushing, as local, separate, differentiative, divisive, dissociative, and
explosive. If we translate tension as feminine and compression as masculine, we can see that Fuller's adjectives, derived solely from a theoretical
study of physical systems and the practical development of the geodesic
dome, indeed have more than a surface similarity to the qualities that have
been assigned to "feminine" and "masculine" from biological, psychological, anthropological, or archetypal investigation. The question then
becomes not what causes feminine or masculine qualities, biology or society, (certainly a masculine question) but what is the relationship or inter-

play between the feminine and masculine principles (a more feminine way of putting it).

Seen from this vantage point, both women and men have both feminine and masculine qualities. Biological gender and social sex role may be isomorphic with these principles, but there is no invariable biological or social determinism. Women represent the embodiment of the feminine and men the embodiment of the masculine, but it is possible for a woman to develop her masculine attributes without becoming "mannish," and a man to develop his feminine qualities without becoming effeminate.

Our culture has overvalued the masculine and denigrated the feminine. This is reflected both in the treatment of women and in the tendency of both men and women to more highly prize assertive, controlling, imposing, objectifying, focal, exclusive, explicit, "doing" ways of being over receptive, allowing, unfolding, relational, diffuse, inclusive, implicit, "being" ways of being. Mastery is sought rather than mystery or ms-tery. This state of affairs is actually the reverse of the "natural order" of things in which the feminine principle is primary and the masculine principle is secondary. Evidence for the primacy of the feminine comes from investigation in many areas, including Fuller's work with physical systems, biological work in parthenogenesis and embryology, and anthropological evidence for the worship of the Goddess as the supreme aspect of divinity in many "primitive" cultures (Eisler 1987).

It may appear to some that I am advocating substituting female superiority for male superiority. That conclusion would be a projection of a patriarchal way of thinking which posits the superior-inferior dichotomy as innate rather than as an unfortunate artifice in our culture. Eisler points out that matrilineal or matricentral societies have not been matriarchal: "the primacy of the Goddess—and with this the centrality of the values symbolized by the nurturing and regenerating powers incarnated in the female body—does not justify the inference that women here dominated men" (p. 27). Rather, when the primacy of the feminine is recognized, the relationship or partnership between feminine and masculine is prized or valued, and the "'feminine' power to nurture and give [is] the normative ideal, the model to be emulated by both women and men" (p. 28).

THE SHIFTING VIEW OF POWER

The evolution, or imposition, of a patriarchal way of thinking and the organization of a society in which masculine qualities are seen as primary and superior has distorted our view of what power is. *Webster's New World Dictionary* gives the first definition of power as "ability to do, act, or produce," derived from the Latin "to be able." The way we have come to view power is summarized by Webster's fourth definition: "(a) the ability to control others; authority; sway; influence (b) special authority assigned to or exercised by a person or group holding office (c) legal ability or authority." An intrinsic ability or state of being, *power-to* has become an extrinsic action or state of doing, *power-over*.

Several feminist writers have commented on these two very different notions of power. French describes how control or power-over gets to be abstracted and valued for its own sake: "any form of control seems good simply because it is a control. It is valued simply because it exists more than for what it accomplishes or creates (p. 68). . . . life is the highest value for 'feminine' people; whereas control is the highest value for 'masculine' people" (p. 93). French further sees that "power-to primarily increases pleasure, and power-over increases pain. Power-to involves expressiveness and a degree of autonomy, whereas power-over involves structure, coercion, fear, and sometimes violent cruelty" (p. 444).

Eisler distinguishes between *actualization power* and *domination power*. She also describes how twentieth-century feminist literature has been probing alternative ways of perceiving and using power, as viewing power as affiliation or linking (p. 193) and quotes Jean Baker Miller as distinguishing between "power *for* oneself and power *over* others. . . . The power of another person, or group of people was generally seen as dangerous. You had to control them or they would control you. But in the realm of human development, this is not a valid formulation. Quite the reverse. In a basic sense, the greater the development of each individual the more able, more effective, and less needy of limiting or restricting others she or he will be" (Miller, 1976, p. 116).

Evelyn Fox Keller (1985) describes how what has come to be seen conventionally as scientific thinking is characterized by the connections among autonomy, masculinity, objectivity, and power. The linkage and interplay between them leads to *autonomy* that "connotes a radical independence from others," *objectivity* that "implies a reductive disjunction of subject from object," *masculinity* "denying all traces of femininity," and *power* "defined as domination" (p. 97). This is not to say that autonomy, objectivity, masculinity, and power intrinsically have these attributes but that they acquire them when they are linked to each other, having been stripped or isolated from the enclosing feminine context or matrix. Keller provides a different view of the possibility of science, and its relation to power, in her discussion of the work of the biologist Barbara McClintock: "To McClintock, science has a different goal: not predic-

per se, but understanding; not the power to manipulate, but empowerment — the kind of power that results from an understanding of the world around us, that simultaneously reflects and affirms our connection to that world (p. 166)."[2]

THE RECOVERY FROM ADDICTION
AS THE RECOVERY OF POWER

Addiction is so far the main arena where the masculinized notion of power as manipulative control or domination has come to grief. Gregory Bateson (1972) describes the alcoholic as having adopted an unusually disastrous variant of "the strange dualistic epistemology characteristic of Occidental civilization" (p. 321), separating his "self" or "will" from his environment in an effort to exert control over it. French appears to be speaking of the same phenomenon when she describes what she calls the theorems of patriarchal ideology:

1. Man is distinct from nature — not a unique species within it, but a species separate from it.
2. What makes man separate is his kinship with a higher power (God, rationality, systems of control) that grant him control over the rest of creation.
3. If man ceases to control the rest of nature, he loses his transcendent position and slides back to the position of intermediate beings like women, workers, blacks. . . . or even below them, under *their* control. (p. 304)

Combining and extrapolating from Bateson's and French's views, we can describe the alcoholic's process as paradigmatic for a wider societal process: The alcoholic has bought the notion of power as domination or power-over and sets about trying to control his environment at the cost of an increase in his level of pain. Alcohol or any other addictive substance or behavior gives him temporary pleasure or escape from pain while maintaining the illusion of control. As the addiction develops, higher doses are required to achieve the same effect, and/or his behavior starts to get out of control. If he admits he is out of control, he would be admitting his powerlessness and would therefore see himself as weak, bad, unmasculine, and at the risk of being controlled by others. He therefore has to deny what is happening and continue to defiantly and pridefully try to impose his willpower. In spite of the increase in pain he will continue to try to maintain the illusion of control. Eventually, if the external consequences become too severe or if he can let in the emotional impact of his behavior, his denial may break, and he may come to see that he is indeed powerless, that his life has become unmanageable. Only at this point is there the possibility of a shift back from power as the masculine power-over to power as the feminine power-to. He goes from "I can control my drinking," through "I can*not* drink," to "I *can* not drink."[3]

Inextricably linked to the notion of power is the notion of will. In struggling with an addiction we exhort ourselves or others to use more willpower, and Friedreich Nietzsche made the "will to power" the cornerstone of his philosophy. Much as we have come to see power almost exclusively as control, we have come to see will almost exclusively as a conscious, masculine, instrumental faculty. Leslie Farber (1976) writes that we live in an "'Age of the Disordered Will.' It takes only a glance to see a few of the myriad varieties of willing what cannot be willed that enslave us: we will to sleep, will to read fast, will to have simultaneous orgasm, will to be creative and spontaneous, will to enjoy our old age, and, most urgently, will to will." He directly ties the modern disability of the will to the increasing dependence upon drugs in our society. Drugs "offer the illusion of healing the split between the will and its refractory object. The resulting feeling of wholeness may not be a responsible one, but at least within that wholeness—no matter how willful the drugged state may appear to an outsider—there seems to be, briefly and subjectively, a responsible and vigorous will" (p. 32).[4]

Farber delineates two domains of will that may further clarify our exploration of powerlessness as potentially liberating. He distinguishes between what he calls *technical* or utilitarian will and *existential* will. Technical will refers to exerting mastery or control over objects, focusing on ends, while existential will speaks of an orientation toward possibilities and relationships, an opening to means. I prefer to substitute the words willfulness for technical will and willingness for existential will. While willfulness is conscious, masculine, and instrumental, willingness is unconscious, feminine, and contextual. Some examples: We can willfully go to bed, but it takes a certain willingness to fall asleep. We can willfully congratulate someone or give thanks, but willingness is needed to feel genuine admiration or gratitude. We can willfully go on the wagon, but it requires willingness to achieve lasting sobriety. We can achieve what is useful through willfulness but can only receive what is valuable through willingness.

The process of recovery from addiction is a process of recovering a different, more feminine, sense of power and will. It entails in many respects a kind of figure-ground reversal, from seeing the masculine principle as primary (an I-It mode) to seeing the feminine principle as primary (an I-Thou mode), a shift from willpower as the control of objects to power-of-will as the creation of possibility or context.[5] The transition between these two different ways of functioning or of organizing reality can be profoundly disorienting and even disheartening. There is almost always a gap in which the old mode no longer works, and the new mode is not yet functioning. Here's how Martin Buber (1965) describes that gap: "illumination cannot be accomplished in any other place than in the abyss of I-with-me. . . . it is in its most real moments not even a monologue, much less a real conversation. . . . all speech is exhausted; what takes place here is the mute shudder of self-being" (p. 137). This transitional state to which Buber speaks is what Alcoholics Anonymous refers to in phrases like hitting bottom, coming to see that one is powerless, deflation at depth, and surrendering to a Higher Power. Optimally powerlessness is a way-station between control and empowerment. Table 1 schematically seeks to present the journey I have been discussing.

Emotions play a central role in this transition from masculine willpower to feminine power-of-will. Willpower, technical will, willfulness, power-over tries to exclude, deny, or suppress emotions while power-of-will, existential will, willingness, power-to includes, allows, or embraces them. As one recovers the ability to experience emotions, one also recovers the ability to create possibility (power-of-will) rather than continuing to modify forms (willpower). Emotions are an unfolding process, an Ariadne's thread, that lead one through the maze of confused thinking and impotent willfulness characteristic of addiction.[6]

Table 2, what I have called the Map of Emotional Recovery, seeks to provide more detail on the journey to, through, and beyond powerlessness. In examining it the first distinction that is useful to make is the difference between emotions and moods. Emotions are always felt in spe-

POWER-OVER	POWERLESSNESS	POWER-TO
TECHNICAL WILL, WILLFULNESS	SURRENDER, "TURNING IT OVER"	EXISTENTIAL WILL, WILLINGNESS
WILLPOWER	BANKRUPTCY OF THE WILL	POWER-OF-WILL
I-IT	I-WITH-ME	I-THOU

TABLE 1

The Map of Emotional Recovery

	LOVE	COMPASSION	NEUTRAL	NOTHINGNESS
	JOY	BEAUTIFUL	WITNESS	ALONENESS
SPACES	SERENITY	SADNESS	DISPASSION	NOWHERENESS
	GRATITUDE	AMUSEMENT	CURIOSITY	
	ANGER	HURT	FEAR	POWERLESSNESS
	RAGE	PAIN	TERROR	EMPTINESS
EMOTIONS	FURY	GRIEF	DREAD	DESPAIR
	ENVY	LOSS		FAILURE
				SHAME
	BLAME	SELF-PITY	ANXIETY	CONFUSION
	GUILT	SUFFERING	PANIC	LONELINESS
MOODS	RESENTMENT	VICTIM	WORRY	DESPERATION
	REVENGE	MARTYR	DOUBT	RESIGNATION
				DISGUST, PRIDE

TABLE 2

cific locations in the body while moods are not directly experienced so-
matically, being created and maintained by thought in an attempt to control and numb out the intensity or impact of emotions. Thus, if you create
the feeling of anger, you will feel specific body sensations, often in your
belly, chest, or shoulders while the mood of blame will revolve around
thoughts of being right or justified and have no body sensations.

Another way to understand the difference between emotions and moods
is to observe how a three year old child expresses her feelings. Her emotions are like a swiftly flowing stream, and in the course of a few minutes
she may go from "I hate you," to "I love you," from tears to laughter.
Most grown-ups have been conditioned out of directly experiencing and
expressing their emotions. The stream has become a swamp. Instead of
allowing the flow and unfolding of feelings, they try to control the process
through thought, focusing on whether the emotions are right or wrong,
justified or unjustified. In many respects moods are totally artificial.
Much as plastics are non-biodegradable, moods can be said to be non-
psychodegradable. If you try to express or process worry, or self-pity, or
resentment, they will simply be reinforced and lead to other moods. On
the other hand, if you get directly in touch with the experience of anger, it
will almost immediately start to move, shifting its intensity and body loca-
tion as well as changing to other emotions.[7]

On the map the emotions are arranged from more external or "safe" on the left to more internal or vulnerable on the right. It is less vulnerable to say to someone "I feel angry at you" than "I feel hurt by you."[8] Being recurrently angry at or hurt by someone, staying focused on the external, is in turn usually preferred to encountering the fear and terror associated with shifting attention to the more internal. At one's core are the seemingly intolerable feelings of powerlessness or emptiness, despair, failure, and shame. Thought takes transitory emotions like anger, rage, and envy and converts them to the persistent moods of blame, guilt, and resentment. In the same way it changes the hurt and grief to self-pity and suffering, and switches the fear, terror, and dread to anxiety, worry, and panic. Similarly desperation gives one more of a sense of control than does despair, while chronic resignation feels more manageable than acute failure, and self-disgust or pride seems more tolerable than shame. Thinking will race around and around in a confused way, reinforcing loneliness as a way to avoid the fundamental sense of powerlessness or emptiness.

The transformation from willpower to power-of-will occurs as the powerlessness and emptiness, often manifested through feelings of shame, despair, and failure, is accepted rather than resisted. People describe a shift to a "sense" of nothingness, aloneness, and nowhereness, frequently accompanied by drowsiness, dizziness, and disorientation. They may say, "I don't feel good, and I don't feel bad. I just feel nothing." This state is at first unfamiliar and uncomfortable but is not acutely painful. If people do not reorient themselves with their familiar suffering, resignation, resentment, or anxiety, a "self-healing tautology" (Bateson and Bateson, 1987) starts to unfold. The nothingness becomes no-thingness, the aloneness opens up to all-one-ness, and the sense of nowhereness transmutes to now-here-ness.

Within the nothingness thought becomes quiet, and the next space of neutrality or the witness state emerges, accompanied with a beginning sense of peace and well-being. Having felt their emotions passionately, people notice an interesting dispassion and become curious about the process that is evolving. The dispassion consistently transforms into compassion, manifested either as beautiful sadness, being deeply touched or moved, or as amusement, a good-natured acceptance of oneself. The process then culminates in the awareness of the pervasive presence of love, joy, peace, and gratitude that flowers spontaneously and serves as a backdrop or matrix for one's entire life. AA refers to this presence as a Power greater than ourselves, Higher Power, spirituality, or God. It can equally be called Higher Self, higher consciousness, or the sacred.

In a previous article (Berenson, 1990) I have suggested that spirituality is inherent in the between or relatedness and that Twelve Step programs are uniquely organized to be consistent with this systemic view of spirituality. The relationship may manifest between an individual and a sense of Divine presence, between individuals, between feminine and masculine, or between human beings and Supreme Being. Once one has accessed the between, functioning in an I-Thou mode, one also accesses power-of-will and can effectively respond to situations to which one previously was unable to respond.

BUT HOW VALUABLE AND USEFUL IS THIS JOURNEY FOR WOMEN?

So far this article has only partially addressed the feminist criticisms of Twelve Step programs presented at its beginning. To restate and summarize the objections, some feminists view the recovery movement as incorporating and reinforcing the following characteristics:

1. *An emphasis upon the private and personal at the expense of the public and political* – While the experience of powerlessness may be liberating for some women in some respects, it does nothing to address the very real social, political, and economic power inequalities that exist. Focusing on their private growth may distract many women, and men, from questioning and changing oppressive power arrangements based upon gender.

2. *A denigration and pathologizing of traits associated with femininity* – The very development of terms like codependence and "women who love too much," the labeling of behaviors and relationship patterns as diseases, combined with the focus upon powerlessness as a key component for healing, have all served to increase stigmatization and to reinforce women's social conditioning. Women wind up blaming themselves for personal and relationship problems instead of getting angry and taking assertive action to change their situation.

3. *A tendency toward self-abnegation and the unquestioning acceptance of authority* – While Alcoholics Anonymous and its Twelve Step offshoots give theoretical lip-service to spirituality as non-dogmatic and non-hierarchical, in practice they wind up asking women to be subservient to male authority. The AA Twelve Steps refer to "God *as we understood Him*," and women who are working the steps are called upon to make amends for damage done to them.

To fully respond to these objections, one would need to examine in some depth and at much greater length the interaction of the stated principles of the Twelve Step programs, the variations in their actual practice, the personal characteristics of recovery program participants, and the enclosing social context and mind-set. With both addictive problems and the recovery movement we are currently in much the same position as the blind men and the elephant, taking a part of the overall picture and using it to try to describe the whole. One individual, interacting with a particular sponsor and a specific group, may find the experience of powerlessness and the practice of the Twelve Steps liberating while another person, interacting in the same or different context, may view the entire experience as oppressive and confining.

While a full response to the feminist critique cannot be presented here, the following addresses each of the specific points of criticism:

The preoccupation with the private: The overvaluation of the masculine principle in our culture has polarized and dichotomized attributes that are more accurately seen as complementary when the primacy of the feminine principle is recognized. Thus the mind has become opposed to the body, the spiritual to the material, and the public to the private. People feel called upon to take a position in favor of one side of the dichotomy against the other side instead of looking at how best to integrate the two. The AA Serenity Prayer and the Twelve Steps recognize the need to function both in a private domain and in a public domain, using both willingness and willfulness: "God grant me the Serenity to accept the things I cannot change" speaks to the receptivity required to shift from power-over through powerlessness to power-to. "Courage to change the things I can" addresses the assertiveness required to take decisive action to correct external problems. Similarly AA members working the Twelve Steps distinguish between surrender steps and action steps. The entire thrust of Twelve Step programs is that an inner transformation be expressed in changed external behavior.

A phenomenon I have observed clinically is that when people start taking decisive action to change problems to which they have become chronically resigned, there are strong feelings of emptiness and powerlessness as they give up the self-image that developed as a consequence of family, social, or political oppression. The experiencing of the acute feeling of powerlessness paradoxically often leads to a longer term empowerment and effectiveness in actively correcting power imbalances. Once men and women have seen the primacy of their feminine, accepting side, there is more room for them to express their masculine, assertive side.

The pathologizing of the feminine: The labeling of behaviors as diseases is not intrinsic to the AA program. In fact *Alcoholics Anonymous* does not use the word disease, utilizing the terms allergy and illness in a more metaphorical sense.[9] Over the years the label disease has come into more widespread use, initially as a way to destigmatize problem drinking and to promote responsibility, though the critics of the disease model see it as stigmatizing and promoting irresponsibility. In adopting much of the substance of the AA program other Twelve Step programs have also adopted and expanded the disease concept even though the behaviors that are being dealt with in no way resemble what has conventionally been seen as medical disease. One participant in a recovery program may ignore the disease model, another may use the term as a useful metaphor, and another may actually believe she has a concrete medical condition.

The pathologizing and denigration of the feminine may be more a function of the prevalent social conditioning than a specific product of Twelve Step programs. Until now, the recovery movement has more adequately addressed the self-perceived needs of a large population than have either family systems or feminist theory and practice. So far I have found it more clinically useful to work with clients on removing labels like codependent after they have used them for awhile rather than to try stopping them from labeling themselves in the first place, as a pure systems therapist might.[10] In addition many people who are participating in Twelve Step programs are aware of the difference between the feminine quality of nurturing and its perversion as caretaking, as well as the difference between the masculine quality of assertion and its perversion as domination. The task for both family systems therapy and feminism is to present these distinctions more clearly and explicitly and to provide an alternative way for people to move toward empowerment without feeling the need to first accept a potentially stigmatizing label.

The acceptance of authority: Kasl's criticism of the Twelve Step movement seems quite relevant on this point. AA's initial members were argumentative, self-willed men who needed to accept limitations upon their behavior and then subsequently make amends for the damage they had caused. It does not make sense to ask women who have been overly submissive to follow the exact same steps.

In actual practice women who are working the steps are making some unofficial changes. One woman described to me how she went about making amends by standing up for herself more frequently. Melody Beattie (1990), in *Codependents' Guide to the Twelve Steps*, suggests taking an inventory of character assets, as well as defects, during the Forth Step and making "a list of those who have harmed or wronged us" (p. 120), in addition to a list of "those we have harmed," as part of the Eighth Step. However, she immediately apologizes: "I understand this is a controversial idea and not what the Step says. But I have a plan for the list and some ideas about helpful amends."

In summary the experience of powerlessness can lead to a new sense of empowerment from which gender, social, and political inequities can be more effectively addressed. However, the theoretical understanding of powerlessness and spirituality, their clinical application in therapy, and the actual practices of the Twelve Steps have lagged, in large part due to the overvaluation of the masculine principle. The Twelve Steps, including the initial emphasis upon powerlessness, provide a foundation for an empowering, non-dogmatic, spiritual practice that is supportive of feminist goals, but there is certainly nothing sacred about their form. They will hopefully evolve to suit particular needs and times. Following is my own version of them that seeks to retain their essence, while expressing them in language that may be more appropriate for our time.

A NEW VERSION OF THE TWELVE STEPS

1. We saw that trying to control and manipulate our feelings and relationships only led to a sense of feeling out of control and powerless.

2. Recognized that our willingness to experience anger, hurt, fear, and shame could free us from blame, guilt, and self-pity and open us to help from a Higher Power.

3. Were completely willing to surrender our pain, letting it be transformed into peace and compassion, then into love, joy, and gratitude.

4. Made an honest, searching inventory of our personal principles and character, encountering both our strengths and limitations.

5. Explored with ourselves and, as appropriate, with our Higher Power and another person, the emotional impact, positive and negative, of our actions.

6. Were entirely ready to forgive ourselves and be forgiven and to congratulate ourselves and be congratulated.

7. Asked our Higher Power to help us make lasting changes.

8. Made a list of people who had hurt us and whom we had hurt and became willing to forgive them or make amends to them.

9. Reclaimed our power and accepted responsibility for our lives, standing up for ourselves, letting things be, or making direct amends.

10. Continued to act with self-respect, honoring our emotions and those of others.

11. Sought through meditation and prayer to create our destiny and to be empowered by the will and love of God, Goddess, All That Is in unfolding that destiny.

12. Having had a spiritual awakening from taking these steps, we seek to share this reality with others and to deepen our spiritual awareness in all aspects of life.

NOTES

1. Whitmont (1982) points out that the Eros-Logos polarity has been oversimplified and is inadequate for covering the wide range of feminine and masculine dynamics. Mythologically, Eros or Cupid was a male phallic deity. I have retained the terms here as an introduction to the concept of two complementary, interacting principles. In developing a fuller understanding it would be useful to explore not only the Eros-Logos polarity but also those of Psyche-Eros, psyche-techne, and Eros-Thanatos.

2. Much of Gregory Bateson's work and some of Humberto Maturana's work can be viewed as consistent with Keller's and McClintock's more "feminine" view of science. While Leupnitz has trenchantly criticized Bateson's avoidance of gender issues and history and Maturana's "call to political acquiescence", there are other aspects of their thinking which are compatible with the primacy of the feminine principle, in particular their views on power. Bateson's vehement attacks on the "myth of power" and Maturana's dismissal of instructive interaction move beyond power as power-over or unilateral control.

3. I have referred to the alcoholic as he both because the majority of alcoholics are men and because of my view of alcoholism as paradigmatic of a pathology of masculine thinking. In examining more closely the connection of problem drinking and gender it is interesting to note that David McClelland et al., (1972) and Sharon Wilsnack (1982) found in their research that men drank to feel more powerful and women drank to feel more feminine while Claudia Bepko and Jo-Ann Krestan (1985) observed clinically that drinking allows men and women to access feelings and behavior usually associated with the opposite gender. Niels Bohr's aphorism may be appropriate here: "The opposite of a trivial fact is plainly false. The opposite of a great truth is also true" (New York Times, Oct. 20, 1957).

4. Farber's view has a decided resonance with Bateson's "surrender to alcoholic intoxication provides a partial and subjective shortcut to a more correct state of mind" (Bateson, 1972, p. 309).

5. One might argue that so many pejorative connotations and preconceptions have become attached to the terms masculine and feminine that it is hard to use

them in a fruitful way. If that is so, Buber's distinction between I-It and I-Thou and his discussion of "the between" are useful alternatives and may have the advantage of being more compatible with family systems thinking.

6. In the Greek myth Ariadne, a symbol of feminine archetype or anima, gives Theseus a ball of thread to trail behind him as he enters the maze to kill the Minotaur. He is thus able to find his way out instead of getting lost.

7. Many therapists do not distinguish between moods and emotions, and what has been called the expression of anger may often be the venting of blame and resentment. Carol Tavris (1982) points out that therapy that asks clients to express their anger may serve as a behavioral rehearsal that reinforces the anger.

8. Within our culture women are prone to initially access feelings of hurt and men feelings of anger. This then can devolve into the stereotypes of the overtly self-pitying codependent and the overtly blaming alcoholic. This difference seems to me largely a function of social roles expectations. Until recently men have been given permission to channel all expressions of feeling into temper outbursts while women have been conditioned to express all emotions through tears.

9. Trying to adequately address the disease concept of alcoholism is enough to drive one to drink. The standard recovery-oriented view is that alcoholism is a disease and that spiritual factors are important in treatment. Critics of the recovery movement tend to criticize both the disease model and the spiritual emphasis. However, there are other variations of these positions. For example Jean Kirkpatrick (1987), the founder of Women For Sobriety, argues that if alcoholism is a disease, it should be treated as such, with less emphasis on spirituality. On the other hand a book which presents the Twelve Step programs as *The Answer to Addiction* (Burns, 1990) attacks the abuses of the disease concept and questions the very notion of treatment, stating that spiritual awakening and fellowship are the main elements in recovery.

10. A large part of the unlabelling process entails helping couples get in touch with, own, and release their anger with each other, rather than following the thread of emotion back to an inner sense of powerlessness. The theory behind this approach is that once people learn to be responsible for, and responsive to, their emotions, they can directly transmute the anger, rage, and envy into love, respect, and admiration. In doing this exercise women most frequently need to learn how to stay with their anger instead of automatically moving into their hurt, and men need to learn to feel the anger rather than automatically trying to control it and their spouses through the expression of blame and resentment.

REFERENCES

Bateson, G. (1972). *Steps to an ecology of mind.* New York: Ballantine.
Bateson, G., & Bateson, M. C. (1987). *Angels fear: Towards an epistemology of the sacred.* New York: Macmillan.
Beattie, M. (1990). *Codependents' guide to the twelve steps.* New York: Prentice-Hall/Parkside.
Belenky, M. F., Clinchy, B., Goldberger, N. R., & Tarule, J. M. (1986). *Women's ways of knowing.* New York: Basic Books.

Bepko, C., & Krestan, J.-A. (1985). *The responsibility trap: A blueprint for treating the alcoholic family.* New York: The Free Press.

Berenson, D. (1990). A systemic view of spirituality: God and twelve step programs as resources in family therapy. *Journal of Strategic and Systemic Therapies, 9*(1), 59-70.

Buber, M. (1965). *The knowledge of man.* New York: Harper and Row.

Burns, J. (1990). *The answer to addiction.* New York: Crossroad.

Eisler, R. (1987). *The chalice and the blade.* San Francisco: Harper and Row.

Farber, L. (1976). *Lying, despair, jealousy, envy, sex, suicide, drugs, and the good life.* New York: Basic Books.

French, M. (1985). *Beyond power: On women, men, and morals.* New York: Ballantine Books.

Fuller, B. (1975). *Synergetics.* New York: Macmillan.

Fuller, B. (1979). *Synergetics 2.* New York: Macmillan.

Hare-Mustin, R. C. (1987). The problem of gender in family therapy. *Family Process,* 26, 15-27.

Johnson, S. (1989). *Wildfire: Igniting the she/volution.* Albuquerque, New Mexico: Wildfire Books.

Kasl, C. D. (1990). The twelve-step controversy. *Ms.,* 30-31.

Keller, E. F. (1985). *Reflections on gender and science.* New Haven: Yale University Press.

Kirkpatrick, J. (1987). *Goodbye hangovers, hello life.* New York: Ballantine.

Luepnitz, D. A. (1988). *The family interpreted: Feminist theory in clinical practice.* New York: Basic Books.

McClelland, D. C., Davis, W., Kalin, R., & Wanner, E. (1972). *The drinking man.* New York: Free Press.

Miller, J. B. (1976). *Toward a new psychology of women.* Boston: Beacon.

Robertson, N. (1988). *Getting better: Inside alcoholics anonymous.* New York: William Morrow.

Tavris, C. (1982). *Anger: The misunderstood emotion.* New York: Simon and Schuster.

Walters, M. (1990). The codependent Cinderella who loves too much . . . fights back. *The Family Therapy Networker, 14*(4), 52-57.

Wehr, D. S. (1987). *Jung and feminism: Liberating archetypes.* Boston: Beacon Press.

Whitmont, E. C. (1982). *Return of the goddess.* New York: Crossroad.

Wilsnack, S. (1982). *Alcohol abuse and alcoholism in women.* In E. M. Pattison & E. Kaufman (Eds.), *Encyclopedic handbook of alcoholism.* New York: Gardner Press.

PART TWO:
FEMINIST APPROACHES
TO TRAINING AND TREATMENT
OF THE ADDICTIONS

Chapter Five

Challenging General Patton: A Feminist Stance in Substance Abuse Treatment and Training

Patricia Pasick
Christine White

SUMMARY. Despite the wide acceptance that substance abuse is in part a family and cultural disease, few clinicians are trained to reconcile traditional addiction treatment with systems therapy. This picture seems to hold true for both addiction counselors and family therapists. Substance abuse clinicians, with their focus on an individual's addiction, do not always widen their lens to include the context of systems. Systems therapists do not always narrow their lens sufficiently to focus on substance abuse. An integrated, feminist approach to bridging these differences is discussed, emphasizing a non-hierarchical, respectful, and curious therapist stance which can effectively challenge denial. This paper outlines how this therapist stance can be explored in a training program. Emphasis is on the person of the therapist and on the many systems in which therapists are embedded, such as family of origin. Included is a discussion of systems therapy techniques that help maintain a curious and non-hierarchical therapeutic stance.

Patricia Pasick, PhD, and Christine White, MSW, are each in private practice as clinicians and family therapy trainers. They are affiliated with the Ann Arbor Center for the Family, 2300 Washtenaw Avenue, Suite 203, Ann Arbor, MI 48104. This paper was developed out of a training grant from Southeastern Michigan Substance Abuse Services (SEMSAS).

Brian is a therapist-trainee with nine years of experience in child protection services and substance abuse treatment. In an opening session, trainees described what famous entertainer or actor most captured their "person as a therapist" with substance abusing clients. Brian chose George C. Scott in his role as World War II's General Patton. "Someone who is in charge, protective of his troops, and determined to destroy the enemy," Brian described. At the start of training his mode of treatment for substance abuse was individual counseling. His therapeutic goal with clients was maintenance of sobriety and education about addiction.

There is wide acceptance that substance abuse is in part a family disease requiring a specialized treatment approach (Bepko & Krestan, 1985; Berenson, 1979; Heath, 1990; Steinglass, 1987; Treadway, 1989). Despite this view, few clinicians are trained to integrate the theory and practice bases of both traditional addiction treatment and family therapy. Some family therapists find it difficult to directly address substance abuse. The crisis of the presenting problem, like severe marital conflict or adolescent acting-out, can draw attention to symptoms which may mask an underlying addiction somewhere in the family. At the belief level, many systems therapists operate with a set of assumptions that direct the therapy away from a sharp focus on an individual family member. Some of these beliefs organize the therapist to (a) refrain from identifying "patients"; (b) work toward changing the family, not the identified client; and (c) ask good questions instead of imposing opinions.

Many clinicians from the addiction field organize their behavior within what seems like an opposing framework. The referring context is very different from the one in which family therapists operate. Many substance abuse clinicians see clients referred by courts or in hospitals because they are actively and dangerously abusing substances. The framework for treatment is to challenge denial and promote personal responsibility for recovery. Twelve-step self-help groups, and not therapy, are often seen as the best context for recovery, for both the addicted person and the family. In contrast to family therapists, most substance abuse counselors hold a belief system in which their therapeutic goals are to: (a) address the substance abuse before any other problem; (b) focus on the addicted client; and (c) unravel denial.

At first glance, a marriage of two belief systems which seem to be in such different camps looks formidable. Our view is that a treatment approach to addictions built on a "both-and" model is possible and essential. Such a model adheres *both* to principles from the addiction field *and* integrates systems ideas and techniques. The goals of treatment are to support the addicted client while challenging the chemical use, and to support the family's recovery while challenging the under-and overresponsible behavior of its members. The centerpiece is a therapeutic stance founded in part on feminist ideals, one which is collaborative, respectful, non-hierarchical and appropriately responsible.

The purpose of this paper is to discuss notions of therapeutic stance in addiction treatment through a description of a training project for family therapists and addiction counselors.

THE TRAINING PROJECT

Ideals and Goals

The language of training is inherently hierarchical, judgmental, and controlling. What it means to train in dictionary terms is to "instruct," "make fit," "condition," or "discipline." The words have the ring of military boot camp. Coming to training often activates assumptions that trainers know more than trainees and are better therapists, that trainees' work will be judged deficient, and that the trainers have a treatment model which they think is best and wish to promote. Implicit is the idea that trainees should change. No wonder then that reactivity and anxiety are high as "training" begins for both trainers and trainees.

We sought to develop a training program in substance abuse and family therapy which challenged these usual assumptions and promoted a set of values more associated with a feminist perspective. One idea was to "live" the model. As trainers we sought to mirror a therapeutic stance we hoped clinicians would explore, one in which the therapist is collaborative, respectful, curious, and appropriately responsible. Another value was to guard against imposing our map of therapy with substance abusing clients onto trainee/clinicians who had their own belief systems about their work.

The goal was not just to teach and model. Instead, we took the responsibility to metaphorically "open flows of conversation," to converse about topics which would enable therapists to understand how a variety of contexts influence how they think, react, and behave as therapists. Change was a possible outcome of conversation, not just a goal of training or of the trainers. We also wished to promote a non-judgmental atmosphere for training. In live supervision, for example, instead of implementing supervision, trainers and trainees combined to become a non-hierarchical reflecting team (Andersen, 1987) to the therapist/trainee seeking our opinions about her work. Throughout training we asked trainees to explore three questions:

1. What is your therapeutic stance and how is it most/least helpful to you in substance abuse work;
2. What connections are there between your role in your family of origin and your stance with addicted clients, especially with regard to patterns of substance use and over- and underresponsible behavior?
3. What are the connections between your therapeutic stance and your work system? How could that system influence the work you want to do?

Process and Procedures

Our mandate was to train the staff of an entire state-funded managed care system for substance abuse, from intake workers and clinicians to supervisors and administrators. Seventy-five persons in smaller groups of 7-15 attended half-day workshops for a total of about 20 hours. Some later chose to take part in agency-based case consultation groups for follow-up training. A small group of clinicians received an additional 72 hours and were trained as consultants to provide ongoing support and further training within the managed care system.

Trainees were heterogeneous in background and training. They came with expressly mixed motivations. Like many of their clients referred by the court, most were there because training had been mandated by a managed-care system for anyone receiving state reimbursement for client fees. They worked in public or nonprofit mental health settings, doing primarily outpatient treatment in poor or working-class regions. Referrals came from courts, managed-care, schools, inpatient drug treatment centers, other therapists, or were self-referred. About half of the therapists were trained in the addiction field; the others were social workers from degree programs. A number voluntarily identified themselves as recovering from chemical addiction, codependency, or as adult children of addicted parents.

THERAPIST STANCE IN THE TREATMENT OF ADDICTIONS

Literature Review

The issue of therapist stance has come under much scrutiny in family therapy (Cecchin, 1987; Heath, 1990; Hoffman, 1990; Real, 1990). In the field we are evolving toward a fuller appreciation of the complexities within the therapist-client system. A feminist critique has focused on the problems inherent in adopting a neutral, multipartial stance, one which does not encourage us to address power imbalances in the family (Hare-Mustin, 1987). As Cecchin notes, neutrality for many therapists has been understood to be "one of noninvolvement, of not having strong opinions, and of not taking responsibility when necessary" (1987, p. 405). We add to the critique with the opinion that a so-called neutral stance, as originally described by the Milan group (Selvini-Palazzoli, Boscolo, Cecchin, & Prata, 1980), does not allow sufficiently for the therapist to challenge denial in substance abusing clients.

Recent ideas from constructivist systems therapy (Allen & Laird, 1991; Anderson & Goolishian, 1988; Hoffman, 1990) have relevance for an effective therapist stance in substance abuse treatment. The central premise is that both clients and therapists construct their own realities within a set of stories or premises. Therapy is about exploring families' belief systems and the interactive patterns which follow. Through conversations, the therapist invites clients to become observers of their own reality, to understand patterns of belief and behavior in relation to the perceived problem, and explore alternatives. More simply, therapy is about helping the client or family to change its current way of changing (Allen & Laird, 1990). The goal of treatment is not to interpret and then intervene but, rather, to create a context for change which enables clients to "restory" (White & Epston, 1990) their lives.

The implications of constructivist ideas for therapist stance are numerous. Instead of becoming neutral observers of the family at work, we are "participant observers" (Anderson & Goolishian, 1988) of the therapist-client system. We seek not only to discover with our clients the beliefs and stories that underlie their behavior; additional task is to understand our own beliefs as well, and our own position within the therapeutic system. With those ideas in hand, therapy may become a mutual conversation in which all participants can express their opinions and even disagree. As Real notes, ". . . the therapist need not necessarily agree at all times with all views. He may choose, at times, to share his own. But he is always respectfully engaged with the multiple realities that greet him" (1990, p. 260).

Many ideas about therapist stance which come from systemic therapy are in concert with premises of traditional addiction treatment. For substance abusers, the belief system that has evolved about the effects of the chemical on thinking, feeling, and behaving is an important focus in treatment. Moreover, it is imperative that therapists come to terms with their own beliefs about addiction and loss of control (Bepko & Krestan, 1985; Brown, 1985). For example, the therapist who believes that alcoholics can recover through controlled drinking may block and confuse a client who is moving toward abstinence within Alcoholics Anonymous. Challenging denial is an important part of addiction treatment. Therapists are urged to offer their opinions about the presence of addiction when they see it, provide education, and recommend treatment. At the same time, an effective stance is one of non-judgment, non-responsibility for change, and powerlessness. This is not unlike the stance described by constructivists who argue that therapists cannot bring about change, but only the context for it (Hoffman, 1990). In any event, clients and not therapists must take personal responsibility for their choices (Jenkins, 1990). Certainly treating an addicted client requires being flexible and able to switch roles (Brown, 1985), like the stance of the constructivist therapist who practices being "multiply engaged" (Real, 1990) with clients. Finally, it is important in addiction treatment for therapists to avoid becoming controlling and over-responsible in the therapist-client system, to guard against an "incorrect complementarity" (Bepko & Krestan, 1985) which counterposes an out of control client with an in control therapist. A collaborative stance described in constructivist therapy is highly useful to avoid the one-up, one-down relationship which is often endemic to addiction treatment.

Respect and Challenge:
Ideas for Therapist Stance
in Substance Abuse Treatment

Our treatment approach proposes that it is possible for a client to peel away the layers of denial necessary for sobriety in a therapeutic context that is respectful rather than controlling or power-oriented, collaborative rather than hierarchical, and curious instead of judgmental. Andersen writes, "If the relationship . . . is 'safe' enough, nonintrusive enough, interesting enough, the mutual exchanges that carry new ideas may trigger new modes of relating" (1987, p. 416). At the same time, this change process must include what one of our trainees called "The Art of Keeping the Alcohol Issue on the Table"; a process of challenges by the therapist to denial.

The task of presobriety and early sobriety stages of treatment is to dismantle the denial system of both the addicted person and his/her significant others. Stephanie Brown (1985) states that denial is embedded in a thought disorder that consists of the following: (a) I am not an alcoholic, and (b) I can control my drinking. The challenge of therapy is to help the client shift that belief system to (a) I am an alcoholic, and (b) I can't control my drinking. In the training project we found that for some therapists, challenging denial meant becoming confrontative and hierarchical. For example, "You've admitted that you have a major problem with alcohol, Barb, but you think you can control it without stopping altogether. I think you're fooling yourself. I don't think you can control your drinking. Think about what happened last weekend. You need AA where the message is abstinence." Such a client may have lived in an atmosphere full of abusive, unpredictable, and overcontrolling behavior on the part of adults. To become confrontative with her may trigger her to go to AA, but it also may mean colluding with behavioral patterns from her family of origin, and, ultimately, undermine her move toward abstinence.

Our position is that challenging denial can be done respectfully and collaboratively. A less confrontative statement to Barb is, "I agree with you that drinking is a major problem in your life. I can hear that you want to consider stopping but that you're scared. I wonder if drinking isn't a solution to some memory or problem that you keep hidden away from yourself and others. Right now I'm curious about what kind of support you'll need to get a good sobriety, to adjust to life without self-medication. If we can figure out in these sessions what support you need, then you may be less worried about what will come up for you as you stop drinking." This statement: (a) puts the alcohol issue on the table; (b) speaks to ambivalence about sobriety; (c) brings in affect; (d) introduces the idea of addiction as a protection against experiencing some painful issue currently unacknowledged; and (f) begins to build in the importance of support.

Other examples that contrast confrontative versus challenging statements are as follow:

(Confrontative) I don't like the sound of this at all, Barry. It seems to me that you are deliberately coming up with excuses to avoid going to meetings. Do you really think you can stay sober this way?

(Challenging) I must be honest with you, Barry, and say that I'm worried about you not attending AA. No one I've worked with has ever been able to sustain sobriety just with a weekly therapy appointment. I'm glad you're here and that you've been sober this week, but I'm curious, do you think you're more similar to or more different from other alcoholics in early recovery?

(Confrontative) To a spouse: What I hear is that you are protecting Dick from the fact that his pot use got out of control yesterday. You say that it's been worse before yet you know and I know that that's not the point, Jan. You need to stand up to Dick and let him know that you won't go out with him when he's using.

(Challenging) On one hand, Jan, you are reporting that Dick used a lot of pot yesterday, so I assume that means you are concerned. On the other hand, you seem to be telling yourself that it's been worse so don't worry about it. Lots of people who worry if their spouses are addicted to substances tell me they have lots of inner conversations like these. They care about their spouses and want to support them, but are worried, upset, and angry when drinking or smoking gets to be excessive or regular. I don't know if that's you or not, but I do wonder what difference you think it would make if you were to tell Dick directly when you had feelings about his smoking?

Part of challenging denial is to assert our opinions with clients about addiction and treatment without insisting that they agree with us. It also means having disagreements without getting caught in power and control struggles. For example: "It sounds like you drink more than you plan to almost every weekend. You and I have a disagreement about whether that means you are addicted to alcohol and therefore need to be abstinent. But if you can imagine that sometime in the future you'll be able to consider not drinking, what difference do you think that would have on your weekend, on your ability to relax and enjoy your friends?" This example illustrates a respectful disagreement with a future-oriented question that invites clients to begin to think about how not drinking might influence their lives.

Often addicted clients have had little experience with a parent figure that modeled safe differences of opinions. The therapist has the opportunity to demonstrate that different opinions are an essential part of relationships. The client in the following example had a lot of pride in her ability to control her drinking. She was experiencing difficulty in not buying and drinking a bottle of wine every night after work. She stopped every night after work at the same store: "I'd be driving home and see the store. Before I knew it, I'd have pulled in the parking lot, bought the wine and went home and drank it." If the therapist had told her what she should do she might have done the opposite in order to maintain her pride. Instead, she was asked, "What do you think would happen if you turned left instead of right when you left work?" She was delighted with this question because it had never occurred to her to go in a different direction.

DISCOVERING THERAPIST STANCE
IN TRAINING

Brian was observed in a session with an adult client, Mark, a recovering cocaine addict. The therapy focused on a topic chosen in a previous session, Perfectionism. Brian reiterated parts of the twelve-step philosophy and Mark compliantly nodded. It unfolded that Mark had skipped two of four Narcotics Anonymous meetings the prior week. Mark explained that some scheduling problems around a new job had kept him from his meetings. Brian reacted:

Brian: I'm concerned if you haven't gone to four meetings. I think you agreed on the importance of this, right?

Mark: Oh, sure, you're right. I could have challenged my boss I guess. Maybe I'm asserting my will again, thinking that I don't need all those meetings.

Brian: That's taking that control again . . . That's real dangerous. The Mark I knew six months ago wouldn't have missed those meetings. You need to work on that. Recovery's got to be Number One.

At a break, while meeting with the team behind the mirror, Brian heard from the observing team that clearly he had supported Mark through a difficult recovery. They did experience him as overactive and somewhat scolding, however. It is possible, the team suggested, that Mark doesn't need four weekly meetings given his stable recovery. What might be more central is his struggle with being a perfect client for Brian while still asserting his idea that four meetings are not as necessary as they once were. He might be testing this idea with Brian. Brian was coached to ask about perfectionism and Mark's family of origin, in particular, about his alcoholic brother and father. Moreover, Brian was gently coached to take a more collaborative, less hierarchical position and talk less. Mark responded quickly to this change in stance. He told moving stories about growing up with a sense that he could never please his father. As Brian stayed quiet, Mark raised important issues about the challenge of recovery in the context of his family with whom he lived. It was the first time in nine months that he had talked openly and emotionally about the family. The team wondered if the greatest roadblock to recovery lay not in missed meetings, but in Mark's choice to live with his alcoholic father.

Techniques to Explore Therapist Stance

Our goal as trainers was not to shape trainees into our image, but to invite them to explore their own therapeutic stance with substance-abusing clients, to experiment as a way of learning more about themselves as therapists. We used several techniques:

As-If work. One technique to facilitate self-as-therapist discovery was to ask participants to role-play a stance which runs directly opposite to the stance they usually take with substance abuse clients and exaggerate it. As Schwartz (1988) notes, asking trainees to play "as-if" they are taking a certain stance is often helpful with problems of self-consciousness. Our exercise seemed to free them from responsibility to be good trainees and from rigid stances, ones that developed as a way to defend against feelings generated by difficult clients and issues. As one alcohol counselor remarked, "I decided in this exercise to join very hard with the controlling woman in this family, since I usually don't. I was surprised to find that the reason I usually steer away from these women is because they remind me of my mother. Now that I know that, I can probably let myself engage more with them as people."

Metaphor. We agree with Madanes (1988) that "when teaching must take place at many levels, a teacher must rely on metaphors, symbols, and narratives that will influence the audience directly and indirectly." Another way of helping trainees discover their stance was to ask for metaphors which capture the essence of the therapist-addicted client relationship. We heard an astonishing range of images. The metaphors seemed to differentiate between (a) alcohol counselors who spent their hours seeing high denial, court-referred clients or recently discharged addicts from treatment centers, and (b) mental health therapists who had less training in substance abuse. Some alcohol counselors (like Brian with his General Patton metaphor) had themselves positioned very centrally. They felt like: ". . . a power company and my clients are the customers. I turn on the light for some, the heat for others; . . . a gearshift which controls how smooth and fast my clients get into recovery; . . . a mother bear with unruly cubs, very protective of outside influences." Family therapists seemed to see themselves positioned in somewhat perilous or draining places: a moat built into shifting sand, a soldier walking in a minefield, a trampoline subject to incessant bouncing, a pliable sponge confronting an addicted client who is a large, hard rock.

As training ended, trainees appeared to have invented metaphors which captured a more collaborative, appropriately responsible stance.

I'm the plane pulling a glider, my clients, into the sky. I can control how high we go, but the flying is up to them.

I see my clients sitting in a tall skyscraper and unable to see out because of filmy smudgy windows. I'm the window washer, taking a risk to climb up high on a scaffold. Working outside, I carefully open up their view and, at the same time, protect myself from falling from the scaffolding.

I'm a cab driver and they are passengers in a new city. They know where they want to go, but I point out other choices. Sometimes we both get lost either because they've given me bad directions, or I'm driving in new territory myself.

Family of origin work. In many cases, therapists' fears of unraveling denial are related to family of origin issues. Some come from alcoholic families and are still in denial about the effects drinking has had on their growth. Others fear that raising conversation in therapy sessions about substance use will feel like repeating the behavior of their critical, blaming parent. They worry about bullying their clients into change, like some members of their abusive, controlling family of origin. Moreover, some therapists are active substance abusers themselves and in their own denial about addiction problems. Some addiction counselors in their own early recovery are reluctant to risk being overwhelmed by doing family therapy with their clients. Still others have negative opinions about family therapy which seem related to unresolved cutoffs with dysfunctional families of origin.

Our approach to family of origin work with trainees engaged with us over a short period was to keep it focused and structured, and therapeutic without becoming therapy. Trainees filled out genograms and considered possible interfaces between their own families and their clients. They were asked to especially address family of origin patterns of over-and underresponsibility and attitudes and behaviors related to addiction. In conversation as a group we chose not to ask trainees to share their family stories. Instead, we asked questions like, "Given your family of origin, what kinds of clients do you think you are most/least reactive to as a therapist"? and "Answer this question: I am not the kind of therapist who would (behave how) _____ because then I would be most like _____ (who in your family)?" (Bepko & Krestan, 1985). For many participants, these small slices of family of origin work were powerful emotionally and influential in their thinking about their stance as a therapist. The convergence of family of origin issues from both the therapist and the recovering client is seen clearly with Brian:

Viewing the tape after his session with Mark, Brian was struck with changes in the therapy as he, as therapist, took a less hierarchical and judging stance. His client was able to surface many important family issues related to recovery and to express much of the pain cocaine had kept hidden. The team asked Brian to reflect on his own family of origin for information about his earlier "General Patton" stance with Mark. He drew parallels to a hero role he played within his family of origin. As a child and youth he would often get caught between his parents in an effort to stop their fighting. With Mark he speculated that perhaps he was re-enacting that same story, over-responsibly getting between Mark and cocaine by worrying about missed meetings. In another sense he might be inadvertently playing out the role of Mark's perfectionistic father. The team also speculated that by focusing on addiction jargon, Brian modulated the expression of emotion in the session to levels he was used to from childhood.

Work system interfaces. Therapists are embedded in a work system that makes a difference in how they do therapy. Most of the participants in our training program were treating clients in active denial, who were court-referred and still actively abusing substances. Caseloads were large and overresponsibility was the norm. Some agencies had specific mandates for therapists, for instance, to require that clients attend 90 AA meetings in 90 days as part of outpatient treatment. While some settings were expressly supporting a systems-oriented treatment approach for substance abuse, they were not providing adequate space, evening hours, differential reimbursement for family sessions, and paper work compatible with a systems approach (e.g., only one file for each family). Moreover, supervisors were not necessarily trained and supportive of a family-centered approach.

We sought to co-develop a curriculum with our trainees that addressed this context. A challenge was to generate enthusiasm for a collaborative, non-hierarchical, appropriately responsible and respectful treatment model within a work context which, for some trainees, seemed directly opposite in structure and mandate. We found that once the training directly addressed this larger systems context, trainees became more open learners. They found systemic and constructivist family therapy fresh and useful because it provided a different set of choices.

MAINTAINING THERAPIST STANCE

Our premise is that evolving and maintaining a therapist stance which is respectful and collaborative, yet challenges denial, is central to effective substance abuse treatment. As practitioners, however, we are not always sufficiently prepared for the range of feelings and reactivity that confront us as we face a family and drinker in active denial about a serious addiction problem. As one therapist described, "Working on addictions within a family feels like surfing on a rough sea. One minute, I'm on my board with them beside me. The next moment, a sudden shift pulls me down under." Brown notes that "alcoholism provokes feelings of basic helplessness, powerlessness, and ultimate inability to control that characterize all human beings" (1985, p. 297). We urged therapists to borrow techniques from family therapy as a way to (a) maintain their role as therapist without becoming overwhelmed, overresponsible, or controlling; and (b) challenge denial without becoming confrontative. Some of those techniques are as follows:

Have Conversations in Which You State Your Opinions. We coached trainees to make statements about addiction and recovery in the context of conversations which allow for opinions. As trainees shifted their thinking away from "treatment" and more toward "conversation," they tended to become less overresponsible and more collaborative. For example,

> My opinion, based on experience with clients, is that you may be addicted to alcohol. If you are, my experience tells me that marital therapy will not be successful until the addiction is dealt with.

> As we have conversations about what happens to you when you drink, it seems to me that we have different opinions about how that affects you. We may have different definitions about what problem, drinking looks like. Let's try and make our disagreement clearer in future sessions.

> In answer to your question, I'm not sure what you "should" be doing about your drinking. In my professional experience, people who are concerned about their alcohol use often find an educational series or AA useful sources of information.

Use Circular Questions. Since its introduction to family therapy (Selvini-Palazzoli et al., 1980) the concept of circularity has evolved, partly as a result of the feminist critique which holds that concepts like circular causality mask underlying inequalities in relationships which are abusive or non-egalitarian (Hoffman, 1985). In training we placed emphasis on the circular process of the interview, the idea that answers to questions only give rise to new questions (Anderson & Goolishian, 1988). Part of creating a context for change is introducing the development of multiple perspectives and voices (Cecchin, 1987). Like Treadway (1989), we find circular questions to be very useful in substance abuse treatment (see Fleuridas, Nelson, & Rosenthal, 1986 for a thorough description of the technique). They open the way for the client, along with the therapist, to make connections, draw patterns, and think about differences.

Examples are: "Even though you and I have discovered that I don't agree that you have a serious drinking problem, I'm curious about other people in your family: who would most agree with you that you don't; who would most agree with me that you do?" or "If you chose to stop drinking, what would be most different for you in how you relate to your spouse and children?" or "Who would react most strongly if you decided on inpatient treatment?" Trainees reported that circular questions: (a) allowed them to "step back" from taking too much responsibility; (b) helped fan their reflexes to chide or scold their clients for drinking; and (c) generated lots of useful information for the therapist-client system.

Ask Larger Systems Questions. We also found that substance abuse work benefits enormously from a larger systems focus (Imber-Black, 1988), particularly in relation to the therapist's stance. Especially when feeling overwhelmed or controlling, trainees were encouraged to converse with clients about the systems which interfaced with substance use: typically, work, family, social, religious, ethnic, political, spiritual, biological systems. What difference will continued usage, abstinence, or recovery mean for the ways clients relate within these systems? Where are potential supports for recovery or triggers for relapse? What messages does the client get from each of these systems about drinking? What are the client's beliefs and experiences with helpers?

To illustrate a larger systems view, one group of trainees represented the larger system and formed a ring around a second group. Trainees sitting in the center ring were role-playing a couple or family being interviewed by a trainer. As the conversation proceeded, a second trainer unravelled a ball of string held by the trainer-interviewer. Each interaction in the interview and each reference to someone in the larger system was underscored by a string element. It became visually clear that in interviews which focused narrowly on the client(s), the segments were thick and lent themselves easily to overresponsibility and over-control by the trainer-interviewer. In interviews which circulated questions around the larger system, the picture was of a complex web. In that frame, the therapist became only one inventor, someone who through questions can weave a picture of interrelatedness for clients to ponder and draw upon.

CONCLUSION

The ideas presented in this paper for both training and treatment are meant to contribute to an already rich arena of knowledge in both the family therapy and addiction fields. We are advocating that a feminist-informed stance means giving our opinions and direct feedback as well as asking questions. It means being collaborative as opposed to hierarchical, and being challenging instead of confrontative. As feminists, we also endorse the idea that appropriately responsible support towards abstinence and recovery is important to treatment. Similarly, peer support for therapists treating addictions is essential to maintaining an effective therapeutic stance.

The exploration of therapeutic stance in addiction treatment needs to continue. For instance, when is it appropriate to take a "hard-line" stand and terminate outpatient therapy for a chronic substance abusing client? How can this be accomplished in a respectful way? Moreover, what difference does gender make in a curious yet challenging stance? Are female therapists more likely to be comfortable with this model than males? How do female versus male clients experience a collaborative stance? The conversations around these questions will contribute to an ongoing dialogue about changed ways of being for both clients and therapists.

REFERENCES

Allen, J & Laird, J. (1990). Men and story: Constructing new narratives. *Journal of Feminist Family Therapy. 2*, 75-100.

Andersen, T. (1987). The reflecting team: Dialogue and meta-dialogue in clinical work. *Family Process, 26,* 415-428.

Anderson, H., & Goolishian, H. (1988). Human systems as linguistic systems: Preliminary and evolving ideas about the implications for clinical theory. *Family Process, 27,* 371-393.

Bepko, C., & Krestan, J. (1985). *The responsibility trap: A blueprint for treating the alcoholic family.* New York: Free Press.

Berenson, D. (1979). The therapist's relationship with couples with an alcoholic member. In E. Kaufman & P. Kaufman (Eds.), *The family therapy of drug and alcohol abuse.* New York: Gardner Press.

Brown, S. (1985). *Treating the alcoholic: A developmental model of recovery.* New York: John Wiley & Sons.

Cecchin, G. (1987). Hypothesizing, circularity, and neutrality revisited: An invitation to curiosity. *Family Process, 26,* 405-413.

Fleuridas, C., Nelson, T., & Rosenthal, D. (1986). The evaluation of circular questions: Training family therapists. *Journal of Marital and Family Therapy, 12,* 113-127.

Hare-Mustin, R.T. (1987). The problem of gender in family therapy. *Family Process, 26,* 15-27.

Heath, A. (1990). Stages of family therapy in treating addictions: An integrative model. *Presentation at the 1990 American Family Therapy Conference,* Philadelphia, PA.

Hoffman, L. (1985). Beyond power and control: Toward a "second order" family systems therapy. *Family Systems Medicine, 3*(4), 381-395.

Hoffman, L. (1990). Constructing realities: An art of lenses. *Family Process, 29* (1), 1-11.

Imber-Black, E. (1988). *Families and larger systems.* New York: Guilford Press.

Jenkins, A. (1990). *Invitations to responsibility.* South Australia: Dulwich Centre Publications.

Madanes, C. (1988). Family therapy training—it's entertainment. In H. Liddle, D. Breunlin, & R. Schwartz (Eds.), *Handbook of family therapy training and supervision,* (pp. 379-385). New York: Guilford Press.

Real, T. (1990). The therapeutic use of self in constructionist/systemic therapy. *Family Process, 29,* 255-272.

Schwartz, R.C. (1988). The trainer-trainee relationship in family therapy training. In H. Liddle, D. Breunlin & R. Schwartz (Eds.) *Handbook of Family Therapy Training and Supervision.* New York: Guilford Press.

Selvini-Palazzoli, M., Boscolo, L., Cecchin, G., & Prata, G. (1980). Hypothesizing-circularity-neutrality: Three guidelines for the conductor of the session. *Family Process, 19,* 3-12.

Steinglass, P., Bennett, L., Wolin, S. & Reiss, D. (1987). *The alcoholic family.* New York: Basic Books.

Treadway, D. (1989). *Before it's too late: Working with substance abuse in the family.* New York: W.W. Norton & Company.

White, M. & Epston, D. (1990). *Narrative means to therapeutic ends.* New York: W.W. Norton & Company.

Chapter 6

Are We Keeping Up with Oprah?
A Treatment and Training Model
for Addictions
and Interpersonal Violence

Dusty Miller

SUMMARY. Addiction treatment trauma theory and the connections between female addiction patterns and interpersonal violence are central clinical issues in current practice. This paper argues for the inclusion of these specialized areas in family therapy and other professional training. An account of the author's personal, political and professional route toward an understanding of interpersonal violence culminates in her model of clinical assessment and treatment. This training model integrates family systems and psychodynamic theory as well as advocating the uses of self-help groups.

Addictions and interpersonal violence (physical and sexual abuse) go hand-in-glove. There are several obvious connections: (1) interpersonal violence against women and children is often perpetrated by men who are abusing chemical substances; (2) women substance abusers are especially vulnerable targets for violence and sexual assault; (3) women who are victims of childhood abuse and/or current violence are at high risk for substance abuse.

Dusty Miller, EdD is Director of clinical mentoring in the Clinical Psychology Department at Antioch, New England College. Correspondence may be addressed to her at 24 Franklin Street, Greenfield, MA 01301.

Portions of this article are excerpted from Miller, D. (1990). The trauma of interpersonal violence. *Smith College Studies in Social Work,* 61 (1), 5-26.
Reprinted by permission.

103

Despite the clinical implications of these connections, family therapy training does not adequately address the treatment of addictions and/or interpersonal violence. My intention in this paper is to argue for inclusion of these specialized areas in family therapy and other professional training. To illustrate how this can be operationalized, I will describe how an integrated treatment model, that I have incorporated in training mental health professionals, uses a feminist perspective to join systemic, intrapsychic and peer support models. In advocating for inclusion of addiction treatment and abuse-related trauma theory and intervention, my emphasis is on the non-hierarchical narrative (story-telling) aspects of feminist and systemic treatment. I will suggest how this can optimally occur in various formats and levels of the healing process and be incorporated in professional training.

We are currently experiencing a multitude of "pop psychology" approaches to the trauma of child sexual abuse. We also know that the realities of violence against women and of female substance abuse are problems of epidemic proportions. All of these situations are more frequently addressed by the media, in women's shelters, and in the peer support/recovery movement than in training programs for helping professionals.

For family therapists, children and adult female victims of interpersonal abuse represent an enormous client population. Abuse survivors also appear to be substantially over-represented among helping professionals. It is surprising, therefore, that family therapy training does not yet adequately prepare clinicians to address this growing challenge. The same gap occurs in exposure to addiction-focused recovery models.

There are several locations for training in Family Systems paradigms:

1. the academic realm, including Social Work, Psychology and Psychiatry departments;
2. externship or institute programs where clinicians get one- or two-year part-time additional training;
3. inservice training for agencies, hospitals and private practitioners.

In each of these areas, the assessment and treatment of addictions and Post-Traumatic Stress Disorder related to abuse and violence tend to be minimal.

Both feminist and systemic models of clinical practice have much to contribute in these training domains. Clinically-based graduate programs should include trauma and addiction treatment and theory in the following courses: developmental theory, feminist theory (psychology of women), hypnotherapy, individual psychotherapy, family systems theory, assessment, psychopathology, human diversity, cognitive behavioral theory, and psychopharmacology. Clinical supervision and consultation components of family therapy and other professional training should include clinical training in treating addiction, child and adult abuse, and other relevant trauma. Inservice training may emphasize addiction treatment or victim-perpetrator models of abuse treatment, but rarely is there an integrated feminist and/or family systems approach.

CURRENT CONTEXTUAL INFLUENCES

The traumas experienced by victims of sexual and physical abuse, battering and sexual assault, as well as the suffering of substance abusers, are the traumas surrounding us in everyday life. Simultaneously we are surrounded by a world in transition.

Some of the changes we witness in other countries suggest a global shift towards more self-determination and a turning away from hierarchical power structures. Here in America, women are voicing our demand for self-determination in the right to control our bodies, our health care, our lifestyles. These shifts are paralleled by efforts in many quarters to democratize health and mental health care.

In the domain of mental health, for example, self-determination is evident in people's changing beliefs about "experts." Out there in the world of TV talk shows and 12-step recovery meetings, ordinary people are moving from a "not-knowing" or "one-down" position in regard to problems and are becoming increasingly confident in their own expertise. Clients who once waited patiently for years to gain mind-altering insights from professionals now turn to Oprah and/or to peers in the Recovery Movement where everyone is considered expert.

Institutions are changing separately and collectively, moving towards greater degrees of self-determination for clients. Although there are notable exceptions, we have seen the following trends:

- Both medical personnel and mental health providers now are more likely to invite clients to be actively involved and informed regarding their physical and mental health care. The theories and practice of psychotherapy and psychiatry have been evolving towards a more democratic and interactive process.
- The legal system has changed. Legal Aid offices are more accessible. The disenfranchised, as well as the middle class, are potentially more informed about their legal rights and more frequently militate for these.
- School systems have implemented less hierarchical forms of teach-

ing: open classrooms, more participatory learning methods, satellite programs and educational TV programs that reach out to engage isolated communities.
- Television shows idealize "user-friendly" hospital personnel, police, lawyers, judges — even therapists!

Related to the move towards self-determination, or egalitarian systems of healing, is the belief in self-disclosure. The sharing of one's story with others, in an effort to establish common ground and relationship, is moving millions towards interdependence in the healing process. Certain questions arise in relation to these evolutionary currents:

1. Can family therapy training support the positive aspects of the current move away from experts, especially in regard to peer vs. professional helping systems?
2. Are we integrating the power of peer story-telling with various feminist and family systems paradigms and interventions?
3. Might we ask of ourselves and our students the same openness and trust in sharing painful stories that we expect from our clients?
4. Can we accept that our existing "ways of knowing" as professionals may be only partially useful to survivors of violence and abuse, especially when there is related substance abuse?

Professional Training and "Pop" Psychology

As we look around at the sea of recovery groups, peer support resources, and self-help literature, we may wonder how our skills as professionals are congruent with or even relevant to alternative approaches to violence and abuse. What kind of listening and guidance can we give that goes beyond what is plentiful — and seemingly less costly — out there in the Real World?

I think that we can, as systems thinkers and feminists, offer a theory and language rich in complexity. We have the capability of moving beyond shorthand prescriptions.

For instance, the talk show host tells an abused woman, "You shouldn't feel guilty, it wasn't your fault." The woman smiles appreciatively but subsides into uneasy silence, her internal experience of shame having been invalidated by this oversimplified injunction.*

Not only has her story been silenced, but her emotional experience has

---

*Dr. Jill Harkaway (Center for Family Studies, Cambridge, MA), is the originator of this example.

been distorted. She deserves the kind of listening and re-storying process that we have been trained to offer. She needs to feel safe and understood in her exploration of how shame pervades her experience, how she has perhaps internalized aspects of the abusive parent. She needs language to articulate how complex her feelings are towards her mother who could not or would not protect her, towards siblings or relatives who conspire to maintain secrecy, towards the father, uncle or grandfather who abused her.

We need to look, however, at what we may not be including in our family systems training. There are a variety of theoretical models and clinical competencies pertaining to violence and abuse which are central in expanding family systems training. Feminist theory and trauma theory have both offered challenging reformulations regarding symptom formation (Brickman, 1984; van der Kolk, 1988).

In specific areas of training, such as assessment and psychopathology, we should be offering an alternative understanding of symptoms (and perhaps even diagnoses), framed as the victim's survival mode or adaptation to negative circumstances. Developmental theory should address the impact of trauma in creating primitive ego defenses like denial, projection, splitting, avoidance and the distortion of the abused child's object world.

Cognitive restructuring of distorted beliefs and stress responses to abuse trauma (Jehu, Gazan & Klassen, 1985) should be included in cognitive theory. Grief or loss theory, attachment theory, and family systems theory (Gelinas, 1983; Miller, 1989) are paradigms in which the impact of childhood abuse traumas has, at least partially, been addressed.

Treatment approaches to both past and current abuse require that professionals become better versed in the language of trauma theory. A diagnosis of Post-Traumatic Stress Disorder versus Borderline Personality Disorder versus "member of a dysfunctional system" affects our preferred theoretical orientation theories as well as the techniques and interventions we teach. Similarly, we need to understand more about addictions in terms of individual physiology, as well as factors in the social and interpersonal context.

Whether we use clinically-focused internship and externship supervision, or incorporate this material in more academic training components, we need to expand our training models to include the social, ethnic, gender and sexual orientation issues relevant to these areas.

For example, in the clinical component of our training, we might focus on the problem of how gender affects the way the female victim of abuse responds to the therapist. Supervision of male therapists presents special issues and challenges in working with abuse survivors. This particular issue could be addressed both in clinical training and in academic courses which include the psychology of women and trauma theory.

Similarly, special issues arise when clients affected by abuse and/or addiction are from a different ethnic or class background from the therapist. This is an area to be addressed both in clinical supervision and in courses dealing with diversity.

Family therapy training can also be influenced and enriched by the current changes in the lay person's approach to recovery from abuse. The influence of story-telling and participatory healing (vs. the passive healing of the "identified patient" by the professional "expert") can reinforce for us the importance of focusing on client narrative rather than emphasizing client symptomatology. I see a parallel process of change and mutual influence between the recovery movement, specifically its emphasis on communal or collaborative telling and reworking the personal story, and the current emphasis in systems theory on narrative, or co-constructing the "therapeutic conversation" (Miller, 1990a). In the tradition of village story-telling, we can develop our trainees' capacity to co-construct both individual and family narratives with their clients, once we as teachers and supervisors become comfortable with our own stories and the way they influence authentic connection and conversation in professional life.

From Self-Help to Systemic Discourse

Clearly there is much that we can learn from popular culture self-help trends and from the Recovery Movement, which have provided solace and healing in a sharing context for countless numbers of women. These contexts have offered women places in which to tell their stories and to participate in an active, mutual healing process.

Self-help leaders from the beginning have emphasized the power of the story, of the personal narrative, in healing, rather than an emphasis on "curing" symptoms. Family therapists, too, have developed new interest in narrative and story (Laird, 1989; White & Epston, 1990), so that there is a parallel process of change and mutual influence between the recovery movement with its emphasis on telling and reworking the personal story, and the current emphasis in family systems theory on narrative, or co-constructing the "therapeutic conversation" (Hoffman, 1990; Davidson, Lax, Lussardi, Miller & Ratheau, 1988).

In addition to providing a forum for women coming together to empower each other through storying their lives, there is another important aspect of the recovery movement which is also empowering, namely the spiritual aspect of healing. As clinicians we often feel constrained when we enter the domain of spirituality. The language of spirituality generally has been edited out of our training. Unlike healers in other cultures—the shaman, the medicine woman—we do not usually perceive ourselves as channeling healing from a greater spirit to our client. Many therapists have, however, in recent years developed much greater respect for alternative healing approaches and for the power of belief in promoting change. It has become clear that traditions of spiritual healing have the potential for creating an energy and connection to others which empowers the spirit, the heart, and the mind.

Another aspect of the "recovery" phenomenon recently has come under increasing scrutiny, namely the widespread practice of labelling women, in particular, as "codependent" (Kaminer, 1990; Krestan & Bepko, 1990; Lerner, 1990). My own questions include:

1. Is the concept of *codependency* incompatible with women's ways of being connected, of being "selves-in-relationship?"
2. How can we, as therapists, support the client's recovery without colluding in stigmatizing that connectedness, interdependence, or mutuality?

In the following letter to the editor of the *Women's Review of Books,* the writer expresses concerns relevant to us as feminists and psychotherapists:

> . . . It is a sad truth that women have to declare themselves sick and in recovery these days in order to find community with other women. Instead of consciousness raising groups, assertiveness training classes, or feminist political action organizations, women looking for company have to go to Adult Children of Alcoholics or one of the myriad groups focused on illness and so-called addictions. This is most unfortunate because it diverts individual women from constructive, empowering activity, and dissipates the strength of the women's movement.
>
> . . . I'm not judgmental about this phenomenon; I understand it. . . . The trend towards talking things over in groups may, in fact, have better results for women than the isolating one-on-one therapy that has been so popular in the recent past. . . . I had a devastating addiction to alcohol for 20 years and got sober in AA. What enabled me to stop drinking was not the Steps but the other people I met in AA who had gone through the same difficult withdrawal from alcohol as I. AA is free of charge, available every day of the week, and a place to go when the urge to drink strikes. . . . Other people who had been through the same painful process gave me the help I needed. I was aware that the Steps didn't speak to me as a woman and a femi-

nist, but I was told to use what I wanted and leave the rest. . . . Let us hope those women now in groups focused on sickness will soon be able to move on and direct their energy into positive, freeing efforts to get rid of patriarchy and its oppressive institutions. (Singer, 1990, pp. 10-11)

While we need to encourage our clients to use the supports and empowerment potential recovery groups can offer, as well as to question some of the risks, it is clear that we, as professionals, have theory and language, rich in complexity, that allow us to move beyond the limitations of popular culture and self-help. This is particularly the case in working with survivors of family violence and child abuse, where we have an important role to play in how the problem and treatment are conceptualized.

As therapists, we must move beyond simplistic criminal justice language through which we divide people up into "victims" and "perpetrators." As we know, language determines behavior. The language of systemic thinking allows us to conceptualize and respond to the complex and often paradoxical elements of interpersonal violence. For example, one Western Massachusetts family therapy team, People's Bridge Action in Athol, has devised a new symbol for the genogram. To designate sexual abuse, a line is drawn between the abuser and the child. Superimposed on the line is a heart with a jagged line through it—a broken heart. The implication is that both the abuser and the child share, at some level, the pain of a violated relationship.

As therapists, we need to reach across the boundaries of our sometimes constricted medical-model training, our safety shield of DSM-III diagnostic distancing. We must find ways to connect our forms of healing with the spiritual dimensions of healing recognized by the lay public, from the Higher Power invoked by 12-step believers to the Goddess or shamanic healing associated with New Age crystal practitioners. There are more ways of knowing than our professional paradigms encompass. The vision offered by those who are spiritually affiliated may bridge the language gap between the linear notion of cause and effect and the more systemic view of connectedness and paradox.

If we are groping for language to express the pain and loyalty of the abuse victim's story, we are almost mute when it comes to the language of those who commit violence. Part of the problem is that we are angry, frightened, and judgmental towards those who inflict violence on children or on women. We don't *want* to listen to the story of the "perpetrator." We prefer to view him as "criminal." We relegate him to behavior modification. He is viewed as someone who will contain his behavior only through the use of deterrents, be they educational, behavioral, legal or social.

The situation is obviously more confusing for us if the "perpetrator" of sexual or physical abuse is a woman. When she has a history of childhood abuse, we view her as a victim as well as a perpetrator of violence. But can we tolerate the use of that "double description" when it is a man who both abuses and was abused?

My strong feeling is that we have to hear the full depth and complexity of the abuser's story, whether we are listening to a man or a woman. Otherwise we silence the "wounded child within" once again, just as he or she was silenced in childhood. It is in this silencing that we replicate old family behaviors and then misinterpret client responses as pathologic.

The following is an excerpt from a remarkable book called *The Bone People*, written by a New Zealander (Hulme, 1984). Keri Hulme tells the story of a Maori child, his father, and a woman who became involved in their agonizing relationship. It is a unique and overwhelming story, told from the perspective of each member of the triangle. The boy, Simon, is probably seven or eight. He is an abandoned child taken in by the father, Joe, and Joe's wife, who later dies. Joe is an overwhelmed single parent, bereaved, tortured by his situation. The boy Simon is deeply intelligent but because of past and current abuse is trapped in the silence of elective mutism. We get to know this strange and fascinating pair through the eyes of the woman who befriends them, as well as through their own narratives.

Joe often beats his son when he has been drinking. Later he is overcome with remorse. Here is an excerpt from his story:

> . . . The air is sweet, but his lungs hurt as he takes in great gulps of air. There is no other sound than the persistent ringing chorus of treefrogs. No lights.
> No questions.
> No more cries.
> O, what did you do that for?
> You must be sick, man. He says it aloud, experimenting with a statement of guilty excuse.
> I must be sick, but who can I tell?
> And abruptly his noisy breathing changes to sobbing.
> A grown man down on his knees beneath the cool moon, crying out the pain in his heart and the guilt in his hands, with no one to hear him anymore.

("Except me now," whispers Joe. "Nearly two years later, I can hear me cry . . .")

It left a gap. It made a wound, for all the child's reacceptance of him. He'd gone back inside and cared for the boy as best he could, all apologies and endearments and tender loving care . . . and curiously Simon hadn't reacted with his earlier extreme fear at being held or thwarted in anything. It was almost as though he had been expecting it for a long time, and was now dully relieved that the worst had happened. The odd marks, the man remembers, the marks which had puzzled the people at the hospital . . . maybe even before . . . but he looked at me without resentment or fear, just looking. Observed me without communicating. He seemed to understand that time, how close I was to the breaking point . . . but now? He must think it's just me taking all my woes out on him. That's not what it is, but he gets punished so often he probably doesn't believe I'm belting him just for wrongdoing. Or does he think he's that wicked? Good for nothing else?

. . . Joe shudders.

At the moment he'd rather cut his throat than hurt his son, but he knows from broken past resolutions, that come the morning if the child is sulky or rude or balks at doing what he's told, he'll welt him with a cold and righteous intent. You've been bad, Simon, and you're sure as hell going to learn . . . do I hate him then? But how can you hate someone and not know it? I love him. I just get wild with him every so often. Like I told him, it doesn't even seem like him I'm hitting. His disobedience or something, I don't know. (p. 173)

The complex languages of systemic *and* intrapsychic theories can enable abusers as well as victims to tell their stories. Violence committed against partners and children is multidimensional. Sexual assault, battering and child abuse are all behaviors both criminal *and* relational. Interpersonal violence is both an external *and* an internalized relational pattern.

The story of violation, shame, rage, and broken hearts, then, must be told on several levels. The context for this storytelling must provide for the safe and gradual emergence of these different levels in ways that do not retraumatize clients.

TELLING THE STORY

The telling of the story of personal victimization and/or substance abuse may begin with a therapist or in a hospital, in a classroom or in a peer support group. It may follow a distressing film, play, or dream which evokes threads of memory recounted to a friend. In focusing here on the importance of story-telling as basic to treating violence, abuse, and addiction, I have chosen to use the personal narrative approach, integrating the development of my professional perspective and treatment model as constructed within the context of my individual story.

My developing clinical perspective derives from social action paradigms as well as from personal experience, psychotherapy and intellectual insights.

Both my own history as a victim of child abuse and my training as a therapist have expanded my understanding. I know, affectively and cognitively, that problems of interpersonal violence are extremely complex, reflecting a systemic interplay of loyalty, love, anger, lust, and betrayal.

I was very much affected in my early adult years by the Civil Rights Movement, the Peace Movement, and the Women's Movement. The themes of self-determination and self-disclosure shaped my thinking both personally and professionally.

My social action experiences in these various political movements helped me to experience the power of both individual and collective story-telling in the struggle for group self-determination and in individual growth and healing. The Women's Liberation Movement had an especially powerful influence in my personal and professional life. Gender issues were suggested by feminists to be at the root of domination. Language changed to emphasize connectedness rather than conflict.

I began scrutinizing my own experience as a girl and as a woman. I joined thousands of other women in the task of re-storying our lives, reinterpreting ourselves in a more positive and self-affirming way. I was telling my own story, experiencing my own voice as it joined with voices of other women, some of them black, some white, some poor, some privileged. We were learning together that we had to change our lives from the inside out. The telling of our individual stories and the hearing of each other's stories drew us together and strengthened us to commit to the lifetime work of gender-centered self-determination.

As a feminist, I was likely to think about problems of interpersonal violence in terms of *power and hierarchy*. That is, I viewed interpersonal violence as a problem of domination: adults believing in their right to exert ownership and control over children, men believing in their right to exert power over women, mental health professionals believing in their right to exert control over disenfranchised clients.

As the honeymoon phase of feminist activism ended, I began approaching the issue of gender oppression more intellectually. I worked in a Yale-based research project on women and global economics. I went back to school and got a Master's Degree in Women's Studies. By the late 70s I was seeking more mainstream professional credentials. I was also very much affected by my own journey through the silences and pain of childhood abuse. Psychotherapy and the support of peers and mentors greatly bolstered me in deconstructing my own story so as to find a voice of my own. I went back to school in the late 70s and completed a Doctoral program in Counseling Psychology at the University of Massachusetts.

I developed a professional interest in the problems of addiction and interpersonal violence. I was concerned with the effects of child abuse on adult survivors and their relational network. I was specifically interested in how related patterns of substance abuse involved the larger professional helping system in relation to such families.

I combined my graduate training in counseling psychology with my personal and political concerns. I was especially influenced by my concentration in family systems theory and practice. Systemic theory attracted me because of its conceptualizations of ideas, situations, and relationships from a "both/and" perspective vs. an "either/or" one. For example, the adult who had lived through the trauma of child abuse could be seen both as a "victim" and as a "survivor"; if she or he had also abused a child, the conceptualization could include the identity of "abuser" while also holding the equally useful identities of victim and survivor. This "both/and" paradigm made it possible to integrate several different treatment paradigms when approaching the complexity presented by the traumas of child abuse, incest, and woman-battering.

My experience as client has been as vital to my process as my training as a professional, as central as my political affiliations. Over the past twenty years I have had several therapy experiences. Each was distinctly different in theoretical orientation, yet each relationship moved me along through my healing journey, helping me tell my story in all its levels of complexity.

I am currently teaching Doctoral students in the Professional Psychology program at Antioch/New England, as well as Social Work students at Smith College and Counseling Psychology students at University of Massachusetts. In my work as teacher, supervisor, agency consultant, therapist, and writer, I have many daily opportunities to listen to and reflect on other peoples' stories of personal, family, and institutional abuse.

I have also reflected on my own story. For me, healing the wounds of child abuse has taken several forms. I experience healing in my present professional empowerment, bearing witness to the development of women's and children's voices, bearing witness to "re-storying." I have experienced steadily increasing connection between the voices of my personal, political, and professional lives.

WORKING WITH VIOLENCE AND ABUSE IN THERAPY

Following my ideas about the need for storytelling, the need for a healing which incorporates spiritual dimensions and more self-determination or shared "expertise," I now continue my own story by telling you how I work with interpersonal violence.

My career as a therapist and teacher has positioned me in the midst of some of the most painful problems in family life, including violence, incest, and addiction. I have had to learn to shift among multiple levels of the micro family system, the macro larger systems, and the wider social context.

The model I am about to describe emerged from my collaboration with several different colleagues: Jill Harkaway from the Center for Family Studies in Cambridge, Massachusetts; my work with my colleagues at the Brattleboro Family Institute, Mardie Ratheau and Judy Davidson; and discussions with Carolyn Dillon of the Boston University School of Social Work. Other influences of primary importance have been two therapists who have participated in my personal journey, Denise Gelinas from Northampton, Massachusetts and Judith Jordan, one of the five women who have developed the Stone Center's "self-in-relation" theory of women's development.

Gelinas (1983), in her benchmark article in the incest literature, "The Persisting Negative Effects of Incest," emphasizes the centrality of family loyalty in the experience of incest. My training with Evan Imber-Black provided the frame of the larger system context which shapes a part of this model. Collaborations with the Brattleboro group and with Lynn Hoffman guided my development of circularity and reflection in beginning the therapeutic conversation with those involved in family violence.

Jill Harkaway and I have shared a clinical interest in the treatment of eating disorders and substance abuse and the effect of these problems on our female clients. We recognized certain common patterns among these clients, and began to develop treatment approaches which helped us avoid the "stuck helper-client" relationships experienced so often in these women's past therapies.

A THREE-STAGE TREATMENT MODEL

The model Jill Harkaway and I use in working with self-abusive behavior is conceptually identical with the model I use in work with systemic violence. It integrates both levels, the systemic and the intrapsychic, and moves sequentially through three major stages, the Outer, Middle, and Inner "Circles" of conversation. Moving from the outer, or systemic, circle, the therapist gathers information about family rules, myths, beliefs, and sequences which provide information necessary to construct a new, more trust-based relationship with the client.

In the middle circle, the problematic behaviors are addressed directly. The clients are helped to connect with relevant peer support resources, like Twelve-Step recovery groups and other professional systems such as hospitals, legal systems, or school personnel. Then, within the inner, or intrapsychic, circle, the therapist can work with the client on reconfiguring the internalized schema. The use of sequential circles also allows the client time to observe the therapist and engage at her own pace. Each stage of treatment is described in greater detail in the following pages.

The Outer Circle of Therapy

In this stage sessions may or may not include significant others, but the process and the schema constructed are always systemic. The sessions essentially follow the format of the circular interview consistent with the ideas of the Milan team (MacKinnon, L., Miller, D., 1987). The therapist is not just obtaining history, she is attempting to elicit a picture of the context of beliefs, behaviors, relationships, events, and feelings in which the client has lived and which have been internalized. The therapist explores, in particular, family myths about power, violence, loyalty, anger, boundaries, and secrecy. Here the emphasis is on the patterns of communication and secret-keeping, not on the content of the secrets themselves. Together we are beginning to create a new "story," but the emphasis is still on cognition, not affect. In other words, we are helping the client to think differently about the story, but we are avoiding too early uncovering of the emotional traumas of the past.

Another major goal within the outer circle is the creation of a new model of connectedness. The therapist assumes the position of a naturalist, approaching slowly and allowing herself to be observed by the client over time. A nonintrusive, nonjudgmental context is established, whereby the client is allowed to experience her own story without the imposition of the therapist. Boundaries are established and asserted for the well-being of both client and therapist. The therapist is clear about her own limits and boundaries.

The issues we talk about in the outer circle are quite purposely not the issues of abuse.

Guidelines for work in the "outer circle" include:

1. The format for the conversation can include the client and others who are part of her life or are connected to the problem she has brought to therapy. The therapist may also wish to include a team of colleagues.
2. The problems discussed should be expanded beyond the abusive behavior to include other life problems of significance to the client.
3. The questions purposely avoid the problems of abuse, even if the client has addressed the abuse or self-abuse directly herself. This is because the therapist is allowing some space and time to occur in which the client can be observing the therapist and making some internal decisions about whether it really feels safe to discuss abuse. The therapist also is learning the client's story as it pertains to the issue of retaining control of secrets to the experience of shame and fear. The therapist is learning how close other people can come to this client without overwhelming her and taking control away from her.
4. Premises about power, control, and age or gender privilege are explored.
5. The use of secrecy as a form of protection is of special interest for conversations held in the outer circle.

The Middle Circle of Therapy

As the empathic relationship deepens between therapist and client, the time comes to approach the silence (or the untold story). More direct questions about abuse and self-abuse are asked. Such questions are less invasive if they take the form of wondering what it would mean to the client to ask about self-abusive behavior. For example, the therapist might wonder aloud, "Who would be most relieved if I were to ask Carol questions about violence in her family?"

Other questions might include:

- Would it be easier for Carol to talk about the problem of drinking or cutting herself?
- Would she think it would be easier for her partner to listen to a conversation about drinking or about cutting herself?
- Would she prefer such a conversation to take place with her partner present or absent?
- If there were secrets about Carol being hurt in some way when she was a child, would it be easier or harder to talk about those secrets in her partner's presence?

In the Middle Circle, self-help groups, 12-step programs, and other formal or informal support systems are used. This expands the therapeutic system to incorporate others, develops positive connections, makes the therapy relationship less isolated, and helps the therapist avoid overresponsibility and burnout.

The Middle Circle is where I also incorporate the spiritual possibilities of transcending the trauma of interpersonal violence. Here, too, it is important for the client to make the connection to others who have suffered and survived various experiences of interpersonal violence.

The Inner Circle of Therapy

Despite careful preparation for both therapist and client about what it will mean to tell secrets of both self-abusive behavior and of being abused as a child, it is still a large and threatening step to take. In stepping into the Inner Circle, I have been very influenced by the work of Gelinas (1983) and of Judith Jordan (1984; 1986; 1987).

Gelinas emphasizes the importance of family loyalties and family resources when working with survivors of incest or physical abuse. Even when the client has decided to give up control of the secret, she is generally tormented by the feelings of guilt engendered by being disloyal to the family.

Jordan and her self-in-relation colleagues (e.g., Surrey, 1984) provide a model which offers the deepest level of empathic connection, or mutuality, between client and therapist. In the self-in-relation model connections are made between the client's shame and the therapist's shame, the client's pain and the therapist's capacity to experience and hold that pain. When the client triumphs over the fear or silence, the therapist's pleasure is almost inseparable from that of the client.

To arrive at the Inner Circle, it is vital to move slowly, deepening the empathic relationship which anchors and empowers the client. It is here that the work which connects and reconstructs the client's experience of separation and individuation within her place in the family is done. It is in the Inner Circle that the client comes to understand abuse and self-abuse as forms of connectedness played out in current relational contexts.

This part of the storytelling in the presence of an accepting other moves beyond the ventilation or validation of recovery groups, into a reframing of the meaning of past and current behaviors. The therapist deconstructs the old abuse story by unpacking confusing meanings which have clustered around it over the years. It is here that the "both/and" paradigm of constructivist thinking (Hoffman, 1990) allows us to help clients move beyond linear "victim-perpetrator" thinking and towards a realization that interpersonal violence has been experienced both as an abuse of power and as an ongoing form of relational connectedness. It is here, too, that much work is done to deconstruct personal feelings of shame, and defenses such as avoidance and isolation of affect which in childhood aided survival but now may get in the way of connectedness.

This work must be done very carefully. Central to it is the integrity of both client and therapist. The work takes time, for as Adrienne Rich muses:

> . . . Truthfulness . . . is not something which springs ablaze of itself; it has to be created between people . . . Truthfulness anywhere means a heightened complexity. But it is a movement into evolution. The politics worth having, the relationship worth having, demand that we delve still deeper. (1979, p. 193)

This last stage of treatment is best done in individual therapy. Individual therapy facilitates trust-building so that new forms of connectedness can be developed. Despite my systemic persuasion, when I am working in this sacred and sometimes frightening place, I am drawing on traditional clinical concepts such as transference and countertransference to guide me.

In order to allow the full, three-dimensional picture of the client's past and present relationships to emerge, I begin by once again exploring the kinds of questions I asked in the earlier stages of therapy. This time the questions pertain to the meaning of telling shameful and painful secrets in the present—that is, telling these secrets especially to me. I refer to the information I have about the client and her family (past and present), reviewing the rules about secrets being shared outside the family.

As I refer to these rules and premises, I am reminding the client that I understand what it may mean for her to reveal parts of herself to me. Just as I have done in earlier stages of the journey towards this Inner Circle, I am careful to remind her of the resources she brings with her. I may, for instance, encourage her to talk about both the ways her father hurt/abused her and *the ways he might also be a positive figure in her life.* (Perhaps he was a tender, loving father in other ways; perhaps he made her strong and capable of great endurance; perhaps she inherited his sense of humor.)

I also encourage conversations about her mother's gifts, her ways of caring, as well as her incapacity to protect. I may spend considerable time helping the client to tell her mother's story when it is, like her own, the story of mother-as-victim: the mother may also have been abused in child-hood or overwhelmed with family responsibilities.

An important part of the Inner Circle work is my conceptualization of the "tripartite selfsystem." The theory is triadic. The child's internalized self-other relational system includes three essential schemes oscillating between concept of self and concept of other:

- the victim, an image reinforced constantly in experience
- the internalized abuser
- the nonprotecting parent or bystander.

This tripartite selfsystem manifests in the adult client as an ambivalent, rapidly oscillating, often unconscious set of relational beliefs and patterns frequently enacted in abusive relationships and self-abusive behaviors. I believe these behaviors really express three-part internal conversations be-tween the split self-schemas. For example, a woman who is drinking and drugging might experience this conversation between her internalizations:

1. "I need a drink." (voice of abuser)
2. "I don't want to drink. It hurts me. It's bad for me." (voice of victim)
3. "I have to drink. I don't care if it hurts me." (abuser)
4. "I wish I could stop myself from drinking, but I can't. It's too strong for me." (voice of nonprotecting parent or bystander)

Treatment involves helping the client to make conscious, and clearly identify, these separate voices or parts of the self, both in relation to the current abusive or self-injurious patterns and to the historical dynamics being re-enacted. Having learned to separate and externalize these voices, she is then able to develop her own protective presence in place of the nonprotecting bystander, to eventually feel in control of the internalized abuser and, with that, the self-abusive behavior.

The work with self-abusive behaviors goes far beyond the behaviors themselves. Focusing only on the behaviors can leave clients feeling si-lenced, similar to the ways they have been in the family. Evaluation of outcome is based on more global manifestations: the management of healthier relationships, the development of a bounded self, the ability to defend against abuse and neglect and, eventually, the ability to eliminate self-abusive behaviors.

The same theory of the tripartite selfsystem can apply to patterns of abusive relationships as well. The tendency to move towards abusive patterns and the feelings of powerlessness to stop the abuse dynamics stem from the same internalized or introjected presence of the abuser and the same absence of an internalized soothing and protecting presence.

Because the self-abusing client has so deeply internalized the cycle of abuse enacted in childhood, she perceives herself now to be the abuser *and* the abused in her self-abusive rituals and/or relationships. She may feel a desperate degree of self-loathing generated by her anger at the abusive parent. She may also be furious at the part of herself which is re-enacting the nonprotective parent or bystander. The need to remind her of her mother's strengths (vs. her deficits) is vital in helping her begin to trust and respect her own attempts to protect herself. Lending of the therapist's strength, concern, and soothing at this point is critically important in providing new positive sources for introjection to alter the balance in the internal conversation.

Transference and countertransference issues become very important in the Inner Circle of work. As I become a guide for the client in her reliving and reshaping a history of abuse and self-abuse, I can readily succumb to the temptation to rescue, to become the client's "good mother." I may also be tempted to be the "avenging angel," the judge who finds her parents guilty of abuse and neglect. The client may also begin imagining me as the good mother, the savior, or the avenging angel, or as one of the tripartite introjects. She may see me as judging her as well as her parents for being abusive. She may see me as becoming the dangerous parent who will use and abuse her; she may try to finagle me into oppressing her in some way or accuse me of nonprotection when I elect not to act in some particular way she wants me to. She is in danger of re-experiencing the pain of being unprotected if she starts to believe that I have magic powers as the good mother/protector.

There are several ways to work with these potential problems. I use guided imagery, although I never suggest that the client close her eyes or induce a deep trance while she is in my office. This technique is powerful and often too frightening, or may be sexually stimulating for a client who has been abused by a parental figure. I make suggestions about benign "guide" figures who will help us both do the work. It is safer to suggest that "guide" figures take the form of a child or animal, since suggesting a "Big Person" as guide might remind the client of either dangerous or ineffectual parental figures.

Because there may be quiet resistance to the use of other resources beyond the one-to-one therapy, I remind the client periodically of the usefulness of self-help groups where she can connect with others who can also take this journey with her. They can provide lifelines at the many moments in a week when I am obviously not available. I make it a rule to talk about other significant and helpful current relationships, especially at the end of a session. I try to diminish the possibility of my being too powerful or parental by opening and closing sessions with references to minor daily occurrences which make us more equal as "mere mortals."

The ending stages of work may involve members of the client's current support system (current family, supportive members of family-of-origin, friends) and also in some cases face-to-face meetings with the abusive and/or nonprotecting parents. The goal at this stage is to work through past unresolved relationships, to confront the past abuse, and to build connections to current members of the client's ongoing life. It is at this point that other therapists may be introduced to aid in the conversations of confrontation or of healing. This is also a helpful way to move the therapist back from center stage and to encourage the client to continue to move beyond this central relationship.

I have said nothing yet about the use of medication and the recent developments in trauma theory. Responses to the traumas of violence and abuse occur not only in the client's emotional and cognitive systems, but also in the basic biological and neuro-hormonal systems. Bessel van der Kolk (1988) and others who specialize in research and treatment of the psycho-biological level of post-traumatic stress, have noted that restimulating the old trauma wounds can activate extreme physiological responses, even when the current stimuli appear to be quite minor.

The client with Post-Traumatic Stress Disorder may have a complete absence of reaction (constricted emotional response) or an extreme over-reaction. Prevalent symptoms include sleep disorders, anxiety symptoms, self-medication with alcohol and drugs, and chronic passivity, alternating with uncontrolled violence or rage, flashbacks, nightmares, and intrusive disturbing thoughts.

Medications including benzodiazepines, tricyclic antidepressants, MAO inhibitors, Lithium, antipsychotic agents and beta blockers have all been found useful in helping alleviate the troubling symptoms associated with P.T.S.D. I am an advocate of the timely use of medication; it can be very helpful in allowing the client to live a more manageable life, to sleep at night, to endure the terrors of uncovered traumatic memory. But—medication does not resolve the underlying problems. It does not take the place of connection with others, nor does it take the place of the storytelling. It does not substitute for the building of healing relationships or the development of daily life pleasures and competencies.

I worry that we will rush off to find yet another "quick fix" or solution to the problems of interpersonal violence. Ingesting something to feel better is very much part of our societal lifestyle. For the sake of our clients and ourselves, we need to resist the temptation to try a medical short-circuiting of the pain and complexity of violence and abuse.

ENDING THE STORY

This story would not be complete without connecting my present ways of approaching violence with my historical and present learning experiences.

My own experience of child abuse compelled me to develop a complex and often paradoxical understanding of human mysteries. This was also the experience that propelled me towards others who struggled for self-determination. I learned the power of storytelling for survival, the power of collective action to achieve individual freedom, and the power of spiritual knowledge. I learned these things from the Civil Rights Movement, the Peace Movement, the Women's Movement. I have experienced the healing power of love from my teachers, friends, colleagues, therapists, and perhaps most of all, from my clients and students.

I celebrate in these loved ones what Keri Hulme did in *The Bone People*.

> They were nothing more than people, by themselves. Even paired, any pairing, they would have been nothing more than people by themselves. But all together, they have become the heart and muscles and mind of something perilous and new, something strange and growing and great. Together, all together, they are the instruments of change. (p. 4)

Implications for a Model of Training

How does this treatment model challenge the "traditional" training offered in family systems and other therapy models? One obvious change is the inclusion of peer support models as a viable adjunct to individual psychodynamic and family systems therapies. Another implication is to integrate systemic theory and intervention (circular questioning, the therapeutic stance, the involvement of family members) with various forms of intrapsychic theory and practice. Perhaps the most important overarching theme is the focus on narrative, the co-constructed story which serves to uncover, to review and relive, to unpack meaning, to create connection with others, to invoke empathic attunement.

Feminist therapy and systemic therapy share a central interest in narrative and story-telling as primary intervention. Conversation is co-constructed and serves to manifest the intersubjective empathic connection. This emphasis on story-telling is also central to peer support and the recovery movement format. In all three of these paradigms, non-hierarchical relationships are favored: everyone contributes to the construction of the healing narrative.

We may not be completely comfortable with the simplifications offered in "Twelve-Step" problem formulations and interventions, but we need to work with what we can accept and value in this form of collective story-telling and spiritual empowerment.

We are surrounded by women supporting other women in responding to violence and abuse. Whether it is in battered women's shelters, in incest survivor groups or on Oprah, women are formulating the problems of violence and abuse in terms we must reckon with. Power dynamics are juxtaposed in a complex analysis which goes beyond intrapsychic pathology or allegedly neutral systemic formulations.

Training will change in each of these areas if professionals and students recognize the serious gaps in what is now offered. The feminist family therapy training program of the future should include the following:

1. Assessment and treatment of addictions, including familiarity with the traditional Twelve-Step recovery model as well as with the feminist criticisms and revisions of same.
2. Exposure to current approaches to Post Traumatic Stress Disorder, especially those approaches focusing on P.T.S.D.-related to interpersonal abuse and violence inflicted on children, adult survivors of such, and violence against women (battering, rape and other terrorist activities). Training should include both individual and systemic assessment of P.T.S.D., including diagnoses of psychobiological effects, common symptoms associated with P.T.S.D., relationship problems, repressed or occluded memory, flashbacks, etc.

   This training component should also include treatment approaches to P.T.S.D., including hypnotherapy, bibliotherapy, psychopharmacology, group therapy, individual therapy (both long-term and brief).

3. Learning to work with narrative-centered treatment approaches, including systemic models like the Reflecting Team (Davidson et al., 1988: Hoffman, 1990) and the 12-step recovery program.
4. Integrating valuable intrapsychic or psychodynamic concepts, such as "self-in-relation" theory (Jordon, 1984, 1986, 1987; Surrey, 1984) with systemic (or couples and family) therapy.

My hope is that we will begin to formally address these possibilities as we revise our training programs to include both critical analysis of and collaboration with major influences in the public domain. I think we will find our students to be willing colleagues in this process; many of them can, in fact, be our teachers.

REFERENCES

Brickman, J. (1984). Feminist, nonsexist, and traditional models of therapy: Implications for working with incest. *Women and Therapy, 3*, 49-67.

Davidson, J., Lax, W., Lussardi, D., Miller, D., & Ratheau, M. (1988). The reflecting team. *Family Therapy Networker,* (Sept./Oct.), 44-46, 76-77.

Gelinas, D. (1983). The persisting negative effects of incest. *Psychiatry, 46,* 312-332.

Hoffman, L. (1990). Constructing realities: An art of lenses. *Family Process, 29,* 1-12.

Hulme, K. (1984). *The bone people.* New York: Viking Penguin.

Jehu, D., Gazan, M., and Klassen, C. (Eds.) (1985). Common therapeutic targets among women who were sexually abused in childhood. In *Feminist Perspectives on Social Work and Human Sexuality,* New York: The Haworth Press, Inc.

Jordan, J. (1984). *Empathy and self boundaries.* Working paper, Wellesley College, Stone Center for Women, Wellesley, MA.

Jordan, J. (1986). *The meaning of mutuality.* Working paper, Wellesley College, Stone Center for Women, Wellesley, MA.

Jordon, J. (1987). *Clarity in connection: Empathic knowing, desire, and sexuality.* Working paper, Wellesley College, Stone Center for Women, Wellesley, MA.

Kaminer, W. (1990). Chances are you are codependent too. *New York Times Book Review,* February 11.

Krestan, J., & Bepko, C. (1990). Codependency: The social reconstruction of female experience. *Smith College Studies in Social Work, 60,* 216-232.

Laird, J. (1989). Women and Stories: Restorying women's self-constructions. In M. McGoldrick, C. Anderson, & F. Walsh (Eds.), *Women in families: A framework for family therapy.* New York: W.W. Norton.

Lerner, H.G. (1990). Problems for profit. *Women's Review of Books, 7,* 15.

MacKinnon, L. and Miller, D. (1987). The new epistemology and the Milan approach: Feminist and sociopolitical considerations. *Journal of Marriage and Family Therapy, 13,* 2.

Miller, D. (1990). Women in pain: Substance abuse/self-medication. In M. Mirkin (Ed.), *Social and political contexts of family therapy.* Boston: Allyn and Bacon.

Rich, A. (1979). *On lies, secrets, and silence.* New York: W.W. Norton.

Singer, A. (1990). Letter to the editor. *Women's Review of Books,* 7(10/11), 10-11.

Surrey, J. (1984). *Self-in-relation: A women's theory of development.* Working paper, Wellesley College, Stone Center for Women, Wellesley, MA.

van der Kolk, B. (1988). The trauma spectrum: The interaction of biological and social events in the genesis of the trauma response. *Journal of Traumatic Stress, 1,* 273-290.

White, M., & Epston, D. (1990). *Narrative means to therapeutic ends.* New York: W.W. Norton.

Chapter Seven

Treating Women Drug Abusers Who Were Victims of Childhood Sexual Abuse

Mary Jo Barrett
Terry S. Trepper

SUMMARY. Clinicians are becoming increasingly aware that many if not most drug dependent women were also childhood victims of incestuous abuse. This fact requires substance abuse therapists and those specializing in the treatment of adult incest survivors to understand more fully the interaction between incest and drug abuse. This chapter explores the development of incest using the vulnerability to incest framework, and proposes a treatment program based on the Multiple Systems Model. A case study exemplifying the program and some specific interventions are also offered.

One of the most consistent findings in the child abuse literature is that children who experience childhood sexual abuse, particularly with a parental figure, are more likely than non-abused children to experience emotional problems in adulthood (Rew, 1989). A number of very recent studies highlight this phenomenon. For example, among hospitalized inpatient women, those who were sexually abused[1] were more likely to experience suicidal ideation, self-mutilation, borderline personality disorder, serious sexual problems, more frequent hospitalizations, and more anti-social per-

Mary Jo Barrett, MSW, is Executive Director of Midwest Family Resources, Inc. Correspondence may be addressed to her at 320 North Michigan Ave., Suite 1801, Chicago, IL 60601. Terry S. Trepper, PhD, is Professor of Psychology and Director of the Family Studies Center, Purdue University Calumet, Hammond, IN 46323.

127

sonality disorder than inpatient women who were not abused (Briere and Zaidi, 1989; Shearer, Peters, Quaytman, and Ogden, 1990). Among out-patients, significantly elevated MMPI profiles were found for women who were incestuously abused (Scott and Stone, 1986). And even when women who are not in therapy (i.e., from a non-clinical population) are sampled, they consistently show more psychosocial problems, such as marital disorders, sexual dysfunctions, lower self-esteem, distorted body images, and poorer social relationships than non-abused women (Finkelhor, Hotaling, Lewis, and Smith, 1989; Jackson et al., 1990).

One specific problem found far more often in adult women who were incestuously abused as children is that they are more likely to abuse sub-stances (including alcohol) than are non-abused women (Kaufman, 1985). Clinicians working in the field of substance abuse have also become aware that large numbers of their drug dependent women clients were also inces-tuously abused as children. Why this is being noticed more now than before is open for speculation. Perhaps it is that clinicians, along with our society as a whole, are more sensitized to the possibility of sexual abuse, and thus ask their clients if it has occurred. Perhaps the clients themselves, because of increased media exposure, are more willing to admit (or re-member) that incestuous abuse happened to them. In any event, this in-creased awareness of the possibility of incest in their clients' past makes for increased responsibilities for drug abuse counselors and other thera-pists, but also opens up important treatment opportunities, especially for cases previously considered "therapy failures" (Root, 1989).

Given the apparent inter-connectedness between incestuous abuse in childhood and adult drug dependence, it is important that clinicians work-ing with either population understand the origins of both, and how they relate to and amplify one another. The purpose of this paper is to provide a model for recognizing how vulnerabilities to and experiences of being incestuously abused can interrelate with the development of drug depen-dency. We will then describe a treatment model for women[2] "survivors" of incest who are also drug dependent. Finally, we will present a case study which illustrates the treatment program and some specific interven-tions.

WHY DO INCEST SURVIVORS
ABUSE SUBSTANCES?

While people abuse substances for many reasons, there seem to be un-derlying factors that make women who were incestuously abused as chil-dren more likely to become drug users and then drug dependent as adults.

It has been found that many, if not most, girls experience their incestuous abuse as traumatic at the time (Russell, 1986), and that most deal with the overwhelming anxiety, guilt, fear, and anger associated with this trauma in ways that may be "functional" within their family systems but maladaptive in the long run (Herman, Russell, and Tracki, 1986). Incest is a social/political problem that serves to keep children, particularly female children, powerless. Females tend to blame themselves for the perpetration and their families and society often concur. Male children on the other hand often do not acknowledge the abuse but rather view it as just the beginning of many sexual experiences even though it is at the hands of an older caretaker. Consequently, females feel victimized and powerless while the male translates the experience into one in which he has power.

Many abused girls develop personality and behavioral patterns that make them prime candidates to become substance abusers, including low self-esteem (Rew, 1989; Hart, Mader, Griffith, and DeMendonca, 1989); self-derogation, self-destructiveness, and self-mutilation (Dembo et al., 1989); and psychological and interpersonal dissociation from the incestuous events and from those people closest to them (Hartman and Burgess, 1986).

How do these patterns lead to substance use and then abuse in adulthood? Most adolescents experiment with alcohol and many with marijuana. What usually mediates against this experimentation turning into abuse is a personal sense of self-protection and good family relations (Kandel, Treiman, Faust, and Single, 1976), both of which are lacking for the incestuously abused girl. In the incestuous family, children's voices are not heard, generational boundaries are not well defined, and parents use children to meet almost all of their needs. The girl may increase her drug use to increase her self-esteem and reduce feelings of isolation by being a member of a peer group which supports such activities without requiring the interpersonal closeness that often represents potential abuse to the child (Singer, Petchers, and Hussey, 1989). After a while, though, the drugs themselves may become negatively reinforcing, by helping her to avoid negative internal states and painful memories (Root, 1989). Further, drug use in adulthood may be part of a progression in the coping mechanisms of sexually abused children, encouraging them to seek out the dissociation-causing effects of drugs in a way similar to those in which they psychologically dissociated when they were children (Singer, Petchers, and Hussey, 1989). Finally, in the more extreme cases, adults who were incest victims as children may have such powerful self-destructive leanings that they abuse substances not for relief but for personal punishment (Briere and Zaidi, 1989) and perhaps even to toy with death (Stanton and Todd, 1982).

From the view of the adult woman who was incestuously abused as a child, then, substance use and abuse certainly does serve important functions. However, the woman's solution to her problem may now have become the problem (Watzlawick, Weakland, and Fisch, 1974). That is, her substance abuse, which originally served the function of reducing the pain caused by the incestuous abuse, may now cause as much or more trouble for her than the problem it supposedly "solved." Of course, that is because drug use was never an adequate "solution" in the first place. In any event, the therapist should keep in mind that, for women incestuously abused as children, drugs serve a powerful function beyond those usually attributed to them for non-incestuously-abused drug-dependent individuals. To forget this (e.g., to encourage complete abstinence immediately) will certainly lead to early relapse and ultimate treatment failures (Root, 1989).

TREATMENT CONSIDERATIONS

Vulnerability to Incest

Although it is easiest to explain the origins of incest within a perpetrator-victim framework — that is, a disturbed, sick, deviant, etc., father[3] perpetrates incestuous acts upon an uninvolved victim daughter — we feel that a more comprehensive model must be used if an accurate understanding is desired. The Multiple Systems Model (Trepper and Barrett, 1986) attempts to integrate the more salient features of the perpetrator-victim, family systems, and ecosystemic explanations of incest.

This model explains incest as resulting from the interaction among various external, family, and internal systems rather than focusing only on one. Accordingly, there is no one cause of incestuous abuse. Instead, all families are endowed with a degree of vulnerability based on socio-environmental, family, individual, and family-of-origin factors, which may be expressed as incest if a precipitating event occurs and the family's coping skills are inadequate. This does not supplant the fact that the ultimate responsibility for the abuse rests with the offender who after all, is the older of the two and is responsible for the well-being of his children. It merely recognizes that responsibility is not cause, and that to fully understand the cause of incest, so that we may effectively intervene, we must accept that complex interactions among various systems make a family more or less vulnerable to the development of incest (Trepper and Barrett,

1986). Therefore in our assessment and treatment of incest we examine and treat all the above-mentioned variables.

For example, we would explore with a woman how she views her role in the world as a woman, her view of how her offender and non-offending caretakers deemed her powerless. We'd explore with her how she sees violence in intimate relationships and how this reality was created. We attempt to incorporate an understanding of the ways society views women and children as powerless and the ways a patriarchical society contributes to the abuse and the woman's sense of self (Brickman, 1984). We examine the client's parents' family history of abuse or other dysfunctional patterns, and we explore the individual dynamics of both victims and perpetrators, i.e., sense of self, behavioral patterns. In all these systems we also search for strengths and try to examine attempted solutions.

When working with families with ongoing incest, the treatment model derived from the Multiple Systems Model dictates that the various factors contributing to the family's vulnerability to incest be evaluated and then be lessened, along with reducing the likelihood of precipitating events, and increasing the family's coping skills. When working with an adult survivor, the vulnerability factors present within her family-of-origin at the time of the abuse are assessed by the therapist and client together so that she has a clear understanding of those factors. Then specific interventions, to be described in the next section, are offered within the Multiple Systems framework.

Overview of the Treatment Program

Our therapy, although individually developed for each woman, does follow the general program for treating ongoing incest (Barrett, Sykes, and Byrnes, 1986; Trepper and Barrett, 1986). We attempt through our treatment to empower women to stop blaming themselves for past abuse and to stop all aspects of any future abuse. Our model helps them define their own learned position of powerlessness and then to break free of this position and regain power in their own lives (Barrett et al., 1990). Since the purpose of this article is to discuss treating drug-dependent women who were incestuously abused, our focus here is primarily on that part of the program that deals with the substance abuse. It should be kept in mind that the majority of our interventions do not deal specifically with drugs, and that many other interventions are offered which are designed to increase a woman's functioning in all aspects of her life.

Our treatment is conceptualized in three stages. Stage I, "Creating a Context for Change," is the stage during which a cooperative client-therapist allegiance is established, where a positive frame for change is offered, and the initial resistances to therapy are dealt with. It is also during Stage I where dysfunctional patterns, both internal and interpersonal, are identified. Stage II, "Challenging Behaviors and Expanding Alternatives," is the stage where those identified dysfunctional behavioral and interpersonal patterns are interrupted through a variety of interventions. Stage III, "Consolidation," is the stage during which, through a series of interventions, the client integrates the changes she has made during Stage II within her own personality and style.

Our interventions are designed based on a multiple systems perspective. Consequently, during all three stages, sessions would include individual meetings, sessions with her partner (if she has one), sessions with children, and possibly sessions with her family-of-origin. We even have therapy sessions with extended-family members and friends when they can provide information or reinforce a particular dysfunctional sequence-breaking intervention. We also are fortunate to have enough women in our program to have ongoing groups for adult women survivors, and most of our clients attend these.

Most of our women are in therapy at least one year, and many for as long as two years. And while the authors' therapeutic preferences lean toward briefer models of therapy, we are cognizant that drug-dependent women who were incestuously abused as children can rarely make significant changes in their dysfunctional patterns of behavior in less than one year.

Stage I: Creating a Context for Change

Denial of abuse of alcohol

Once we have assessed the client's use of alcohol or drugs and have determined with the client that it is of a problematic nature, we attempt to work on both abuses conjointly. Over the years, we have very successfully integrated the addiction model into our work and use both inpatient treatment and Twelve-Step programs consistently. Sobriety is not a condition of treatment. We hope to avoid the power struggle that would be created by a hierarchical demand. Such a requirement could represent a repetition of the abusive relationship experienced by the client, i.e., someone in a position of authority, professing that they care, demanding something of the client much too close to their childhood trauma. In Stage I we help clients to explore the self-abusive nature of their use of alcohol/substances and to understand how this maintains them in the victim role.

Denial of the sexual abuse

Although the therapist might suspect that the substance-abusing client had been incestuously abused as a child, the client may not have fully accepted, remembered, or openly disclosed it at the beginning of therapy. One of the first "interventions" at the beginning of treatment is for the therapist to create a context where the abuse can be disclosed. First and foremost, the therapist must display caring, compassion, unconditional positive regard, and empathy. The therapist during the initial assessment should also directly say something like:

> In my experience, many women who have problems similar to yours had sexual relations when they were children, usually forced or co-erced, with an adult, and usually a family member. This might not make any sense to you now, but if over time you have a memory or feel safer telling me about any scary sexual experience, I want you to know that it is pretty common with women.

The client may not disclose experiences at this time, but the subject is now in the open. The main concern from then on is for the therapist to maintain an atmosphere of safety and protection so that, when she is ready, the client will feel safe to disclose.

It is imperative that the therapist remember that denial of abuse is protective for the incest survivor. Denying the abuse — whether it is denial of the actual facts, denial of the awareness of the episodes, denial that the responsibility lies with the caretaker/offender or denial of the impact the abuse had on her — helps a woman deal with the overwhelming intensity of the abuse and a deep sense of shame. To expect her to shed this protection immediately to a relative stranger is unrealistic. Instead, the therapist should think of the disclosure and acceptance of the abuse as a Stage I goal.

Identification of the sequence of dysfunctional feelings and behaviors

Once a woman has disclosed her past sexual abuse, the next step in Stage I therapy is for her to understand the dysfunctional sequences contributing to her drug or alcohol dependency. The pattern that we have identified is: (a) she has some problem in her current relationships with her partner or family; (b) this problem stimulates primitive feelings that she experienced during the time of her sexual abuse such as feelings of powerlessness, anger, and a need to dissociate or escape into fantasy; (c) she then uses a drug or alcohol as a way to alleviate those feelings; (d) this use of drugs then may exacerbate problems in her relationships to recursively begin the process all over again.

To help the client identify this sequence, we usually ask a number of questions, such as: "What happens with the two of you that makes you feel out of control? What does he do that makes you feel safe, not safe, or feel at risk? What happens in your relationship that makes you feel most powerless?" To get a more complete picture, the converse should also be asked; for example, "What does he do to make you feel the most safe or the most powerful?" Finally, we ask, "When you feel powerless, afraid, angry, etc., what do you do?" We, of course, encourage the client to look at the ways that her use of drugs may increase her feelings of power and control, and help her dissociate from those painful feelings dragged up from the past during the dysfunctional sequence.

Another way to help the client identify the sequence is to assign the keeping of a journal. Every time she uses a drug or takes a drink, she is to write it down, along with all of the events and the feelings that occurred before and after. We go over the journal in session, again with the goal of her developing an insight into the circularity of the dysfunctional sequences.

Negative consequences of change

Once the client accepts the premise that her drug use may, at least partially, serve some psychological and interactional purposes related to her prior incestuous abuse, we then ask her to tell us all of the reasons she should not give up drugs. This intervention has three purposes. First, it highlights the fact that change will be difficult, and that her therapist understands and accepts that. Second, it focuses on the potential stumbling blocks before they occur, so that both the therapist and client are alert to them. Third, it offers the paradoxical message that therapy should go slowly; that is, change may cause her to suffer as much as doing the drugs. For example, she may then suffer more painful memories about her incestuous abuse when her husband tries to have sex with her while she is straight. Usually the client argues with the therapist that, in spite of these negative consequences of change, she really wants to stop abusing drugs and that she wants to do so as soon as she can.

Stage II: Challenging Behaviors and Expanding Alternatives

The major goal of Stage II is for the client, who has clearly identified the cycle of drug use as being based in feelings of victimization, powerlessness, and an inability to protect herself in her relationships, to develop strategies to disrupt that cycle. The therapist's job is to offer ways for her to succeed in this. We use a combination of individual and couple sessions to help each person understand how each of them might contribute to a problematic relationship. Many couples enter therapy with the world view that the sexual abuse survivor is the problem and the spouse is the powerful helper or healer. Having each spouse attend in her or his own individual sessions begins to redistribute this power differential more equally. The spouse or significant other of the survivor is forced to observe her or his own family-of-origin and problematic behaviors. Both members are redefined as clients. Family sessions are offered where the client is encouraged to protect herself emotionally while still being a strong and assertive spouse and parent. Also, we may have family-of-origin sessions where the client is helped to confront old patterns of interaction and replace those patterns with functional behavior. The family-of-origin work may be accomplished through tasks assigned to the client or the client may be encouraged to bring various members of her family into session in order to possibly confirm her realities, or to practice changed styles of interactions. If her own sexual abuse has not been confronted, she *may* prepare at great length and then be encouraged to confront various members of her family about the abuse.

Stage III: Consolidation

When the woman is able to identify the point at which her feelings of victimization and powerlessness emerged, then disrupt internal and interpersonal sequences that would lead to her using drugs, Stage II is complete and she is conceptually in Stage III. During this stage, the client assumes more and more responsibility for her own therapy, for example, by designing her own assignments. Sessions are reduced and ultimately check-up or booster sessions alone are scheduled. A final session is offered with structured exercises intended to help the client experience the difference between the way she feels in the present, as compared with her feelings when she abused drugs; i.e., these feelings should include being more in control of her life, feeling less victimized, or feeling more powerful, for instance.

CASE EXAMPLE

To demonstrate the clinical use of the primary treatment themes we have discussed—protection, power, and control—let us consider the following case example:

The family was referred by the school for family therapy treatment. The fifteen-year-old son, Tim, was engaging in delinquent behavior in school and in the community, and the thirteen-year-old daughter, Sue, was acting out at home. The ten-year-old daughter, Leigh, was symptom free. The mother, Lynn, was divorced from the children's father, Skip. Skip saw the children frequently but on an irregular basis, as he traveled and was out of town much of the time.

The school social worker reported that Lynn was cooperative about treatment for her son and daughter but was apprehensive about any treatment for herself, either individually or in family therapy. The school felt that the mother abused alcohol, and during times that she was drunk became extreme in her discipline of the children.

The therapist was able to get Lynn in for a session alone ostensibly to discuss the family problems. The therapist effectively joined with her, and she agreed to periodic sessions alone with the therapist as part of a family therapy program. Lynn admitted that in fact she had been struggling with alcoholism throughout her first marriage, even though she had long periods of sobriety. She occasionally went to AA meetings. Lynn stated that her binges were extreme and destructive to both her and her children. She was quite concerned about the harm she was doing to herself and to the children. The therapist and Lynn decided that therapy would consist of both individual sessions and family sessions. They also agreed that, besides dealing with her children's problem behaviors, an important goal was to help Lynn stop drinking and get control of her life.

One of the "workable realities" that we create with our clients is to demonstrate how the abuse of alcohol is part of a cycle of victimization that they learned as children. Very early on in Stage I we began to explore this pattern with Lynn.

Therapist: Lynn, you keep telling me that you are worried about hurting yourself and the children.

Lynn: Yes, I am frantic sometimes. I just seem to go into a trance, I don't know, I can't explain it.

Therapist: You know, I have heard similar words from other women I work with. I'd venture a guess that you are no stranger to victimization and hurtfulness?

Lynn: It shows, huh?

Therapist: I guess it is my job to look for hints. I know we don't know each other very well. Maybe we can talk about it without *really* talking about it until you feel safer with me.

Lynn: I am not sure I feel safe anywhere.

Therapist: Ever?

Lynn: Oh maybe, when I have put a few (drinks) back.

Therapist: Many of your relationships in your life have been hurtful?

Lynn: We can start with my parents, move on to my brothers, then of course my husband, and now it looks like my kids are going to join in on the kicks.

A few sessions were spent gathering information about her being victimized by her parents and her husband. As she talked more and more about the violence she experienced, she admitted that she was feeling an increased urge to drink. The therapist and Lynn identified the interactional sequence between self-abusive behaviors and experiences of victimization.

Lynn: It just seems like I don't know how *not* to get myself hurt or to not hurt myself. It just seems that that is all that ever happens to me.

Therapist: Your father sexually abused you for a long time and you don't remember most of it. You told your mother and she just told you to stay away from him, that he had to have sex to feel good about himself. Your brother attempted to have sex with you, and your ex-husband physically abused you. Lynn, tell me, through all of this, when could you have learned to like yourself and to protect yourself? I can think of a lot of other things you would have learned by being in that world.

Lynn: That is what is so confusing. I don't know what I learned. I've spent most of life trying not to remember and now you tell me that it's good to talk about it, and that it's because I'm getting stronger that the memories are coming back to me. Why should I want to get stronger if it means remembering more terrible things? How is this better than drinking to forget? How is this going to help with my kids?

Therapist: I thought you might be feeling this way. It is always difficult for me during this part, because I know someday it will feel better and yet it feels so terrible now. What do you think you did learn from being hurt at such a young age? What messages do you think a kid would get from all that?

Lynn: I learned that no matter what I did or said it was always going to happen to me anyway.

Therapist: That you were powerless?

Lynn: Over everything. There's never been anything I felt I could control. I just watched the world happen around me. Sometimes I could pretend that all those terrible things weren't happening to me, but I always knew something was wrong with me. I must have done something to make the world so bad. It didn't seem to happen to other girls like it did to me.

Therapist: So that little girl knew that she could not stop the abuse, felt like she was doing something to cause it, and no matter how hard she tried to pretend it all wasn't happening, somehow she knew it was. So instead of developing Lynn you were developing _____?

Lynn: One big *loser*.

Therapist: When you see that little girl, is that what you'd call her, a loser?

Lynn: No, when I think of her, me, growing up, I think of a little girl that was victimized, very sad, in a lot of pain, who has to do anything to pretend to be normal.

Therapist: One thing I know is that we all have our little girl/victim inside of us and we naturally try to protect her. The strange thing is, that some of the ways we protect her end up hurting her and others.

Lynn: Like drinking, is that what you are getting at?

Therapist: Yeah, like drinking, but that is only one way of protecting yourself. There are a lot of others. After listening to my clients, I figured out that there are four basic areas that we can use to protect ourselves, sort of like the four basic food groups.

Lynn: Well, I know I use alcohol and if I am not drinking it is sugar.

Therapist: You got two of them. Alcohol or drugs, food, sex, and money. Four sure ways to fill up that empty hole, or pretend the world is okay, or get enough power to attempt to fight back.

Lynn: So if I give that all up, what is left?

Therapist: Over time that is what we will figure out together.

During the family sessions the therapy concentrated on helping Lynn regain control over the kids without being abusive. Like many women who have been abused she was unclear about age-appropriate behavior of children. She was never permitted to follow a normal developmental process; she was treated both like ages five and forty-five her whole life. The therapist continued to work with Lynn during Stage I to help her clearly identify in both the past and present, times when she was victimized. Like many people who have been abused, she was able to dissociate from the abusive experiences.

Lynn: I talked to my brother today and it only took four minutes until I felt completely annihilated by him. He started telling me how I am raising my kids all the wrong way. I knew he'd been talking to my mother. All I had to do was hear the change in his voice and I felt it taking over.

Therapist: Felt what taking over?

Lynn: Like what I write in my journal. I hear his voice and his words, I feel shitty about myself, just like I did when I was younger. Like when he tried to have sex with me. I couldn't decide if he was right and I was wrong, and why me . . . and should I because he loves me and all those confusing thoughts. I was completely overwhelmed. And then I started thinking about vodka. Then I thought, "No I can't let him do this to me."

Therapist: Which is what you thought as a kid. "No I can't let him do this to me." That's great you didn't let him make you drink.

Lynn: No, but then I thought about food and that made me so anxious, I hung up the phone and immediately went to the refrigerator. One of the kids came in and I felt caught in the act, like it was something dirty.

Therapist: Again, like a kid, you always felt like everyone must know that you're doing something dirty.

Lynn: Yeah, and I lost it on her.

Therapist: Hitting?

Lynn: No, but saying some pretty vicious things.

Therapist: So you know the cycle and you're getting really good at identifying when you feel victimized. I know the interaction with your daughter felt terrible, but I am extremely impressed with how you are slowing down the sequence and are able to identify it so clearly. It was only about a month ago that you didn't have a clue.

The therapist and Lynn then drew a picture of the cycle (Figure 1) so that Lynn can have an image of the internal sequence.

Therapist: You know, Lynn, this doesn't happen to you every day with every interaction. Many, many times something happens to you and you don't end up abusing yourself or abusing others. We need to track that, too.

During Stage II, Lynn continued to identify the problem sequence and became proficient at recognizing the ways she protected herself by abusing herself. She slowly mastered other means of care and protection with the result that she felt more empowered and more self-confident. During the following family session the therapist attempted to interactionalize the pattern.

Lynn: You don't seem to understand, Sue always tries to do anything she can to get at me. It's just one constant battle.

Therapist: Has it always been that way?

Tim: Between them, yeah, they're always at it.

Lynn: She uses her father against me. She steals from me, she swears at me. It's getting better with the other two kids, but every time I see a slight improvement with her it's only a matter of days before it reverts back.

Therapist: You feel like Sue has the control?

Lynn: She has all the control.

Therapist: Do you feel like a victim? Is it like Sue abuses you?

Lynn: She used to abuse me. Now she just hurts me. I walk away from her a lot now.

Therapist: And pretend she doesn't exist.

Lynn: I see what you're getting at.

Therapist: Let's see if we can explain it to Sue because I think the same thing is happening to her and that is why you two get into it. Sue, your mom has gone through a lot, as we all know, and what she's figured out is that when she feels like someone is going to hurt her she tries to protect herself.

FIGURE 1

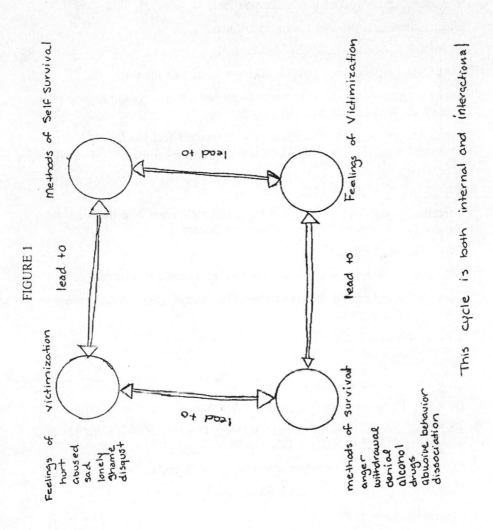

Methods of Self Survival

Feelings of Victimization

lead to

lead to

lead to

lead to

Feelings of Victimization
hurt
abused
sad
lonely
shame
disgust

methods of Survival
anger
withdrawal
denial
alcohol
drugs
abusive behavior
dissociation

This cycle is both internal and interactional

141

Lynn: A lot of the stuff you do and say really hurts me.

Therapist: And how does that make you feel?

Lynn: Completely furious. I want to kill her.

Therapist: Before the fury, how do you feel?

Lynn: I feel hurt, scared, a failure like everyone tells me I am.

Sue: No one tells you that. It seems like everyone always thinks you're special and pays all this attention to you.

Lynn: (Angry tone) How would you know what I feel like? You're too consumed with your own life. You have no idea what my life has been like.

Sue: A hell of a lot better than mine.

Therapist: It just happened. It just happened right now. The two of you just got into it with each other and I saw it happen.

Lynn: I know, I know.

Therapist: How did you feel when she said everyone treats you special.

Lynn: It freaked me out. It was that terrible "special-ness" that everyone saw, and yet I hated it.

Therapist: Victimized?

Lynn: Yes.

Therapist: So what did you do?

Lynn: I yelled at her, anything to make her stop.

Therapist: You yelled at her to make her stop, to make yourself stop. Then what do you think she felt, and then did?

Lynn: She felt abused and then screamed at me to protect herself.

Therapist: You got it!! Are you with us, Sue?

Sue: Yeah, I got it.

Later on in the same session, the therapist attempted to help Sue and Lynn discover the times when they did not escalate in such a negative manner.

Therapist: Sue, we all decided that *your* "victim" and your mother's "loser" parts have to stop triggering the fights. When are there times that you don't see your mother's loser or bitchy protector.

Sue: I do see it, but not a lot.

Therapist: Tell your mother the last time.

Sue: Remember when I took the money from your wallet that night to buy some beer? For some reason, you didn't go crazy. Sure, you were mad, but for some reason you talked to me and it really made me think about the fact I could be an alcoholic too.

Therapist: Somehow that night, Lynn, you did not feel victimized.

Lynn: I did at first when I found the money gone, but I went to an AA meeting, and then I talked with some friends and realized that something must be going on with this kid, and abusing her was not going to help.

Therapist: Great, you interrupted the pattern. Let's figure out how you both can repeat that.

During an individual session, the therapist and Lynn discussed the possibility that Sue was sexually abused by her father and subsequently discussed this in a session with Sue and Lynn. Sue disclosed, during a painful session, that her father had indeed attempted, on several occasions, to sexually abuse her. These episodes occurred during their visitations. This stimulated Lynn's feelings of victimization, but now, with the help of the therapist, she felt empowered to handle the situation differently than her mother had. She also decided to deal with her ex-husband in a different way than in the past.

Lynn decided to contact Child Protective Services on her own, and to help them in their investigation. She talked at great lengths with Sue about her sexual feelings, her confused feelings about her father, and told Sue that, whatever happened, she would believe her. Although her ex-husband tried to use the same bullying tactics as he had in the past, Lynn stood firm with him, and told him that she was indeed going to encourage prosecution (something Sue did not want) unless he began treatment at our Center immediately. He was also to have no further contact with Sue until his therapist deemed it appropriate. This was acceptable to Child Protective Services.

During this entire process, Lynn did not drink. Her therapist reframed all of these actions as evidence that Lynn had "regained herself," had become a woman who was empowered, self-protective, and protective of her children. This was particularly heartening since this crisis evoked a mass of old fears, feelings about her own abuse, and a need to escape.

Consolidation stage of therapy had begun when Lynn asked her therapist how much longer her therapy would be needed. She had a new job, one that was better paying and had more responsibility, but demanded more of her time. She felt in control of her family, and her children were, in fact, doing far better at home and at school. Her relationship with Sue was described as "normal." (We fight once in a while, but it gets resolved.) They both said they respected and loved each other.

The therapist did an intervention with Lynn and Sue during one of their last sessions. She asked them to role play their relationship as it had been when they first came in. It was a difficult and even funny task for them to do. It was apparent how much each had changed, and how different Lynn felt about herself. She was told to let the therapist know when she needed some help on something, but that Lynn's therapy was, in the therapist's mind, complete.

CONCLUSIONS

We have found the treatment conceptualizations described here to be *necessary* when treating drug- and alcohol-dependent women who were incestuously abused as children. However, these conceptualizations are not usually *sufficient* to treat alcohol or substance abuse per se. We recognize that many vulnerabilities to substance addictions exist, such as socio-environmental, family, physiological, etc., and that treatment programs must be planned to address those. We hope that what we have described will sensitize drug and alcohol counselors and other therapists to the possibility of incestuous abuse in the histories of their clients, and that they will feel confident to intervene with their clients so that past abuse does not lead to a lifetime of victimization.

NOTES

1. This paper will tend to focus on women who were abused incestuously or by an intimate extrafamilial other. The authors recognize this is only a portion of women who were sexually abused. Many, if not most, of the treatment considerations will apply to survivors.

2. This paper will focus exclusively on women alcohol or drug abusers who were incestuously abused as children. We recognize that many boys are also incestuously abused, and that many become alcohol and drug abusers. We feel that, while there is clearly an overlap, many of the issues raised here are gender-linked and different for each sex, and that those related to males deserve a separate treatment.

3. For the sake of readability, *father* will be used to mean any father figure, including *step-father*. We understand that the two relationships may be different in a given family; however, in general most of what applies when discussing incest between father and daughter also applies to step-father and step-daughter, particularly if that relationship has existed for a number of years.

REFERENCES

Barrett, M.J., Sykes, C., and Byrnes, W. (1986). A systemic model for the treatment of intrafamily child sexual abuse. *Journal of Psychotherapy and the Family*, 2, 67-82.

Barrett, M.J., Trepper, T., and Stone-Fish, L. (1990) Feminist informed family therapy for the treatment of intrafamily child sexual abuse. *Journal of Family Psychology*, 4, 151-166.

Briere, J., and Zaidi, L.Y. (1989). Sexual abuse histories and sequelae in female psychiatric emergency room patients. *American Journal of Psychiatry*, 146, 1602-1606.

Brickman, J. (1984). Feminist, non-sexist, and traditional models of therapy: Implications for working with incest. *Women & Therapy*, 3, 49-67.

Dembo, R., Williams, L., la Voie, L., and Berry E. (1989). Physical abuse, sexual victimization, and illicit drug use: Replication of a structural analysis among a new sample of high-risk youths. *Violence & Victims*, 4, 121-138.

Finkelhor, D., Hotaling, G.T., Lewis, I.A., and Smith, C. (1989). Sexual abuse and its relationship to later sexual satisfaction, martial status, religion, and attitudes. *Journal of Interpersonal Violence*, 4, 379-399.

Hart, L.E., Mader, L., Griffith, K., and DeMendonca, M. (1989). Effects of sexual and physical abuse: A comparison of adolescent inpatients. *Child Psychiatry & Human Development*, 20, 49-57.

Hartman, C.R., and Burgess, A.W. (1986). Child sexual abuse. Generic roots of the victim experience. *Journal of Psychotherapy and the Family*, 2, 83-92.

Herman, J., Russell, D.E.H., Tracki, K. (1986). Long-term effects of incestuous abuse in childhood. *American Journal of Psychiatry*, 143, 1293-1296.

Jackson, J.L., Calhoun, K.S., Amick, A.E., Maddever, H.M., and Habif, V.L. (1990). Young adult women who report childhood intrafamilial sexual abuse: Subsequent adjustment. *Archives of Sexual Behavior*, 19, 211-221.

Kandel, D.B., Treiman, D., Faust, R., and Single, E. (1976). Adolescent involvement in legal and illegal drug use: A multiple classification analysis. *Social Forces*, 55, 438-458.

Kaufman, E. (1985). *Substance abuse and family therapy*. Orlando: Grune & Stratton.

Rew, L. (1989). Long-term effects of childhood sexual exploitation. *Issues in Mental Health Nursing*, 10, 229-244.

Root, M.P. (1989). Treatment failures: The role of sexual victimization in women's addictive behavior. *American Journal of Orthopsychiatry*, 59, 542-549.

Russell, D.E.H. (1986). *The secret trauma: Incest in the lives of girls and women.* New York: Basic Books.

Scott, R.L., and Stone, D.A. (1986). MMPI measures of psychological disturbance in adolescent and adult victims of father-daughter incest. *Journal of Clinical Psychology,* 42, 251-259.

Shearer, S., Peters, C.P., Quaytman, S., Ogden, R. (1990). Frequency and correlates of childhood sexual and physical abuse histories in adult female borderline inpatients. *American Journal of Psychiatry*, 147, 214-216.

Singer, M.I., Petchers, M.K., Hussey, D. (1989). The relationship between sexual abuse and substance abuse among psychiatrically hospitalized adolescents. *Child Abuse & Neglect,* 13, 319-325.

Stanton, M.D., and Todd, T.C. (1982). *The family therapy of drug abuse and addiction.* New York: The Guilford Press.

Trepper, T.S., and Barrett, M.J. (1986). Vulnerability to incest: A framework for assessment. *Journal of Psychotherapy and the Family,* 2, 2, 13-25.

Watzlawick, P., Weakland, J., and Fisch, R. (1974). *Change: Principles of problem formation and problem resolution.* New York: W.W. Norton.

Chapter Eight

Who's on Top?
Sexism, Alcoholism
and Systemic Therapy with Couples

Donna Laikind

SUMMARY. This paper presents a case study of an alcoholic couple. At the time they were referred for therapy, the male client was recently sober and the female was still actively drinking. The paper describes treatment from a feminist systems perspective. Gender bias and ongoing alcohol abuse are seen as the key variables in treatment. The paper illustrates the ways that certain clinical decisions were made and points to the need for a feminist-based therapy in dealing with similar cases.

The treatment of an alcoholic couple can be seen as the treatment of their assumptions about gender. A couple affected by alcoholism usually holds rigid ideas about gender roles and is either in conflict about the expectations inherent in those roles or feels inadequate about living up to them.

Working from a feminist systems perspective, as suggested by Bepko and Krestan in *The Responsibility Trap,* the family is viewed as a gender-based system imbued with traditional patriarchal assumptions. The most fundamental construct in this approach is that alcoholism is systemic. It is an interactive process that includes the relationship between the drinker

Donna Laikind, MS, is Chairperson of the family welfare agency, *Family Dynamics* in New York City and is a family therapy consultant in private practice. Correspondence may be addressed to her at 165 E. 66th Street, New York, NY 10021.

The author would like to thank Peggy Penn, MSW, and Jo-Ann Krestan, MA, for their careful readings and wise suggestions for this paper.

147

and alcoholism, the relationships between people in the family, and the relationship between the family and other systems. Alcoholism is also seen as a chronological and progressive process that requires an understanding of ongoing patterns of behavior between people.

Alcoholism is perceived of as adaptive and reciprocal behavior, especially around sex roles and gender functions. Over- and underresponsibility are nodal issues and, again, are tied to gender expectations. The underresponsible person feels incompetent; he is cared for but has no power. The overresponsible person is a doer for others but is usually underresponsible for self and secretly feels inadequate. These positions, when rigidly polarized, can lead to feelings of anger on the part of both persons and to a battling for power and control. Each partner may take pride in certain gender-defined behaviors, but these grandiose feelings actually cover a sense of shame about inadequacy in living up to male/female stereotypes. In fact, alcohol abuse signals us to look for gender issues since it serves as an attempt to correct behaviors and appearances when they do not seem to measure up to societal norms. Alcohol maintains illusion. As Bepko and Krestan (1985) argue that an alcoholic system skews the hierarchy of power in a couple. The alcoholic man is allowed for once to be vulnerable and needy; the overresponsible female is allowed to be "on top." The female is sanctioned, for a time, to show her strength. And, when both partners are alcoholic, they vie with one another for one-down dependency, making them more equal.

So, therapy with the alcoholic couple must be feminist-oriented because alcoholism stabilizes the system around rigid sex roles. What are some of these patriarchal assumptions about a woman's "place"? They include the belief that women's needs are less important than men's and more pathological. Women are less adequate and are valid only in relationship to men. Most significant is the reality that "men and women have an 'unequal access to choice of roles.'" (Walters, p. 23).

Accordingly, the goals of therapy with alcoholic couples are to rebalance the family, to correct the complementarity around power and responsibility, and move away from the rigidity of roles assigned by society.

There are three stages of treatment. In Stage One, pre-sobriety, the primary emphasis is on breaking denial and connecting the alcoholic to resources in the community such as AA. The systemic work involves destabilizing the family and disrupting the established reciprocity that maintains the alcoholism. In Stage Two, the goal is adjustment to the change in pattern represented by sobriety. It is a time to calm the system and normalize feelings, with a stress on self-focus. Actually, not much therapy should be done in this stage. Stage Three is a time to rebalance the system. Rigid roles should give way to more flexible and, often, more symmetrical behavior, and the issues of power, control, pride and intimacy should be negotiated with the couple. It is a time to make overt what had been covert—the rigidity of gender roles.

For the last two years, this therapist has been working with an alcoholic couple using this framework. We three have tried to change the black and white world of addiction and gender bias, to remove the blinders, and create a panavision world less constricted by beliefs about gender. Our lens was humanistic rather than sexist, stressing the inherent worth of the individual and the capacity for self-realization. The following is a description of the couple and a description of how clinical decisions were made and goals set, while working from a feminist systems perspective.

DESCRIPTION OF THE COUPLE

Laura and Tim came into couple therapy two years ago. Tim, gentle and lanky, was 40 years old and a moderately successful painter. Laura, 32, a dancer, was a natural beauty with a child-like quality. Both were exceedingly attractive, soft-spoken, bright and creative.

Married five years, Tim and Laura had been actively drinking throughout the relationship until shortly before they came for therapy. Marital conflict had increased since Tim had been sober for nine months—for the first time in his life—and going to Alcoholics Anonymous regularly. Tim was concerned about Laura's continued drinking, and said he no longer wanted to be in control of a dependent wife. Laura saw the problem as her lack of autonomy in the marriage. She felt she could not be her own person in the marriage or stop drinking without doing it for Tim.

There was a history of severe alcohol abuse in both families. Laura's is an affluent California family where both parents are active alcoholics and her sister, five years younger and adopted, has been sober and in AA for 4 years. Tim is the youngest of four children of a Midwestern farm family. His aging father is actively alcoholic; his older brother is alcoholic as well; one of two older sisters is a compulsive eater. Tim's mother, who died one year ago, and had been separated for many years and then divorced from Tim's father, was a Puritan teetotalling schoolteacher. So neither Laura nor Tim had had any model for a sober relationship in their families of origin.

In my initial evaluation, the issues of a gender-based system based on patriarchal assumptions emerged immediately. The reciprocal over- and underresponsibility was clear when they explained how Laura had been assigned the role of dependent female and Tim had felt responsible to meet her every need. Actually, they flip-flopped their roles according to their drinking and drugging, taking turns being depressed and dependent. There was even a period of sadomasochistic activity between them when they literally took turns tying one another up (although Tim usually did the tying and was "on top"). Their mutual drinking kept them both down in a child-like stage of playing at life. Oddly, they were quite symmetrical in their inability to reach out and ask for help, in their fear of expressing anger and their mutual sense of lack of entitlement. Each felt the secret shame of not living up to the expectations of gender roles. Tim suffered from the numb affect typical of early sobriety when old rules about roles and behavior have been stripped of their power to maintain illusions, but new patterns of behavior have not yet replaced them.

Laura and Tim had lived in a fantasy of the traditional marriage with Laura as the perfect homemaker and Tim as the powerful provider. Lots of candlelight dinners fed this sexist idyll (really based on the fleeting "white middle class family life in the fifties") (Goldner, 1985, p. 33). The idyll was bolstered by their drinking and the need for illusion so strong that even on their first date, it overshadowed reality. Laura said that on that first night she saw Tim as a savior, a perfect man, a father figure, although he got drunk on the steps of a church and she had to help him home. So, their original contract was to base the relationship on patriarchal assumptions, and to feed the illusions this preserved about gender and power with heavy and constant doses of liquor and drugs. Laura had been maintaining the illusions for two generations, because her real father could only be seen as a powerful and protecting figure if she used her own drinking to blot out memories of his never standing up to her mother and of his sexual improprieties towards Laura.

Laura and Tim had both bought into many stereotypical assumptions: a woman needs a man and is nothing without him; the man is superior, a savior; he is her access to society and provides her only validation of self; when she acts emotional, she is "crazy". They both came to therapy with confusion over the roles they have been assigned by society, by family history, by gender.

The goals of the therapy for this couple based on a feminist systemic model were:

- Help them to recognize the trade-offs on individuation that had been made for the safety of a traditional marital bargain;

- Help each one to free the real voice from within and feel a sense of entitlement and self-worth unrelated to role;

• Move Tim from the black and white affect of early sobriety; help Laura to become sober;

• Move them both away from the one-down position of alcoholism.

CLINICAL DECISIONS

The decision was made to work equally overtly with Tim in applying the feminist approach. The trap for the therapist, all too often, is to shift the female's thinking away from traditional societal assumptions around gender, but leave the male unchanged and "out in the cold."

One clinical decision I made was to use myself as a female therapist to explore the gender issues between Tim and me. Although transference has long been viewed as not relevant to systems thinking, the here and now of what happened between us in the clinical setting helped Tim to understand his relationships with females.

I decided not to make Laura's drinking a central issue of the therapy. She had made it clear that she had a number of binds around stopping drinking. If she did it to please Tim, rather than for herself, she might lose what small sense of independence she had; if she did it because she felt alone and isolated and needed my approval, she might become again the "best little girl," her survival role growing up in her alcoholic household. I had to respect what few boundaries Laura had been able to maintain, and also not get into the familiar patriarchal position of telling her what to do because I knew best or because it was "for her own good."

Another decision had to be made about how much to pry out childhood memories, suppressed by alcohol, to do the necessary and important family-of-origin work with both of them. Laura, in particular, could remember very little about her past; she had only a vague sense of her father's inappropriate sexual behavior with her. I made a judgment to respect their own timing. Since Laura was in the Pre-Sobriety Stage, we were just beginning to break down her denial of her drinking problem. And Tim was in the stage of early sobriety, the holding phase where you do not want to confront. Again, it would be all too easy, and seemingly expedient, to push them to open up memories of the past so that we could connect their family legacies around alcoholism or sexism to their present behaviors and beliefs. Yet, this confrontation would carry the enormous danger of my being in charge of their therapy, and of replicating their being in the one-down positions they both tended to vie for.

I, instead, had each one, in separate sessions, visualize their resistance. Their symmetry went so far that they each, separately, visualized a wall.

Laura's wall was a large brick structure that she was always trying to climb over or under. But even as we talked, even as she "built" it, she said, to her amazement, it got smaller. It seemed more like a prop on a theatrical set, and she realized that she could actually just go around it. Finally, she realized she could shrink it down to pocket size and use it for her own purposes, taking it out when she needed to put distance between herself and someone or something else. Tim's wall was a three-ply plexiglass one, and he could bump into it without even knowing that it was there.

The work with family-of-origin went smoothly soon after the visualizations. Laura even commented that, in her previous individual therapy, she always felt the therapist had the answers and Laura was unsuccessful because she could not think of them. She said that I gave her the keys to many doors and left her to decide which to unlock and when.

In fact, often metaphors were used by the three of us . . . they were "on an odyssey" . . . he was looking for a "clearing in the woods." It suited the creative manner of this couple, but it was also another way of first seeing the broader, often historic, implications of their understanding of gender. The use of metaphor helped us to move away, through language, from the strictness of roles prescribed by society. As we started to shake up their patriarchal assumptions about their roles, they said that there was no longer a "captain to the ship" and that the "crew had mutinied." We all understood what this meant.

Laura and Tim were going on a brave journey of discovery but their paths would be parallel, not together. They sometimes complained of the loneliness of this, even as they sat together in a couple's session. But their relationship seemed too charged to have them work on interactional issues at this time, and individual work gave them some space to define self away from stereotypes of the male and the female.

One important task of the therapy was to look at purposes served by the symptom of drinking for each of them. For Tim, drinking had allowed him to show his vulnerable "feminine" side that could be receptive to Laura's help. This was the feeling, needy side not sanctioned for a man in a patriarchal society. Drinking seemed to serve three gender-related purposes for Laura. It kept Tim on top. It maintained the illusion of an old-time traditional marriage that gave her acceptance and validity, a status she felt that she as an individual could never have. It blocked her from remembering her father's improprieties so she could still believe that men were "safe."

It is important to mention that not all these clinical directions were conscious decisions, although they were all guided by my assumption about the importance of clarifying gender issues. Many times clinical decisions were made in response to what the couple presented in a session and represented leitmotifs that unfolded naturally. I felt that I could not be rigid if I suggested that they should not be.

THE COURSE OF TREATMENT

The Couple in Treatment: The Early Stage

Initially we met for couple sessions. Just as their lives were moving away from the symmetrical dependency of their mutual alcoholism, so the course of the therapy would be a self-focused but parallel voyage of self-discovery with each witnessing the other's forays out into the real world. But, first, we needed some innocuous barometers of how firmly entrenched they were in patriarchal assumptions that the man is in charge and invulnerable. The simplest of male-domain tasks was suggested for Laura — she should drive Tim's car. Her first reaction was fear, shame, vertigo and fakeness. She admitted that her bind about feeling powerful was that it made her more like her mother, whom she saw as an abuser of power. The task opened a Pandora's Box of uncontrolled emotions. It was safer to "take a back seat." A parallel "feminine" experiment was suggested for Tim. He was asked to look Laura directly in the eye for a moment of intimacy. He could not do it. So, we had an early indication from each of them that it was dangerous or difficult to shift roles.

We also traced the gender-related issues of power and control. These were introduced indirectly in the therapy by tracking "who is in charge of this stage of the relationship? . . . now who is in charge?" We tracked the competition between them for sobriety, for my attention in the therapy, for the favor of fathers, for success in AA.

Competition and power were normalized as part of their relationship. They served to reframe the context of the couple's definitions of dependency and need.

It was important also to allow Tim and Laura to experience loss — the loss of their beautiful fantasy of the perfect marriage, the loss of their old relationship based on patriarchal assumptions, the loss of Tim's important role of caretaker with Laura as she began to articulate a new sense of freedom. We acknowledged their feelings of sadness as the old relationship melted away; we also normalized their depression as mourning for the end of their couple's myth of perfection.

Since they had been so used to the wild swings of sobriety-drunkenness, of grandiosity-shame, it seemed helpful to try to offer them an experience of the area in between. Specifically, to move them away from perfectionistic expectations, they were asked to try for a "B" instead of always trying for an "A"—and ending up with an "F." This appealed to them and they reported that they were able to have a "B" dinner and a "B" birthday celebration soon after.

Tim agreed to go to Al-Anon meetings to help him with his feelings of loneliness and depression. The work started with Laura to understand why she felt like a fake. She described herself as a chameleon, always changing who she was to please the person in charge. It was her ultimate obedience to her parents to stay child-like and malleable. She was very aware of her female dilemmas around changing this persona. She understood the rules of the traditional marriage; husband is the validation of self to society; being married is the reconnection to family; being a couple means that you are not alone. But Laura also began to understand the trade-offs of this deal. As she said "Tim is my key to having friends and my link to family, but he also locks me up." Was it an either-or dilemma of losing herself to have Tim?

Laura also began to realize the problems of being female and alcoholic. "It's tough being a woman and an alcoholic; it seems like a double shame." As Bepko says, drinking is "double indemnity" for women. (1986, p. 70). Often a woman drinks in response to the one-down status imposed by social roles and is then further shamed for being unladylike. We discussed how women are socialized to be caretakers; to see no intrinsic value to self. The female alcoholic relieves the pressures of her caretaking role by becoming dependent on alcohol and is then stigmatized by society for her drinking. A male alcoholic becomes dependent but is seen as macho. The woman drinks alone; the man with his companions. Her shame in both roles is her secret.

We also tried to externalize the role of drinking in Laura's life, in the model of Michael White (1989). Drinking for Laura was very sneaky. It never asked to take over her life totally. It just bargained for a corner and allowed her to do some things independently, so she never felt she had to send it away completely.

Laura needed to learn to put herself first. We did some exercises that literally gave her practice in this. We played a kind of word game where she had to practice a different sentence structure using more "I" words. On every level she needed to move away from seeing herself as the object of others' actions.

Going Home

Both Tim and Laura made visits home around this time, and it made real the issues we had been dealing with in our family-of-origin work.

For the first time, Tim had a very powerful unanesthetized experience in going home. It was really necessary to face his anger and disappointment with his father as part of his growth. He needed to understand his own preoccupation with being "macho." He began to remember more about his past. "I was a child and an adult all at the same time." His strongest memory was of being a little boy left alone, who was rewarded only for being very still and very quiet. Another powerful, pivotal memory resurfaced. He was with his father, around the age of 14, after his parents had split up. His father suddenly asked if Tim would like to move in with him and his girlfriend. Tim felt torn between his Puritan strict mother and this alcoholic father who had abandoned them both. He felt trapped and immobilized, a feeling now he can relate to his affect as an adult. He suppressed the fury that he had to chose between them. The memory had now come alive, and he began to understand the limbo he is in as an adult. Whose son is he? Is it always black and white, good and evil? What will he do with his anger if he makes a choice for himself now? Being male means being drunk and no good. Being female means being alone and abandoned. The gender stereotypes could not have been clearer, and the choices could not have been more grim.

Laura made her visit to California, ostensibly to visit friends. We tracked her fears about seeing her parents and explored the usefulness of these feelings. Her parents might turn her back into a child. Or would it be worse if she saw herself as adult with them as children? Dad and Tim, as always, merged in her head as the "man" who is in charge, but does not really protect. She had a dream where she was swimming among fish, but she does not know if they are friendly dolphins or killer sharks. She returned from her trip on an exhilarating high—a return to a "different Laura." With her friends she had discussed the past and her childhood feelings of being a fake, having to keep the family secret of her parents' drinking. She was able to bring more vivid memories into the session—of her mother's constant criticism, her father's not being strong enough to stop her, of her guilt for bringing her sister Margot (adopted) into the alcoholic family. She understood that she never had a childhood and that she was chosen to be the strong one.

We discuss her leaving Tim. She feels capable of doing it and also knows that others can survive her leaving them, whether they be parents or mate.

The Separation

The therapy reaches a stage where Laura and Tim begin to feel that being together is heavy baggage and is slowing them down from being whole people. The work now is to make separation real. The danger is that this separation from one another represents a ritualized separating from families that never took place. They have moved away from their extreme positions. Laura no longer needs to feel guilty about leaving (as she did about leaving her parentified role in her family of origin). Tim understands that the identification with his mother's role as the one who was abandoned is no longer necessary. We plan a timetable for their separation, and some rules for what they are calling a trial separation. The timetable and rules help them to make their plans concrete and to detoxify the strong feelings they both still have around the issue of separation.

Separate But Equal?

What followed was a time of individual therapy. With Tim, the relationship between him, the male client, and me, the female therapist, is our way to explore his feelings. Alone with me in the sessions, he admits to feeling vulnerable. He is afraid of being himself, with me, a female. If I see what he is really like inside, I will reject him. He announces he is depressed, possibly suicidal. He wonders, if I worry about him, will I connect more with him, but then not be professional? Who's in charge of the session? If he is incoherent, will I make sense of it? Is he entitled to talk about what he wants? He is suspicious that I, like all females, may use witchcraft. He says he never could understand the need for the feminist movement, because his problem is that he always saw women as more powerful than he. He evokes an extraordinary image. When he visited his 93-year-old grandmother in a nursing home, she lay quiet, almost in a fetal position, but still, the power of her eyes captured him, and he felt he could not escape. All these images and realizations point to the value that alcohol had in suppressing his feelings. He always felt inadequate in the traditional male role of being the stronger one, who was always in charge. The gender themes of power and control and who's on top come out; it may be a trial by fire, but he is connecting to a range of feelings as never before.

We looked to his family-of-origin to explain some of his legacy of shame and his binds around changing it. He made an important intergenerational connection between his father and the dilemma of change. If he is a fraud and shameful, then he can maintain his anger at his father and a connection of shame with him. If he is legitimized and his life is real, he legitimizes his father as father but he lets him off the hook in terms of blame and they are less connected. Like his relationship with women, it seems an either-or situation. He either feels left out or as if he belongs to a macho club of drunks and failures like his father.

We also tracked Tim's feelings of inadequacy in relationship to his mother. He could never live up to her expectations — be the best little boy, and the man of the family, and the puritan. Feeling he had failed her, he finally left town and hung up on her phone calls for years, just as he disconnected himself emotionally from all women.

Tim's dilemma was that he often had put his mother's, and other women's, needs before his own. This was framed as a mantra: "I have to give up my needs in order to care for others, to have my mother's approval as the best little boy." He was to repeat the mantra as a bolster, a more appropriate one than alcohol had been, whenever he felt his real self repressed (Penn, 1990).

Tim begins to connect to a range of appropriate feelings and forms a relationship with a woman where he can look her in the eye, even during lovemaking, and feel intimate and equal. He also begins to make changes in his work. He always showed his works with a group but never had a one-man show. This reflected his old role as the quietest and youngest member of his family. Now he has a greater sense of self and wants to be center stage. Being sober, he says, has made him believe that change is possible and makes him available for therapy.

Laura also begins to understand the dual nature of drinking. It connects her to family and it maintains the illusion of perfection by blotting out the bad memories. But, in a strange way, it is more real to drink. Because it shows the world she is not perfect, that her family failed in some way, drinking also makes her not a fake. In any case, drinking is the last link to her parents. She knows that to stop drinking is to betray her family.

Laura's further dilemma is over going to AA. It represents going back to being obedient and doing what she is told. She feels it would return her to a childlike state.

After all the careful therapeutic planning, it is a chance incident with Laura that opens up many feelings. She has come to a session at a wrong time. We spend a long time discussing what her resistance may be. Afterwards, I realize it is *my* mistake and, after a moment's hesitation wondering whether I, as the therapist, can get away with the mistake, I apologize to her at the next session. She breaks down. She knew she was right, but felt, as in childhood, that it was her job to protect those in authority, that she is the keeper of shameful secrets that all is not what it seems. The chance incident opens a flood of feelings. She goes to AA as an experiment. Suddenly the shame is replaced by a small good secret inside her. She remembers how disastrous it was to expose her emotions to her mother, but here she feels a private happiness. She no longer is consumed by the shame that connected her to her mother. She feels a range of emotions never before allowed to her. She has decided to accept messy and real as her life, moving away from the family secrets and the illusion of perfection. She knows that to care for someone else, she has traded herself — it is a woman's age-old dilemma.

Therefore, Laura understands better her conflict about leaving Tim. She makes another visit to California. Ostensibly it is to visit her dearest childhood friends, but it is also to test her new-found clarity about self with her parents, and see, in vito, some of the intergenerational binds we had discussed. Sober and disconnected from what is familiar, she writes back the penultimate woman's cry of lack of self:

> I feel not really here. Semi-transparent. I feel at a standstill. Empty . . . My slate is wiped clean. All the rules, guidelines, expectations, behaviors, don't work . . . It is as if no one can hear me and I have nothing to say . . . I move in very little space . . . I have disappeared . . . I want to go home, but there is no home to go to. I am so desperate for love, but I have run out of presents to give . . . I felt I had no feelings because I didn't think it was proper to feel anger.

Sober at last, and very angry, Laura is learning to be alone with herself. Her feelings of pride dissolve the feelings of shame, she sometimes sees herself as beautiful, not ugly. She says that she is involved in an evolutionary process. She has crawled out of the water, she has started to breathe air, but she is not yet walking and very far from flying.

It's a scary and rough world for them both, but it is no longer built on illusion and archaic notions of how men and women should be with one another.

CONCLUSION

Laura and Tim came in to couples therapy with specific dilemmas related to their stages of alcoholism: Laura was not sober and Tim was in early sobriety. Certain clinical decisions, for example, about how much work would be interactional and how much self-focused, were based on these stages. Some variables examined in working with Laura and Tim were specific to them but could be generalized to other cases. Alcoholism can be seen as a commentary on gender. Its presence serves as a clue to gender issues in working with other alcoholic couples, since one function of the alcoholism in the system is to blur rigid societal sex roles. The dimension of gender is broader yet, for all families are gender-based systems. In fact, it could be said that gender is not a variable but a given in triangulated situations and that systemic therapy, by definition, should be feminist-oriented. As socio-linguist Deborah Tannen points out, "gender does not go away" (1990, p. 28).

Laura and Tim made the therapy an odyssey of discovery. Most of all, this was due to their personal bravery and willingness to examine long-held assumptions about gender and family roles. Possibly other success in the therapy was due to using a humanistic, non-sexist, framework and a wider lens to examine how we feel and act in relationship to the roles we have been assigned by gender, by family history, by alcoholism.

Haven't we all felt the discomfort of the psychic blisters that are formed between the roles we are assigned by a political society and our real selves?

EPILOGUE

A central goal of the therapy for both Laura and Tim was to learn to speak for themselves. It seems only right, then, to end with a message that I suggested each one write for the reader.

TIM: Two years and three months into recovery I can say that I have very different relationships with women than I ever had. I have found out that women are just as capable of being jerks, just as fallible and can be just as divisive as men, i.e., myself. I guess in some ways that means I've taken women off the pedestal. I've also found that can make me closer to them, which makes me very nervous, but I have found there are rewards from sober intimacy — major rewards. I no longer feel the need to imagine myself as a sexual partner for nearly every woman that I encounter. What a relief. Sometimes I still have fantasies of "the conspiracy of women," something that coming of age in the era of feminism, being an alcoholic and coming from an alcoholic family has given me. I feel a lot of progress, more intact inside than perhaps I've ever felt, yet I know I'm just getting started.

LAURA: It is now six months into sobriety and I am still involved in the difficult task of transferring the authority in my life back to myself. I am convinced that only through not drinking have I been able to come as far as I have. I still live with the idea that I am not good enough. I do not deserve. I am not smart enough. I will fail without a man to protect me. . . . .[I sought] validation through a man. If he liked me, I could like myself. He became the authority . . . he became superhuman . . . as I relinquished more and more responsibility for myself to a man the loss of self increased. It matched the nothingness I felt inside . . . Alcohol helped fulfill a prophecy. (1) It helped perpetuate the mask. (2) It promoted the crumbling image of horror I had within. It was a trap. But the fear of walking away from that legacy was so gripping. It felt, at times, as if I could just sneak away while it wasn't looking. There seemed to be only one way. Slowly and deliberately turn around and walk in the other direction. You have no idea where you are going, but you have stopped the progression. And as you walk you can hear all the voices calling to you to come back. Your mother, your relationships, your secrets, but you ignore them and keep walking because it is the one and only thing you can do for yourself. Maybe later on there will be more, but for now it's all you can do to keep walking in the other direction.

REFERENCES

Bepko, C. (1986). Alcoholism as oppression: The dilemma of the woman in the alcoholic system. *Women and family therapy.* In Ault-Riche, M. (Ed.) Rockville, Md: Aspen Systems Corp.
Bepko, C. with Krestan, J. (1985). *The responsibility trap.* New York: Free Press.
Goldner, V. (1985). Feminism and family therapy. *Family Process*, *24*:31-47.
Penn, P. (1990). Personal communication.
Tannen, D. (1990). *You just don't understand.* New York: William Morrow and Company.
White, M. (1989). *Selected papers.* Adelaide: Dulwich Centre Publications.

Chapter Nine

Chemical Dependency Treatment for Lesbians and Their Families: The Feminist Challenge

Deborah J. Bushway

SUMMARY. The field of chemical dependency has recently begun to come to terms with the particular issues of lesbians and gay men who are addicted. The challenges of providing service to this community and their families are complex. Some of these complexities are reviewed in this article.

The field of chemical dependency has recently begun to come to terms with the particular issues of lesbians and gay men who are addicted (Finnegan & McNally, 1988; Kominars, 1989). There are now gay and lesbian AA meetings in most major cities, and a number of treatment programs have realized the need for specialized treatment for lesbians and gay men.

ALCOHOLISM AND THE LESBIAN AND GAY COMMUNITY

These services developed in response to research in the 1970s and 1980s which indicated an increased risk of alcoholism for the homosexual community. Weinberg and Williams (1974) reported that 29.4% of their sample of 2,497 admitted to drinking "more than they should." Fifield,

Deborah J. Bushway, PhD, is Clinical Director of the Pride Institute, 14400 Martin Drive, Eden Prairie, MN 55344.

The author wishes to acknowledge the contributions of the staff at Pride Institute, particularly Jane Levin, PhD, to this article.

DeCrescenzo and Latham (1975) reported that one third of the Los Angeles gay or lesbian population abused alcohol regularly. Similarly, 29% of the men in a sample of Midwestern gay communities were found to be alcoholic as defined by the Michigan Alcohol Screening Test (Lohrenz, Connelly, Coyne & Sparks, 1978). Diamond and Wilsnack (1978) reported finding similar patterns of alcohol abuse among lesbians. These studies generally explain such drinking patterns as a response to the invisibility and stigmatization of the homosexual community by the dominant culture.

Because the dominant culture in our society remains heterosexist, lesbians and gay men must "come out" to themselves and to others. During this process, many people use alcohol or other drugs to medicate the pain and shame of becoming a member of an oppressed and stigmatized group (Nicoloff and Stiglitz, 1987). Most dramatically, white males who "come out" experience a fall from status as members of the dominant culture by having abdicated their position of privilege and betrayed their gender role (Pharr, 1988). For many lesbians and gay men, secrets, hiding and denial have become core defenses in a homophobic and heterosexist culture. These same defenses can allow drinking/drug abuse to develop into an addiction (Glaus, 1989). Thus, the very skills which may have allowed a lesbian or gay male to cope with a hostile environment may now stand in the way of seeing the dysfunctions associated with her or his alcohol or other drug use clearly.

It is important, however, not to assume that homosexuality "causes" alcoholism. Isrealstam and Lambert (1983;1986) have challenged earlier psychodynamic work linking homosexuality and alcoholism with incomplete psychosexual development. Understanding the behavior of members of oppressed groups requires striking a delicate balance between intrapsychic interpretations and sociological explanations. More structured investigation into the sociological and psychological factors influencing the development of addictions in members of oppressed groups is needed before final conclusions can be drawn (Neisen & Sandall, 1990).

CHEMICAL DEPENDENCY TREATMENT

Over the last fifteen years, it has become increasingly clear to treatment programs and therapists working with chemical dependency that we must treat addiction as a family issue (Black; 1981, Finkelstein, Duncan, Derman & Smeltz, 1990). Most treatment programs have developed a "family week" which takes place at some point in each patient's treatment. For lesbians and gay men, these family weeks may represent yet another experience of heterosexism. For women, a husband and children may be assumed to constitute family. The choice to "come out" and involve a same-sex significant other in family week, while crucial to recovery, can be terrifying. The choice to involve family-of-origin in treatment is also more complicated for lesbians. Treatment programs must be sensitive to different definitions of family and to the specific challenges inherent in working with diverse family groups.

Concurrently, most therapists have become aware of the need to expand traditional definitions of mental health when dealing with members of any "special population" (e.g., women, ethnically diverse populations, lesbians, gay men) (Fassinger, 1991). These special considerations, however, continue to feel auxiliary rather than core to most theory and programs. In other words, most "special populations" continue to be seen as "special" and treated as exceptions to the norm of white, middle-class, heterosexual, North American male models of behavior. Treatment programs are commended for being accepting and understanding of cultural diversity, gay or lesbian issues, women's concerns, etc. This is, however, very different from a fundamental shift in perspective which would define the "special population" as the norm and develop theory from that point (Brown, 1989). This fundamental shift in perspective can be approached only by creating a safe community and then uncovering a psychology of a group of people in a community less affected by oppression. This is the challenge and opportunity presented by specialized treatment programs such as Pride Institute.

FAMILY INVOLVEMENT AT PRIDE INSTITUTE

Pride Institute is a freestanding alcohol and other drug treatment program designed specifically for lesbians and gay men. The entire client population is lesbian or gay, and approximately 80% of the staff is lesbian or gay as well. (All of the direct service counseling staff is lesbian or gay.) This unique environment creates a very powerful community and offers families and primary patients an exciting opportunity to explore the possibilities of their relationships.

We, at Pride, believe that chemical dependency has an impact on everyone close to the addicted person. Therefore, we view the family unit as the women and men define it themselves. We encourage equal involvement from families of choice and families of origin, depending on the clinical context for each individual. In this way, Pride is very similar to other treatment programs who have increased their sensitivity to lesbian and gay issues. The primary difference is that Pride is a lesbian and gay treatment community which begins to create the fundamental shift in perspective (Brown, 1989) discussed earlier. In that context, Pride offers an opportunity to discuss the dual secrets of addiction and homosexuality. For many family members, this is the first time they have been able to openly discuss the impact of homosexuality on their lives. This is true for partners as well as siblings and parents. Many of our clients and their partners come from very heterosexist and homophobic environments which have made it difficult to safely review their own internalized homophobia and its impact on their lives. In order to look closely at the impact of homophobia and heterosexism on a relationship, clients must be able to work with therapists who have dealt with their own deeper prejudices and reactivity regarding lesbian and gay couples and families (Markowitz, 1991). This is an important point for all therapists (both gay or lesbian and heterosexual) working with gay or lesbian couples and their families to remember. The countertransference which can occur at this point can be very subtle and extremely damaging.

Many family members bring their own ideas about chemical dependency and homosexuality to family week. These ideas are often directly linked to the heterosexist bias with which they live. Family members may, for example, view homosexuality as an aberration and an illness, and may further view the alcoholism simply as one aspect of the larger "sickness." A crucial part of the program, therefore, is education which allows family members to begin to separate the two issues. Lectures on topics such as the coming out process, heterosexism, gay and lesbian relationships, the disease concept, and family of origin help family members to see that homosexuality has not "caused" the addiction.

Also, in the process of attending lectures, groups and other community activities, family members begin to come to terms with their own heterosexism and homophobia. Much of the recent work on prejudice reduction suggests that genuine contact with the target group is a primary tool in reducing bias and bigotry. The power of being in an environment in which gay is the norm is, in part, the opportunity to look past stereotypes and bias and "know" a variety of lesbians and gay men as people. Non-gay or lesbian family members tend to visibly relax as the family week progresses and as they grow to know and enjoy both staff and other patients.

Family-of-origin members also may need to begin to work through the grief associated with the loss of familial dreams, aspirations and expectations for the identified client (Bradley, 1989). Family plans for our clients often have heterosexuality imbedded in them. This may be the first time that parents and siblings recognize that sobriety will not produce the outcome for which they may have been secretly hoping (e.g., a heterosexual lifestyle). The family group (consisting of other family members experiencing a similar process) offers support and validation for whatever reactions people may be experiencing. Group members are introduced to the P-FLAG (Parents and Friends of Lesbians and Gays) organization as a source of support when they return to their homes. In addition to the work directly related to homosexuality and addiction, family members also learn about relationships and how to begin to build a healthier relationship with the addicted person. The identified client also learns to listen to the experience of those around him or her. In the best of all outcomes, family members leave the program with a sense of hope and mutual understanding.

The power of this environment and the family week is best illustrated in the following case example. This example represents a composite of lesbians seen in treatment at Pride. They are not specific individuals.

CASES

Jill is a twenty-six-year-old woman who has been self-supporting for the last several years. She has a lot of debt now, due to her drinking, but no one close to her knows about this. She is reserved and a bit shy. She lacks confidence in herself and in her abilities. She is very careful in treatment not to break any rules and to be cooperative.

She has come out only recently (within the last year) to her mother, although she has had the same partner off and on for 5 years. She had feared that she would lose her mother in the coming out process, and she now fears that she will lose her if her mother learns about the extent of Jill's addiction and about Jill's behavior while drinking. The thought of losing her mother absolutely terrifies Jill.

Jill explains that she has recently "changed" her relationship with her partner. They are no longer being sexual or exclusive, but they do plan to continue to live together. Her ex-partner (Pam) is in recovery from alcohol/other drug abuse as well. Jill maintained regular phone contact with Pam during her first weeks in treatment. Jill is the one who had asked for a change in the relationship with Pam and feels very proud of that assertion.

As Jill opened up, it emerged that her behavior while drinking was often radically different from that of the Jill we were getting to know in treatment. She reported incidences of rage and violence with Pam as well as verbal assaults on her mother and other family-of-origin members. It also became clear that her internalized image of "lesbian" was quite negative. She saw lesbians as "unfeminine" and "crude." It became clear that this viewpoint was based in a belief in rigid gender roles. In other words, Jill believed that women needed to behave in stereotypically feminine ways in order to be valued and loved in this world. The thought of behaving in a way that strayed from that rigid definition of feminine was paralyzingly frightening to her. She could or would lose everything, including her sense of self (Miller, 1986). Thus, her discomfort with being lesbian was rooted in her own sexism (Pharr, 1988). It also became more clear that her drinking allowed her a temporary escape from the demands of the gender role which she had been taught and in which she so deeply believed (Bepko and Krestan, 1985). Jill was able to see that her mother had been a primary source of her ideas about gender roles. She could also see that part of her fear of losing her mother was rooted in the fact that her drinking behavior had generally strayed from that role and she doubted that her mother could tolerate and accept that "deviation."

It became clear that both Pam and Jill's mother needed to be included in family week. The idea of these two worlds clashing was very upsetting to Jill, but she agreed that this seemed the only way out of the abusive and self-shaming cycle in which she found herself. Both women were invited, and both indicated willingness to attend.

As family week approached, Jill's anxiety rose steadily. She fought her urges to become more reclusive and instead worked to garner support from the community. By the time Pam and Barbara arrived, Jill was almost as shaky as she had been in her first days of treatment.

Pam and Barbara had not spent much time talking with each other at any point in their five years of contact. Each felt obviously uncomfortable around the other. The family group, however, consisted both of parents and of significant others, and each of them were able to connect with others in the group. During the course of the week, Barbara and Pam were able to hear each other's concerns and love for Jill in the safety of this group. They were also able to hear one another's frustrations, pain and confusion regarding the addiction and their respective relationships with Jill.

Barbara was able, over the course of the week, to challenge her own stereotypes about "lesbians" and the lesbian lifestyle. The staff of Pride is a very diverse group, and this diversity helps to challenge many stereotypes about both appearance and behavior of lesbians and gay men. She was able to separate Jill's identity as a lesbian from Jill's addiction. She began to accept that Jill needed to change in order to maintain sobriety, and was able to voice support for those steps toward increasing autonomy and assertion. She was able to verbalize an interest and willingness to maintain contact with Jill throughout the change process, thus addressing Jill's fears that change would threaten her mother to the point of loss of the relationship. Barbara was also able to begin to realize that a heterosexual lifestyle was not necessarily part of recovery for Jill. Barbara voiced as much support as she could for Jill and her lifestyle, although acceptance of this reality was very difficult for her. Jill came to see that her mother was giving her as much acceptance as she was able to, and began to accept that her limitations were not Jill's "fault" or due to some inadequacy in Jill. She began to form a more adult relationship with her mother, seeing her mother as an individual with her own struggles, which did not necessarily result from nor reflect on Jill. This step toward autonomy, while maintaining connection was a critical turning point for Jill.

Also, within the safety of the family group, Pam was able to voice her own vulnerabilities and pain over Jill's abusive behavior while drinking. Pam was encouraged to let Jill know this aspect of her internal life in the session when Pam joined Jill's primary group. Jill was able to hear Pam's experience. She was also able to begin to "own" and integrate that angry and hurt part of her self. This bridge across the pain allowed the forgiveness and healing to begin. Pam and Jill were also able to see how isolated they had been in their relationship, in part due to their internalized homophobia and heterosexism. The isolation had meant that there was no safe place to talk about problems between them and no place to learn about positive options in lesbian relationships. They both became clear, however, that they were not ready for the relationship to end. They also knew that they did not want to return to being lovers, and that they both feared that living together would recreate the isolation with which they had lived previously. They set up some guidelines for their on-going relationship when Jill returned home.

Throughout all of this work, Jill realized that an extended care setting was appropriate for her immediately following treatment at Pride. She realized the intensity and depth of the issues with which she was dealing, and agreed that she needed more time to stabilize. She saw that she could allow selective others to see and know her more fully and genuinely without rejection or shame. This was an extremely powerful experience for Jill. She was able to know herself more fully as she related more of herself to key others in her life (Miller, 1988).

Pam and Barbara came to understand addiction and its impact on individuals and families more clearly. They each also came to realize their own roles in creating the uncomfortable relationships they had been having with Jill and her addiction. Their own recovery plans were interwoven with Jill's continuing care plans.

COMMENTARY

While this example may sound very similar to other forms of family experience in treatment, there are several crucial differences. A primary one is the position that Pride family therapists take in *actively valuing* lesbian and gay relationships. It can be argued that therapists working with lesbian or gay couples and families cannot be neutral. Rather they must be able and willing to struggle against negative messages from wider society about the worth and value of lesbian relationships and their integration into the extended family (Dahlheimer & Feigal, 1991). This message is delivered both overtly and covertly at Pride, and is possible to this extent only in a context which operates from the paradigm within which Pride operates. These valuing messages come in the form of lectures, phone calls from counselors to partners, and role models of successful relationships.

A second difference is the emphasis on "joining" the relationship in treatment. This emphasis interfaces closely with the first point made in this commentary, but is slightly different. In valuing gay or lesbian relationships in which addiction is a factor, we must listen very hard to what the relationship represents to the couple and what its participants are telling us. Using some of the standard approaches of family work in the chemical dependency field would likely result in a loss of the clients. Often, in traditional programs, couples and families are heavily confronted with the "dysfunction" being seen in the family. With lesbian or gay couples, it is crucial to listen even more closely to their definitions of the issues. We need to teach what a healthy relationship would feel like and to support the development of more healthy interactions, but this work must be done from *within* the relationship. Lesbian or gay couples are accustomed to defending themselves and their approach to life to the rest of the world. If family therapists working in treatment fail to join the couple, any feedback or work is likely to generate a response of fortification or fleeing rather than change. This is true with all families, but particularly true for those whose very relationships are stigmatized and oppressed. In this case, families are not protecting the dysfunction as much as they are protecting their right to exist. We must remember that it is not that long ago that professionals labeled all lesbian and gay relationships as dysfunctional and sick. Again, in the case of Pam and Jill, we see that "joining" the relationship allowed the therapist to learn about the violence, and thus to provide opportunity for healing on both sides of the pain. It is likely that the violence would have remained a secret if the relationship had felt "threatened" or had been labeled dysfunctional from the outside.

A third difference is the hesitancy to apply heterosexual norms to the understanding of lesbian relationships (Mencher, 1990). Few heterosexual couples would talk of breaking up while continuing to live together. Few would want or need to maintain a high level of contact with one another throughout the breakup. This behavior is not abnormal in the lesbian community. We can probably best understand it in terms of recent theories of women's development (Miller, 1986; Chodorow, 1989; Luepnitz, 1989). If women know themselves through their relationships, the process of two women ending a romantic relationship will be very different from breakups we have come to expect in the heterosexual world. Therapists must be willing to respond to each case individually and separately in the absence of population-specific norms. To push for premature definition of the relationship (i.e., are we working on breaking up or getting together here?) would likely send this pair of women rushing together out of the terror of premature autonomy and individuation. The isolation produced by keeping their relationship "closeted" meant that neither Jill nor Pam have strong relationships outside of their primary relationship. In order for them to "break up" (if that remains their goal), they must each build other relationships in which they can know themselves as lesbians and as women. Otherwise, the loss of this connection does, in fact, threaten their very existence at a fundamental level.

A fourth point is the need to redefine "codependency" within the treatment field. Traditionally, both Barbara and Pam would have been encouraged to look at their "codependency" and to separate and take care of themselves. Relational models of development would suggest that the developmental challenge for women is to find a separate sense of self within connection—not apart from it. Again, we probably need to be teaching about "healthy" connection rather than focusing on autonomy as a goal for our lesbian clients (and for many of our gay male clients as well). Rather than the traditional caution or prohibition against relationships for the first year a person is in recovery from addiction, we need to be bringing relationships (both current and potential) *into* the treatment process. At Pride, we use Miller's (1988) "outcomes from a healthy relationship" to discuss healthy connection rather than focusing on "codependency" per se. A complete discussion of the concept of codependency is beyond the scope of this article, but it is important to remember that, historically, the term had a very specific utility. "Codependency" referred to the tendency of family members to become comfortable with the addiction's central place in their relationship. This focus has been lost as the term has been applied without rigor or question to any strong connection.

CONCLUSIONS

It is crucial for family therapists in the chemical dependency treatment field to re-examine many of the assumptions and norms from which they have been working. A recent survey of 1,864 lesbians and gay men in Minnesota indicated that 28% of the community belonged to self-help groups such as AA, NA, etc. (Northstar project, 1991). This level of involvement should allow us to begin to establish new paradigms of both recovery and connection for our own community. The work of recent theorists regarding women's development is particularly applicable for lesbians in recovery. It appears, however, that these theories can inform our work with gay men as well.

We must take care to avoid overstating gender differences (Hare-Mustin, 1987) as we work to define new alternative paths of development. It is important to remember that the path of development through connection may not be a relevant context for all women, and that the path of development through separation and autonomy may not be relevant for all men. In our work with lesbians and gay men, it is clear that some men may find their safety in connection while some women find their safety and sense of self in autonomy. As we struggle to shift perspectives and to create new paradigms (Brown, 1989) in treatment, we must also take care to continue to *listen* and to avoid the temptation to create new stereotypes into which lesbians and gay men may not easily fit.

As we work to apply what we know and what we have learned to treatment for lesbians and gay men, it is clear that the field of chemical dependency has truly only *begun* to respond to the needs of the community. This beginning must not be discounted, but neither should we become complacent. The field must continue to confront its assumptions. We must not forget that Twelve-Step recovery programs were founded by middle-class, white, heterosexual men. Family therapists within the treatment field must continue to forge new frontiers, individually and within agencies. In summary, we must not forget to have "the courage to change the things we can" within the chemical dependency field.

REFERENCES

Bepko, C. & Krestan, J. (1985). *The responsibility trap.* New York: Free Press.

Black, C. (1981). *It will never happen to me.* Denver, CO. M.A.C.

Bradley, M.A. (1989). Treatment issues for families of lesbians and gay men. *Our voice.* Pride Institute's newsletter.

Brown, L.S. (1989). New voices, new visions: Toward a lesbian/gay paradigm for psychology. *Psychology of Women Quarterly, 13,* 445-456.

Chodorow, N.J. (1989). *Feminism and psychoanalytic theory.* New Haven: Yale University Press.

Dahlheimer, D. & Feigal, J. (1991). Bridging the gap. *The Family Therapy Networker. 15* (1), 44-53.

Diamond, D. & Wilsnack, S. (1978). Alcohol abuse among lesbians: A descriptive study. *Journal of Homosexuality, 4,* 123-142.

Fassinger, R.E. (1991). The hidden minority: Issues and challenges in working with lesbian women and gay men. *The Counseling Psychologist, 19,* 157-176.

Fifield, L., De Crescenzo, T., & Latham, L. (1975). *Alcoholism and the gay community.* Los Angeles Gay Community Services Center.

Finkelstein, N., Duncan, S.A., Derman, L., & Smeltz, J. (1990). *Getting sober, getting well: A treatment guide for caregivers who work with women.* Cambridge, MA: The women's alcoholism program of CASPAR.

Finnegan, D. & McNally, E. (1988). *Dual identities: Counseling chemically dependent gay men and lesbians.* Center City, MN: Hazelden.

Glaus, K.O. (1989). Alcoholism, chemical dependency and the lesbian client. *Women & Therapy, 8,* 131-144.

Hare-Mustin, R. (1987). The problems of gender in family therapy theory. *Family Process, 26,* 15-27.

Isrealstam, S. & Lambert, S. (1983). Homosexuality as a cause of alcoholism: A historical review. *International journal of the addictions, 18*(8).

Isrealstam, S. & Lambert, S. (1986). Homosexuality and alcohol: Observations and research after the psychoanalytic era. *International Journal of the Addictions, 21,* 509-537.

Kominars, S.B. (1989). *Accepting ourselves: The twelve step journey of recovery from addiction for gay men and lesbians.* New York: Harper & Row.

Leupnitz, D. (1989). *The family interpreted: Feminist theory in clinical practice.* New York: Basic Books, Inc.

Lohrenz, L., Connelly, J., Coyne, L., & Sparks, K. (1987). Alcohol problems in several midwestern homosexual communities. *Journal of Studies on Alcohol, 39,* 1959-1963.

Markowitz, L.M. (1991) Homosexuality: Are we still in the dark? *The Family Therapy Networker, 15,* 26-30.

Mencher, J. (1990). Intimacy in lesbian relationships: A critical re-examination at fusion. *Works in progress series.* Wellesly, MA: The Stone Center.

Miller, J.B. (1986). *Toward a new psychology of women.* Boston, MA: Beacon Press.

Miller, J.B. (1988). *Connections, disconnections & violations.* Wellesly: The Stone Center.

Neisen, J.H. & Sandall, H. (1990). Alcohol and other drug abuse in a gay/lesbian population: related to victimization? *Journal of Psychology & Human Sexuality, 3*(1), 151-168.

Nicoloff, L.K. & Stiglitz, E.A. (1987). Lesbian alcoholism: Etiology, treatment and recovery. In Boston Lesbian Psychologies Collective (Ed.), *Lesbian psychologies.* Chicago: University of Illinois Press.

Northstar Project. (1991). *Out and counted: A survey of the Twin Cities gay & lesbian community.* Minneapolis: Gay & Lesbian Community Action Council.

Pharr, S. (1988). *Homophobia: A weapon of sexism.* Inverness, CA: Chardon Press.

Weinberg, G. & Williams, C. (1974). *Male homosexuals: Their problems and adaptations.* New York: Oxford University Press.

PART THREE:
SPECIAL ISSUES IN TREATMENT
AND RECOVERY:
REFLECTION AND INTERVENTION

Chapter Ten

Women and Shame: Kin and Culture

Marilyn Mason

SUMMARY. Shame, the "master emotion," is taking its place in the therapy literature where we have focused attention on its etiology and the family's influence on early childhood development. We now recognize that we must look beyond the impact of the family of origin to the cultural context of shame. When we examine shame in women's socialization in a patriarchy with its concurrent oppression and abuse of women, we can further understand the perpetuation of shame. This feminist perspective on shame supports the research findings on gender differences in shame—that women experience greater degrees of shame than do men. We can more readily see that addiction is both the cause and the result of women's shame.

How is shame gender-bound? And just what is the link of shame to women's addictions? We have become quite sophisticated about shame; we know shame is systemic—that it is the "master emotion" (Goleman, 1987). We have made great headway in naming and defining shame; we have examined shame in our intrapsychic and kinship systems, our families of origin. But the remaining challenge is to face the overpowering and typically overlooked cultural context of shame. It is crucial to women's understanding and sense of self to explore shame within its cultural roots; we must focus our attention on women's socialization, the ever-present shaper and perpetuator of women's shame. When we focus on

Marilyn J. Mason, PhD, is a Licensed Consulting Psychologist in private practice in Minneapolis, MN. She is Adjunct Assistant Professor, Department of Family Social Science, University of Minnesota. Correspondence may be addressed to her at 1409 Willow Street, Minneapolis, MN 55403.

women's socialization in kin *and* culture, we can understand women's shame and addiction.

THE CONTEXT OF SHAME

We face in ourselves, our clients and our students that which is deeply embedded in our families, our institutions, and our cultural values. We live in a culture of abundance — that is, material abundance. Yet we are spiritually impoverished. Perhaps one reason we feel shame so intensely is that our nation has not faced its shame. Indira Ghandhi, in an interview with Oriana Fallaci, stated "It's a great privilege to have led a difficult life, and many people in my generation have had this privilege. I sometimes wonder if young people today are deprived of the dramas that shaped us" (Fallaci, p. 171). But Indira did not know what we know. We have not had the external dramas but we have had the internal traumas.

If we were going to prevent children from living in the most dangerous places in America, we would protect them from the family. We *have* had the traumas; we have tremendously high rates of family violence. For example we know that 400,000 more cases of father-daughter incest will be reported in the U.S. this year; we know that one in four women will be beaten. One of five women have been sexually assaulted, and 38% of all female children are sexually assaulted by age 18 (Covington, 1986). Every six minutes a woman is raped. And women who are alcoholic or drug-dependent are *twice* as likely to be incest and rape survivors than are nonalcoholic women. We know that we rank eighteenth in the world in infant mortality. We know that 40 per cent of the people living in poverty in this nation are children. And we know that the second highest cause of death in American children is homicide. We carry this national history in our communities, our workplaces, schools and churches, and in our families past and present.

Nationally, we do not live our values. Our values are reflected in areas where we invest our energies — time, caring and money. When we live with many thousands of people who are homeless and in poverty, while spending 67 per cent of our tax dollars for defense, we can see where our nation's dominant energy is focused. We live in a shamebound, racist, sexist, ageist, homophobic, addicted society and this touches all of us (Fossum, 1985). The shame is binding; few escape.

This is the shame of the woman whose hand hides
her smile because her teeth are bad, not the grand
self-hate that leads some to razors or pills
or swan dives off beautiful bridges however
tragic that is. This is the shame of being yourself,
of being ashamed of where you live and what
your father's paycheck lets you eat and wear.
This is the shame of the fat and the bald,
the unbearable blush of acne, the shame of having
no lunch money and pretending you're not hungry.
This is the shame of concealed sickness — diseases
too expensive to afford, that offer only their cold
one-way ticket out. This is the shame of being ashamed,
the self-disgust of the cheap wine drunk, the lassitude
that makes junk accumulate, the shame that tells
you there is another way to live but you are
too dumb to find it. This is the real shame, the damned
shame, the crying shame, the shame that's criminal,
the shame of knowing words like "glory" are not
in your vocabulary though they litter the Bibles
you're still paying for. This is the shame of not
knowing how to read and pretending you do. This is
the shame that makes you afraid to leave your house,
the shame of food stamps at the supermarket when
the clerk shows impatience as you fumble with the change.
This is the shame of dirty underwear, the shame
of pretending your father works in an office
as God intended all men to do. This is the shame
of asking friends to let you off in front of the one
nice house in the neighborhood and waiting
in the shadows until they drive away before walking
to the gloom of your house. This is the shame
at the end of the mania for owning things, the shame
of no heat in winter, the shame of eating cat food,
the unholy shame of dreaming of a new house and car
and the shame of knowing how cheap such dreams are.

(Rutsala, 1986, p. 12)

KINSHIP SHAME

The above poem illustrates many of the sources of shame. Our primary experience of shame has its roots in our families of origin. Our families instill shame in early childhood; they perpetuate shame through secrets — secrets about natural and unnatural life events. Often it is not the event itself — death of a loved one, sickness, incest, suicide, racial secrets, or disabilities — but rather the secrecy enveloping the event that creates shame. Intending to protect themselves and their children from this pain, parents create family myths and obscure the actual sources of pain, which are passed on and cause unresolved grief, denial, addictions and an ongoing sense of shame. Young people learn the "no-talk" rule when they receive the message, "There's nothing going on here and don't tell anyone" (Beletsis and Brown, 1981, p. 189). This is a fundamental rule in the shamebound family.

> A shamebound family is a family with a self-sustaining, multigenerational system of interaction with a cast of characters who are, (or were in their lifetime) loyal to a set of rules and injunctions demanding control, perfectionism, blame and denial. The pattern inhibits or defeats the development of authentic intimate relationships, promotes secrets and vague personal boundaries, unconsciously instills shame in the family members, chaos in their lives and binds them to perpetuate the shame in themselves and their kin. It does so regardless of the good intentions, wishes and love which may also be part of the system. (Fossum and Mason, 1986, p. 8)

Children read parents quite clearly; sensing their parents' buried pain, they attempt to protect them through burying their own feelings or, often, acting out the family pain. This is an attempt to draw parents away from their own pain. Most of this occurs at the unconscious level. In shame research instruments we see adult recollections of childhood memories:

> During the years I was growing up (childhood or adolescence) my father/mother was not very available to me either because of work or perhaps an illness or injury that may have hospitalized him/her for a long period of time, or for some other reason that may or may not have been clear to me.

> My father/mother was a cold, distant person. I had great difficulty talking to him/her and he/she seemed unable to listen to me or understand me. I could not depend on him/her to be there for me when I needed him/her.

> In my family there were certain things my parents would not allow us to talk about or to express, such as feelings of anger or sadness, or thoughts of death or sex, or fears, or whatever might be upsetting to mother or to father. (Cook, 1986a)

This legacy of buried source events in families' lives leaves a reservoir of buried pain and loss. Children normalize this process that is critical to the development of shame. Their relationships with others and with themselves are deeply affected.

Interpersonal Shame

Shame is born in relationship. When parents shut down their vulnerable feelings, they sever the natural interpersonal connection, the "between" link so essential to relational growth. When children's needs are neglected, they grow up with feelings of general inadequacy, fear of rejection or abandonment. Today's researchers are now recognizing the correlation between parental bonding, acceptance and rejection as significant factors in the dynamics of shame. Today we call this emotional abuse — lack of touch, lack of eye contact, lack of positive feedback, lack of attention, or verbal threats or assaults. While child neglect lies at one end of the continuum, violence, intrusion and abuse lie at the opposite end. Many children experience terror and trauma in abusing families. Adults responding to items on research instruments recall:

> During my childhood and/or my adolescence I was sexually abused by one or more members of my family or a close relative (father/mother, stepparent, sibling, grandparent, aunt or uncle).

> Discipline from my father/mother was very harsh. He/she spanked me or beat me or hit me hard enough to hurt badly.

> My mother/father sometimes threatened to abandon me or to send me away if I didn't behave better.

> My father was physically violent toward my mother. He would either shove, push, slap her, hit her with his fist, choke her or beat her.

> My mother was physically violent toward my father or my siblings (perhaps in self-defense against violence).

> I got the feeling from my father/mother I could never do anything right, could never please him/her, or that somehow I was just never good enough for him/her. (Cook, 1986a)

In order to survive the painful scenes above, children resort to denial. They repress memories and form life-essential defenses. The fences a child puts up to survive replace the personal boundary.

A boundary is the invisible screen that encompasses the young, growing ego self—the screen through which we interpret life and make meaning. It is the line between the self and the not-self, or other. Our boundaries exist intellectually, emotionally and physically. And our boundaries protect our souls. For a child to grow naturally, with high self esteem, this line must be respected.

When a child experiences violence or neglect, he or she is unable to develop natural boundaries. The generational line between parent and child is invaded through abuse or overprotection, or underdeveloped through neglect or "affectionless control" (Parker, 1983, p. 12). The degree to which a child's boundaries are violated is the degree to which the self becomes damaged, perceptions become impaired and victimization begins. With these onslaughts, what a child learns relationally in these early years becomes internalized and normalized. The child does not have a clear sense of what she/he thinks, feels or wants physically. These childhood beliefs about the self and relationships accompany the child into adult relationships, often resulting in repeated experiences of abuse and disrespect. When boundaries are disrupted, family shame is instilled, maintained, and passed into the next generation.

In using the metaphor of the screen for the self boundary, I point out to clients that as children they *were* powerless. As we develop, our personal power grows. But when girls have been subject to abuse, they feel powerless as adults. They feel all control is outside them. As if there is a zipper on the outside of their screen around the self, they are subject to others being in control of their screens, often unzipping them and entering their personal space without invitation (Fossum and Mason, 1986, p. 70). Intimacy is terrifying when we don't know where we end and others begin. The degree to which we have known respect for our expressed feelings, respect for body dignity and respect for our thoughts and abilities is the degree to which our boundary zipper will be on the inside. The goal for all of us is to have our zippers on the inside. (See Figure 1.)

Lying at the core of the self, within the boundary, is shame.

Internalized Shame

Shame is about the self. Shame safeguards the spirit. Sartre said shame is the "immediate shudder which runs through me from head to foot without any discursive preparation" (Sartre, p. 82). He has called shame the internal hemorrhage. This fascinated me, since I always knew at some

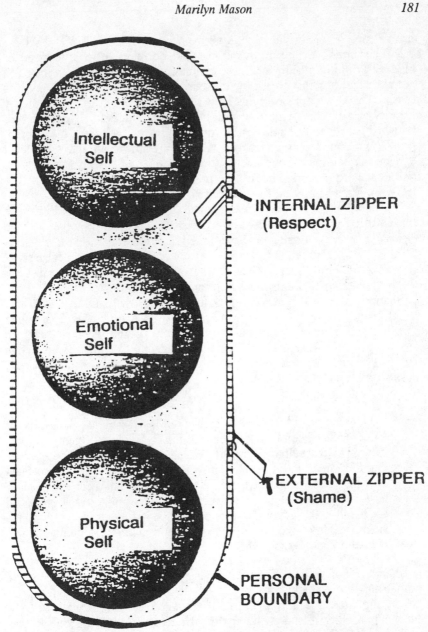

Figure 1. The Boundaries to the Self.

level shame is wired within us, a network wired in our historical selves. Painful shaming events from our past lie dormant, often repressed or blocked in our adult minds. These childhood experiences, with their full range of feelings, become buried in our spiritual core. This is why it is essential to know our history as intimately as possible. A single word by another person can trigger our deeply planted minefield of painful, unknown history; our shame spurts forth within us. We feel the internal head-to-toe shudder. If we are fortunate, we are able to dip into our bucket of survival techniques, our defense mechanisms, and quickly "cover" the risk of the exposure to shame. We may use anger, tears, changing subjects; we learn to rely on these defenses.

The survival patterns become ingrained. They become safety insulation for our true and unmet selves. These defenses don't just dissolve; we take down our fences only after we have turned to our history to learn why they were so essential to our survival. We must recognize how our "false self" was a major form of coping before we can begin the journey to meet our true self. Facing shame is the way through.

Shame is the most powerful block to human growth and development, to intimacy and to spiritual growth known to us at this time. Shame can grip our self in paralysis as our words fall away and we feel frozen in space and time. That is why I tell my clients that facing shame is like Drano. All the jammed gunk has to come up first before our spiritual drains can be cleansed.

So let's define shame:

> Shame is more than loss of face or embarrassment. Shame is an inner sense of being completely diminished or insufficient as a person. It is the self judging the self. A moment of shame may be humiliation so painful, or an indignity so profound, that one feels one has been robbed of her or his dignity, or has been exposed as basically inadequate, bad, or worthy of rejection. A pervasive sense of shame is the ongoing premise that one is fundamentally bad, inadequate, defective, unworthy, or not fully valid as a human being. (Fossum and Mason, 1986, p. 8)

Shame is not guilt, nor the underlying dynamic of guilt. Guilt is our human capacity to make mistakes or violate our values. We may feel guilt for getting a divorce, for having an affair. We feel guilt as we look back on our parenting mistakes, our political naiveté. These are outside us, violations of the cultural myths or personal values. With guilt there is a way back; we can repair. We can say we're wrong, we're sorry, we made a mistake. Guilt is about behavior; about what I *do*. Shame is about who I *am*. While shame is a cul de sac, guilt offers a direction. Guilt is the conduit to our conscience. Our goal is to move from self-consciousness to conscientiousness, from shame to *mature* guilt, to living our own values.

The Cul de Sac of Shame:
Control and Addiction

Shame can become a driving life force. Yevtushenko, the Russian poet, has stated that shame is the most powerful motivator of human progress. This begins with attempts to control. When one's family life seems out of control, a child learns to use control to prevent the hemorrhage of shame. This control becomes at times rigid and perfectionistic. The child hangs on to some corner of life that is manageable for him/her, so he/she can feel good about some aspects of life, and more importantly, escape the shame.

In controlling ourselves we often attempt to control others as well; we think that will make our world safer. While control may have meant survival in childhood, it becomes a cyclical trap in adulthood. Unfortunately, we also live in such a highly controlled society that control becomes normal. With our advanced technology and our ability to control *things* with high efficiency (witness FAX and Polaroid), we live with the illusion that we can control *people* as well.

We do need to be in control; self-control is essential to adulthood. But when shame underlies it, the control becomes a driving force. Often the self becomes fused with our role selves; these become hiding places for our control. We can even feel a sense of competence through these roles — the successful businessman or professional woman, the ideal homemaker, the ever-giving teacher. Roles offer culturally prescribed behaviors; we can lose our selves in our roles (role sleep) and reap external rewards. But often the person feels they *cannot* stop — they are on a treadmill, driven by perfectionism. The intense energy in the behavior covers the anxiety that stems from their shame and lack of developed self; an exaggerated form of shame-driven control leads to essential releases. These cyclical releases are often expressed in the form of addictions and compulsive, secret behaviors. Naturally these release behaviors result in felt shame — from drinking too much, binge eating or compulsive sex. We know what to do for shame; we resume our control. And the shame cycle continues.

We have seen myriad articles embracing the word *addiction*. It has been so broadened that its meaning is confounded. The definition I like best for addiction is:

When you can't control when you start or stop the activity, when it begins to damage you and your close relationships, you're addicted. (Milkman and Sunderwirth, 1987, p. 16)

While we recognize the inherited biochemical and neurochemical aspects of addiction—that we are twice as likely to become alcoholic if we had alcoholic parents—we have recently become more aware of other factors. Addiction has often been a major coping device for women who were abused or rejected by their parents. One recent study of women with eating disorders showed that they suffer significantly higher levels of shame. Studies of their families of origin indicate that these women experienced rejection from parents, most significantly from their fathers (Cook, 1991).

"Alcohol saved my life," said Mary. When telling her life story, she recounted the stories of her ethnic shame (she had a Native-American heritage), her brothers' and father's sexual abuse of her and her mother's beatings and neglect. She was so traumatized that she realized that without medicating her pain with alcohol, she might not have survived. In fact, research on shame and addiction shows that poor childhood relationships with mother and father *and* sexual abuse and abandonment are major predictors of alcoholism (Cook, 1991). Relying on her alcohol use to maintain control, Mary was able to develop a strong "pseudo-self." When she sought alcoholism treatment years later, she looked back on her alcoholism as a life saver. This raises a question: For how many women is addiction a major coping mechanism? Mary's form of coping is surely linked to her family of origin and the alcoholism there. But Mary's shame grew from more than *kin*; it was also *culture*. Mary was soon to learn that facing her alcoholism was clearly not enough; she had to face the fallacies of cultural socialization. Mary later asked the question, which problem came first—the socialization or the alcoholism?

SOCIOCULTURAL SHAME

We cannot heal our shame in psychotherapy, twelve-step groups or family of origin workshops alone. We must examine how women's socialization instills and insures her shame. Since gender is a social construct, we have to become aware of how our social tasks as women are both learned *and* assigned (Goodrich, Rampage, Ellman and Halstead, 1988, p. 22). Until we face the *non*-psychological aspects of shame, we cannot be free. We need to be conscious to be free. We can explore this missing context in five areas: (1) Women and Patriarchy; (2) Women as Objects;

(3) Women in Love/Limerence; (4) Women and Abuse; and (5) Women and Ageism.

Women and Patriarchy — Women as Less

Living in a patriarchal culture yields serious consequences for women. With the onset of the feminist revolution we became clear about religion and the roots of patriarchy and women's place in man's established church. In recent years we have become clear about the effects of the "white male system" and the many power imbalances it creates. Women have always been "less than" in our culture — economically, politically, educationally, socially and physically. Women, in fact, have remained at a preindustrial stage, working for the family with no exchange value in the market place (Hare-Mustin, 1988, p. 39). Politically we have seen what has happened when a woman attempts to run for office; women become targets of "ad hominem" attacks. In addition, women have not learned to support themselves or one another politically. In education we see more women working, yet their salaries remain much lower than males' for the same work. A "working mother" in the U.S. still has an average of 35 hours a week of housework to face, with the least help with childcare of any mothers in the world (Hare-Mustin, 1988, p. 24). Socially women are still referred to as "girls," a reminder that women are viewed as childlike and immature. And, physically, women have had to look up to men, in a culture where only size and strength count. It is only in recent decades that women have legitimately entered the sports world.

Current research findings on shame indicate that a woman still has "less than" status. Dr. David Cook devised an instrument to measure internalized shame, based on the Fossum/Mason definition of shame above (Cook, 1986). He found that there is a definite link in women's internalized shame between a sense of *inferiority* and *alienation* (Cook, 1990, p. 2). His research showed that women's inferiority scores and alienation scores were *consistently* higher than those of men. In fact, he stated that he would have to develop separate instruments because the experiences were so different for women. This strong statistical difference only makes explicit what we have always known. Women enter the world in an inferior place, and women typically show lower self-esteem than males.

At first glance, women's sense of alienation was a surprise; women value connection. But when we recall how women's natural sense of caring has led women to be over-responsible in relationships, we say "of course." When relationships fail or end, many women feel totally responsible and become self-blaming. The cultural prescription for women to be martyrs becomes a way to hide the shame. This alienation, says Dr. Cook, is closely linked to depression (Cook, 1991).

The consequences of women being "less than" have been reflected in the widespread "codependency" movement. Women's caring and over-responsibility have been labeled a "fatal disease" (Walters, 1990, p. 53). Any oppressed group learns to accommodate to survive; our caring is not biologically determined by our sex. It is a gender difference. Women socialized to be pleasers and "good girls" (Bepko and Krestan, 1990) are now being victimized by being labeled codependent, put in groups and pathologized for learning to follow the rules (Lerner, 1990, p. 18). While this rapidly-growing social movement has created an opening for many women to examine their relational over-responsibility, we must be mindful of the capitalistic money-making exploitation that has run rampant in this movement, blaming women for caring and natural nurturing of relationships.

Women as Objects

From the cradle on, women are loved as objects. Girls get positive reinforcement for being cute and highly feminine—sweet and pleasing. Yet we have also learned that pre-adolescent girls have a strong sense of a developing self; it is in adolescence that girls succumb to cultural messages. Carol Gilligan states that when girls enter puberty, a transformation process occurs cognitively, physically and reflectively (Gilligan, 1989). Younger girls find their voices and do speak out. But when these same young girls move away from the family, seeking peer inclusion, they join a world in which human means "white male" (Gilligan, 1988). Adolescent girls become bombarded with the sexist message that women are objects. One longitudinal study of adolescent girls showed that 72 per cent of those with highest scores on "high femininity" (sex-role stereotyped as sweet, demure, and passive), ended up addicted to chemicals (Richardson, 1981). This clearly illustrates how sex-role socialization, promoted by media, is unhealthy for women's natural development. Our sex-role stereotypes have given the message that, to be loved, a woman must be thin, sweet and always selflessly accommodating. I wonder how many women turn to drugs and chemicals because their body images can never fit the media images? And how many young women turn to drugs or chemicals for permission to be sexual? Or how many women turn to chemicals because of the painful secret of a same-sex preference?

Taught to hate all the ways in which they seem inadequate, women medicate. The powerful social stimuli of our addictive culture shape our brains. Young girls, especially girls whose boundaries were violated, are especially vulnerable to absorbing these messages. Turning outside their families for role models, they seek an identity through media. They seek loving relationships. The models for identification are often anorexic models in suggestive clothing. We know that men's appearances in advertising communicate *power* and women's appearances communicate *presence*. Women spend billions of dollars on beauty products to enhance their "marketability." In a desire to be loved, young adults focus on their outside selves, often turning to seductive behaviors to "get him." (Young girls interested in "her" often lie to themselves or bury their same-sex feelings in a homophobic culture.)

Women in Love (or Limerence)

Young women who have grown up in shamebound families often mistake intensity for love. The energy charge of intensity was often the substitute for intimacy in their families. This intensity fits well with society's message that we "fall" in love rather than "grow" into love. What we have learned in recent years is that many young adults enter into intensity—filled "limerent" relationships and label it love (Tennov, 1979). Young girls, observing parents who might have married for "romantic love," often see a "love" that long ago had died. Seeking genuine love, they too turn to romantic love. While I am not indicting romantic love, it is important that women learn about limerence. Limerent relationships involve "being in love." In limerence, our relationship with our chosen love object eclipses all other relationships, most likely because of the intensity of the sexual attraction (Tennov, 1979). Young women with underdeveloped boundaries are especially vulnerable to staying in limerent relationships and enter into fraudulent love relationships because they have no real self-protection.

Researcher Tennov says that, by late adolescence, 97 per cent of American men and women have fallen in love, often more than once (Tennov, 1979, p. 23). Exhilaration and powerfully passionate feelings make many girls addicted to the "highs" they experience and they become "beginnings addicts," repeatedly seeking the intense passion of the early stages of limerence. Fearing rejection and alienation, they begin one relationship before another has ended. Limerent relationships have the following characteristics:

- acute longing for reciprocation
- dependency of mood on the love object's behavior
- fear of rejection
- heartache and uncertainty

• buoyancy when reciprocation occurs, and
• ability to emphasize only what is admirable in the love object while avoiding the negative. (Tennov, 1979, pp. 23-24)

What had appeared to be women "loving too much" is often an inherited maladaptive biochemical response to certain chemicals (Milkman and Sunderwirth, 1985). Today we realize the biochemical and neurochemical aspects of this dynamic, recognizing that we can become dependent on the adrenaline (epinephrine) rush and increased concentrations of phenylethylamine (PEA) in the brain (Milkman and Sunderwirth, 1985). Sadly, many young women make lifelong decisions while in the state of limerence. For girls from shamebound families limerence appears to be the safe haven they have sought, only to often later find it the hiding place for fraudulent love and abuse.

In contrast to heterosexual women, young women who find they are attracted sexually to other women often live with the shameful secret about their preference, often waiting many years to let themselves honestly acknowledge it. Lesbian women have a double jeopardy; they not only have the limerence, but they have to hide it. Many of these women turned to alcohol or other addictions in order to fit into a homophobic society.

Women and Abuse

When women are "less than" and treated as objects, abuse is often the consequence. While our federal statistics on abuse of women are outrageously high, they do not truly reveal the breadth of violence toward women. We all recognize the escalation of violence against women, especially sex murders. When researching abuse, independent researchers consistently find higher rates of abuse. In a recent survey of 4,500 women in *MS.* magazine, three out of four women had survived male violence (Russell, 1990, p. 35). Only seven per cent of the women in the survey could say that they also had never experienced male violence and also that they had never known a rape victim (Seery and Clossick, 1991, p. 37). A random sample of urban women showed that 21 per cent of the women experience marital violence; 14 per cent experienced marital rape (Russell, 1990, p. 35). Also, 44 percent were victimized by rape or attempted rape (Russell, 1990, p. 36). Sixty per cent of rape cases involve a known perpetrator (Russell, 1990, p. 37). In alcoholic families, 60 per cent of women have been victims of rape (Russell, 1990, p. 37).

Fifty per cent of incest victims are from alcoholic homes. Seventy-four per cent of women from alcoholic families have been physically, sexually and emotionally abused. And 47 to 75 per cent of women in chemical dependency treatment centers are incest survivors. In my own consultation with women's halfway houses for alcoholism and drug recovery, I found that 75 per cent of the women were incest victims. In a recent study, almost 50 per cent of women in alcoholism treatment were sexually abused (intercourse and fondling) *before age 14* (Cook, 1991).

We do not need further statistics to understand fully what happens to women who are abused. The damaged self internalizes the shame. This internalized shame becomes manifested in low self-worth, self-contempt, self-mutilation, depression, suicidal ideation, dissociative disorders, and, in extreme cases, multiple personality disorders. Women who feel no sense of control often turn to addictions to medicate the buried pain and rage that truly belong outside them.

What, then, are the results of women's socialization? With women as "less than," as objects caught in limerence and suffering abuse, we see women living in shame. This shame may be manifested in shame about their core being, shame about relationships, shame about their bodyselves and shame about their competence. And when women finally do face their shame and integrate their true selves, they face yet another potential reservoir for shame — aging.

Women and Ageism

Why does ageism belong in this list of the socialization of shame? The woman who was made an object and who was abused takes her buried pain into the later years. What the young adolescent girl experiences in facing a culture, the mid-life woman also faces as she moves into late life. Many lonely women in our ageist, sexist culture turn to alcohol or drugs to cope. One study shows that 62 per cent of women over 60 are on psychoactive prescription drugs (Mandanaro, 1982). Women face the shame of being old and of becoming invisible in our youth-valuing culture. Women spend billions of dollars on cosmetics and medical procedures to buy "youth." This is closely linked to the women who have swallowed all the cultural messages that women are immature and incompetent. Our ageist attitudes constantly remind women that an old woman is a useless woman.

Perhaps one of the most powerful uses of media, such as the Oprah Winfrey Show and other talk shows, is the exposure of what we are living with. Women are given permission to talk — to not feel alone. Workbooks that accompany books such as *The Courage to Heal* offer help to individual women (Bass and Davis, 1988). Women are learning more, talking more, looking for the way through, the way out.

Sadly, the way out involves economics. Upper-class and upper-middle-class and even middle-class women can afford the high cost of necessary help. Women of color and women victimized by our economic caste system struggle to find help. Agencies throughout the country are setting up groups for women, but part of our ongoing shame is exacerbated by the fact that so many of our sisters are in poverty. When we turn to the global community, the view is even more dismal. As I write I feel the downward spiral of shame.

But there is a way up and out. Empowering women to work together is the first step toward the healing process. Women talk with one another; they gain support in myriad groups. Perhaps part of the success of the twelve-step movement is that there women can be mutual in their sharing, they can be anonymous and non-hierarchical. This surely can be a model for empowering women. Many women, who struggle with the "maleness" they see in twelve-step groups, are translating the language of the "steps" to fit the experience of women.

Whether from our families of origin, or from being born female, we face shame. We can, and we do, heal. We heal in relationship.

THE WAY THROUGH –
FROM SHAME TO RESPECT

The healing process can take many years. Whether we get involved in long-term psychotherapy, participate in women's groups or turn to our empathic friends and family members, we face a process. This process has identifiable phases.

Phase One – The Naming Phase

Eventually we need to name our shame, sharing our secrets, our pain, with a listening friend, a family member or life partner. When we can tell our shameful secrets, we can begin to externalize the shame; we can start the movement upward in the spiral of shame. With empathy we realize we are not alone.

This phase might also involve reading about abuse, and recognizing the consequences of agoraphobia, perfectionism, depression, dissociation, anxiety, and obsessive-compulsive patterns. This can happen through attending workshops or watching television specials. No one today needs to recover without the benefit of the psychoeducational materials available. Many find help through writing a memoir, a family history and a sexual history. Many also do family genograms, finding family ghosts as they

decode the sexual secrets, the abuse and the losses (both natural and unnatural) in the family.

In this phase, in which women ask for help, many women face their
addictions—eating disorders, self-mutilation, chemicals and alcohol to
name a few. Support is crucial to this phase. Many women enter Women
for Sobriety groups or twelve-step groups to help with addictions. Others
attend abuse recovery groups.

In this phase women also can identify areas of our shame, identify the
sources of shame, and get validation that their experiences were shaming
ones. They learn about impaired perceptions and begin to understand what
healthy relationships are. They begin the process of bringing the shame
back into the dynamics of the relationships from which they were born,
rather than keeping the shame internal. They see that others were responsible for their childhood shaming experiences.

Phase Two—Affective Reconstruction

As we face our past, it is important to begin the self-empathy process—
the experiencing of compassion for the historical self, the child who shut
down her natural affect. To move from self-contempt to self-acceptance
and forgiveness, I suggest women bring in childhood photographs so we
can study not only the family constellation, but the child's true expressions. Women begin to recall blocked memories through drawings, family
interviews and letters. In this process, deeply buried feelings surface;
women face the rage, the unresolved grief and loss of innocence and/or
childhood bonding. As she unravels the family myths, a woman develops
her own true story, her reality. She often visits graveyards to have unfin-
ished conversations. In so doing, she is also forging an identity. She finds
her false self-survival identity replaced by a growing real self. Often affir-
mations help to reprogram the childhood shame scripts (I am not lovable; I
don't deserve respect). As she finds her feelings, a woman begins to trust
her self, and discovers where she ends and the rest of the world begins.
She enters into the phase of boundary reconstruction.

The Integration Phase

In developing our boundaries, we define our natural self. We become
true to our own values. We break the implicit family rules that imprisoned
our adult behavior and are no longer bound by childhood family loyalty to
myths and secrets. We find our voices and speak out. We leave some
relationships; new ones begin. The shame reduces as we begin to hold
others accountable for what was done to us.

To aid this externalization process, I often ask clients to name their shame. They typically find very creative, honest names ("Svengali" was one). We then talk about when "Svengali" comes, how frequently and what happens to us when "Svengali" comes. I then ask the client to look at any behaviors she knows about that might invite "Svengali." I also asked her to bring in a list of all her life accomplishments *despite* the fact that "Svengali" has been in her life so long. This is typically very validating for a client's self-acceptance, recognizing that, despite the shame, they have achieved. As women find their voices, they find their personal power. Self-esteem grows as we forgive ourselves and others who are deserving. Some say we should *always* be forgiving. We see many women who experienced traumatic violent childhoods who find they do not feel forgiving, and often feel guilty. In cases where the emotionally abusing and/or violent dynamics continue, many women recognize they must have minimal contact and/or say a final goodbye to family members.

In this final ongoing phase, women restructure relationships. By taking risks interpersonally, by living their own values, women continue to regain their selves. In so doing, they often establish new meaningful rituals. They create new friendship families—families with support for their changes. They live with acceptance and self-forgiveness. Flattened spirits become alive. Womens' depths grow; they go deeper. They also feel a connection to the goddess, to all sisterhood, to all women of all time. In guided imagery exercises, women typically can image this wise woman who has been so choked through shame and addiction. This is the realm of the spirit. As author Mary Richards wisely states, "There is a creative spirit deep within you desiring to be free; you may as well get out of its way for it will give you no peace until you do" (Richards, 1964, p. 92).

As women face shame in kin and culture, they face inequality and find feminism. They learn they deserve equality. They also face a monumental challenge—to live with "a new consciousness in which competition will be balanced with cooperation and individualism will be balanced with love." This is the move from patriarchy to partnership. Author Riane Eisler calls for a new partnership way, action based on the higher goals of humanity (Eisler, 1988, p. 345). She states this is ". . . more than a reaffirmation of the dignity and worth of half of humanity. . . . It also offers us a positive replacement for the myths and images that have for so long blatantly falsified the most elementary principles of human relations by valuing killing and exploiting more than giving birth and nurturing" (Eisler, 1988, p. 39).

When we face our shame in kin and culture, we can take the first steps toward change; we can recognize that addiction is the cause and result of women's shame.

This form of relational healing requires feminist therapy; it also requires using our selves. It is imperative that we as professionals have "done our own work." We must be clear about our own boundaries and ghosts from our pasts, as we are vulnerable to countertransference experiences. In working with shame, we often face our own dragons as memories are jarred loose. Our own growth continues. And as we make mistakes through our own natural imperfectionism, we give our clients and ourselves the gift of permission to be authentically who we are and to model the essential caring and provide the necessary holding environment in which our clients can risk exposure in facing their shame.

REFERENCES

Bass, E. and Davis, L. (1988). *The courage to heal*. New York: Harper & Row.

Beletsis, S. and Brown, S. (1981). *A developmental framework for understanding adult children of alcoholics*. Monograph. Stanford University.

Bepko, C. and Krestan, J. (1990). *Too good for her own good*. New York: Harper & Row.

Cook, D. (1991). Telephone interview: results of study of 100 alcoholic women in treatment at Hazelden, MN.

Cook, D. (1990). Draft manual: Clinical use of internalized shame scale. Unpublished manuscript. Menomonie, WI: University of Wisconsin-Stout. p. 2.

Cook, D. (1986a). Internalized shame scale research instrument-childhood scale. Menomonie, WI: University of Wisconsin-Stout.

Cook, D. (1986b). Internalized shame scale. Menomonie, WI: University of Wisconsin-Stout.

Covington, S. (1986). Physical, emotional and sexual abuse. *Focus on family and chemical dependency,* 9 (3).

Eisler, R. (1988). *The chalice and the blade*. San Francisco: Harper & Row.

Fallaci, O. (1976). Indira Ghandi. In *Interview with history*. Boston: Houghton-Mifflin.

Fossum, M. (1985). In personal conversation and training workshops.

Fossum, M. and Mason, M. (1986). *Facing shame*. New York: W.W. Norton.

Gilligan, C. (1988) Exit-voice dilemmas in adolescent development. In C. Gilligan, J. Ward and J. Taylor (Eds.), *Mapping the moral domain.* Cambridge, MA: Harvard University Graduate School of Education.

Gilligan, C. (1989). Keynote Presentation at Family Therapy Networker Conference.

Goleman, D. (1987). Shame steps out of hiding and into sharper focus. *The New York Times,* 15 Sept.

Goodrich, T., Rampage, C., Ellman, B. and Halstead, K. (1988). *Feminist Family Therapy: A Casebook.* New York: W.W. Norton.

Hare-Mustin, R.T. (1988). Family change and gender differences: Implications for theory and practice. *Family Relations,* 37, 36-41.

Lerner, H. (1990). Problems for profit. *The women's review of books.* 7, 15-16.

Mandanaro, J. (1982). Unpublished research. From Wingspread Health Center for Women, Santa Cruz, CA.

Milkman, H. & Sunderwirth, S. (1985). Esalen catalog (K. Thompson, Ed.) Big Sur, CA: Esalen.

Milkman, H. and Sunderwirth, S. (1987). *Craving for ecstasy.* Lexington, MA: Lexington Books.

Parker, G. (1983). Cited in David Cook, Family of origin measures: validating a new scale. Paper presented at the Annual Conference of the AAMFT. New Orleans, LA.

Richards, M. (1964). *Centering.* Middletown, CT: Wesleyan University Press.

Richardson, A. (1981). Androgyny—how it affects drinking practices: A comparison of female and male alcoholics. *Focus on women: Journal of Addictions and Health,* 2, 116-131.

Russell, D. (1990). Femicide: Speaking the unspeakable. *MS. Magazine,* 1:2, 34-36.

Rutsala, V. (1986). *Shame: ruined cities.* Pittsburgh: Carnegie-Mellon Press.

Seery, B. and Clossick, M. (1991). Analysis. *MS. Magazine,* 1, 36-41.

Tennov, D. (1979). *Love and limerence.* New York: Stein and Day.

Walters, M. (1990). The codependent cinderella who loves too much . . . fights back. *The Family Therapy Networker.* July-August, 52-55.

Chapter Eleven

Codependent or Empathically Responsive? Two Views of Betty

Jane Sloven

SUMMARY. This paper contrasts treatment based on two different models of conceptualizing female behavior, Codependency and Self in Relation. It applies each model to the marital problems of one couple, focusing on the female partner. It demonstrates that Self in Relation theory is more consistent with principles of feminist family therapy practice.

INTRODUCTION

An important part of our task as therapists is to choose a theoretical framework through which to view the problems our clients present. Choosing one theoretical framework over another is similar to the use of a camera lens. One can choose a telephoto lens, sharpening the focus on just one part of the picture, or one can choose a wide angle lens and capture the larger picture. The choice of a lens in treatment influences not only our clients' perceptions of their problems and of themselves, it also determines treatment choices and treatment outcomes.

This paper explores the marital problem of one couple by comparing and contrasting two different lenses which are focused on the experience of the female partner in the marriage. One lens is the popular concept of Codependency. Codependency is a descriptive label that emerged from

Jane Sloven, LCSW, is in private practice in Portland, ME. Correspondence may be addressed to her at 10 Machigonne Street, Portland, ME 04102.

The author would like to thank Carol Lohman, LCSW, Nancy Abel, LCSW, and Stephanie Abate, LCSW, for their careful reading of earlier drafts of this article.

195

the field of chemical dependency treatment. It has been adopted by many therapists and clients to refer to women in relationships with addicted or otherwise dysfunctional partners. It focuses very specifically on the women in these relationships and their behavior.

The contrasting framework is the evolving concept of "Self in Relation," a psychological theory of development that has emerged from the work of feminist psychotherapists at the Stone Center for Developmental Services and Studies at Wellesley College. Its focus is broad and inclusive of many aspects of women's lives and relationships.

These two theories or "lenses" provide ideal points of comparison in demonstrating the ways that one's perspective on female experience can radically affect the course of treatment.

Definitions of codependent behavior attempt to establish a paradigm of disease. They pathologize women's experience, labeling a woman's traditional "other focus" as unhealthy while ignoring its value to human relationships. This lens ignores the social, political and economic factors that contribute to women's highly developed skills in these areas.

In contrast, self in relation theory explores the development of women's sense of self and hypothesizes that *healthy* development occurs for women in the context of relationship. This theory values and honors the skills of empathy and attention to connection in relationship. This wider lens incorporates social, political and economic factors into psychological assessment.

Self in relation theory is inherently feminist in perspective, while codependency theory is not. This paper will demonstrate that while the goals of treatment conducted from either perspective are very similar, the means of achieving those goals has a radically different impact on a woman's experience of herself and on the ultimate integrity of any relationship she seeks to sustain. The theoretical stance of self in relation can be integrated much more consistently with feminist family therapy practice.

CASE HISTORY

Betty came to see me on the recommendation of her family physician. Betty was experiencing chronic back pain and neck pain. Recently, she had begun to have episodes of spastic colitis, an illness which was common in her family. At 65, Betty presented as an intelligent, attractive, upper-middle-class woman.

Betty was employed as the office manager for a medium size legal firm. She managed an office staff of five and oversaw all the billing herself.

She'd had the position for fifteen years, received excellent reviews, felt secure, and obtained great satisfaction from her work.

The problem, Betty said, was her marriage. A year previously, her husband, George, had told her he was in love with another woman. Although he had been acting oddly, Betty was unprepared for this as an explanation. They had been married for forty-five years, had three grown children and had lived in the same comfortable community for most of their adult lives. Betty was stunned. She had felt George might have been experiencing a mid-life crisis: he was moody, unpredictable and often working late; nevertheless, Betty expected it to pass.

George had asked for a divorce and was not willing to discuss his feelings. Betty went to visit her oldest daughter. When she returned, George told her he had changed his mind and wanted to stay married. He said he was finished with the affair and loved Betty. Otherwise, he wouldn't discuss what had occurred.

Betty felt greatly relieved but confused. She sought a therapist. She and George began conjoint sessions. Betty felt that the therapist sided with George. "He said I'd just have to get used to George seeing and talking to Hazel (his former lover) because Hazel ran one of the corporate subsidiaries and there was no way to avoid contact if George was to do his job." Betty was threatened by the continuous contact. George would not change jobs; the therapist supported George's position on this issue. Betty felt she and George argued uncontrollably in the sessions and left them as unresolved and conflicted as they began. She and George dropped out of treatment after two months.

Three more months had passed, and Betty and George were still fighting. They got along for a few days, and when Betty tried to talk to George about her feelings or to ask him to talk to her about his, they'd erupt into conflict. George didn't want to talk, according to Betty. He said, "What's done is done," and he was not explaining anything. Betty couldn't understand why George had the affair or why he ended it. She felt that without an understanding of the problems in the marriage that led to the affair, they would be unable to create a secure marriage for the future. She was plagued with the question, "Why? Why the affair? Why end the affair and return?" As George continued to refuse to discuss it, Betty became more obsessed with her questions. She would pursue George with these questions, and George would withdraw further. Betty would cry herself to sleep, and George would sleep in his daughter's old room.

When Betty first came to see me, she said George refused to return for couples counseling and she was unable to continue living as she'd been living. Betty's existence had been focused around her husband and family and now, since the kids had grown and had families of their own in other cities, her day to day life focused on her husband and her job. She was fine at work, but dreaded returning home at night. She felt old, unattractive and uninteresting when she was with George. Betty's sense of herself was deteriorating, work was the only place where she felt self assured.

In looking at Betty's family history, I learned that she was one of five children. As the oldest, she was responsible from an early age for caretaking as her mother was often dysfunctional due to colitis attacks. Betty felt her mother asked to be taken care of by everyone and appreciated little. Betty idealized her father. What affection and attention she received came from him. She described her parents' relationship with each other as distant and unaffectionate. Betty took care of her siblings from an early age and had close relationships with three of her sisters but a distant relationship with her youngest sister, who was closest to her mother and had always gotten much of her mother's attention, according to Betty. Betty had been aligned with Dad while her youngest sister had been aligned with Mom. Something in the mother-daughter relationship hadn't worked here, and Betty still carried feelings of rejection and resentment. She felt no matter how hard she tried, she could never satisfy Mom and no matter how little her youngest sister did, it was always more than enough.

In sessions, Betty had great difficulty focusing on herself. She spoke repeatedly of George, his behavior, her inability to understand his motivations for the affair or for deciding to end the affair and stay with her. She described the repeated attempts to talk with him about the affair, the ensuing arguments, her frustration. She began to consider divorce. Betty could easily focus on her concerns about George but when asked what *she* felt she said she felt confused, she didn't understand why George had the affair, she didn't know how she could feel comfortable in the marriage if she didn't know why he strayed or why he stayed. Betty didn't feel he was paying attention to her, she didn't feel he really cared about her or for her. Betty couldn't focus on what *she* felt about herself or what she *needed* aside from George's saying that he loved her and needed her and had the affair because he was temporarily deranged.

George was invited in for one session. He seemed a self-possessed, rigid man. He spoke of his desire to stay in the marriage and his difficulty understanding Betty. He felt the affair had ended and there was no need to discuss it. He said he had no feelings about it. George also said he couldn't understand Betty's emotional reactions to him; he felt she was emotionally ill. Betty had described George as impervious to her questions about motivation and feelings. It appeared clear that George was not able to experience his own feelings and so was unable to empathize with Betty's.

Considering the factors involved in this case, I wondered which lens to choose. Would a framework defining Betty's behavior as "codependent" work well for her, or would a framework of "self in relation" be more appropriate? What would be the consequences of either choice?

CODEPENDENCY THEORY

The concept of codependency evolved out of the chemical dependency field. Substance abuse counselors working with alcoholics and addicts often found that as their "primary" clients got better, others in the family got worse. They noticed that spouses, oldest children, and others in the family seemed as "addicted" to overfunctioning for the chemically dependent person as the chemically dependent person was to the substance. It became clear that the behaviors of family members were organized around the behavior of the chemically dependent person. The intractability of this focus was labeled as its own disease process, co-alcoholism, para-alcoholism and then "codependency." This allowed everyone in the family to have a "disease" from which they could "recover." The twelve steps of AA and Al-Anon could then be utilized by "codependents" as a way of learning to live their own lives, regardless of the behavior of the chemically dependent person. As children of alcoholics began to receive attention and treatment, and adult children of alcoholics began to identify the consequences of growing up in alcoholic families, the concept of codependency grew. The establishment of The National Association for Children of Alcoholics (NACOA) increased national awareness.

The definition of codependency, however, shortly began to be applied to a variety of people. Anyone who grew up in a family with "dysfunction" and rigid rules could be classified as "codependent" regardless of the presence or absence of chemical dependency. Different definitions of codependency evolved. One early and popular definition was supplied by Melody Beattie:

> One who has let another person's behavior affect him or her, and who is obsessed with controlling that person's behavior. . . . The heart of the definition and recovery lies not in the *other person* — no matter how much we believe it does. It lies in ourselves, in the ways we try to affect them: the obsessing, the controlling, the obsessive 'helping,' caretaking, low self-worth bordering on self-hatred, self-

repression, abundance of anger and guilt, . . . other centeredness
that results in abandonment of self, . . . (Beattie, 1987, pp. 31-32)

Another definition, which focuses on the style of behavior, was offered
by Sharon Wegsheider-Cruse (1985):

> A specific condition that is characterized by preoccupation and ex-
> treme dependence (emotionally, socially and sometimes physically)
> on a person or object. Eventually, this dependence on another per-
> son becomes a pathological condition that affects the co-dependent
> in all other relationships. (1985, p. 2)

Many varied definitions have appeared; all describe similar traits.
These include: external referenting (being other-directed), dishonesty,
control, perfectionism, fear, rigidity, judgmentalism, inferiority/grandi-
osity, self-centeredness, and not dealing with feelings in a healthy way
(Schaef, 1986, p. 42).

Codependents have also been described as having difficulty experiencing appropriate levels of self-esteem, setting functional boundaries, owning and expressing their own reality, taking care of their adult needs and
wants, and experiencing and expressing their reality moderately (Mellody
et al., 1989).

George is not chemically dependent, yet Betty has let his behavior become the focus of her daily life. She is "externally-referented." *Her* behavior can be defined as obsession with controlling *his* behavior. She's
worried he will get reinvolved with Hazel. Her behavior can be defined as
controlling—questioning him constantly, calling him at work, driving by
to see if his car is there. Her sense of her own self-worth at this point is
abysmally low and at times she feels intense self-hatred. She has an abundance of anger and rage and guilt about those feelings. Her focus on
George results in abandonment of her own needs and of her sense of self.
Betty is anxious, she somaticizes, she feels victimized, she is exhausted,
angry and confused, all characteristic codependent traits (Beattie, 1987,
pp. 37-39).

But, she's been in a marriage for forty-five years, and George has had
an affair which he has been loathe to discuss. Is her need to feel good in
relationship with George pathological? Is her need for him, her unhappiness at the change in status of her marriage evidence of unhealthy characteristics of codependency springing out of her own emotional insecurity?
Some of Betty's reactions are normal, expectable reactions to this situation, but Betty isn't able to work through her feelings and move on, and
the feelings are heightened by George's recalcitrance and unwillingness to

engage in dialogue and full disclosure of his feelings to Betty. Nonetheless, Betty's inability to see her own deterioration and to honor her own needs, her inability to detach and her increasing obsession with George could clearly be labeled codependent behavior.

Treatment Implications of a Codependency Model

If I choose to view this situation through a codependency lens, how does treatment proceed and how is Betty asked to view herself? A comprehensive treatment format for codependency has been outlined by Timmen L. Cermak in *Diagnosing and Treating Codependence.* His format labels the four stages of treatment as: Survival, Reidentification, Core Issues and Reintegration. Treatment first involves accepting the label of codependent, which requires a breakdown of denial. "Codependents place a premium on maintaining their behavior as voluntary. While this appears to be in direct contradiction to the compulsivity which runs their lives, it makes sense if it is perceived as a *denial of limitations.* Codependents take pride in believing that they can always draw on their willpower to tolerate one more disappointment. This belief creates the illusion that they are in control while everything around them is out of control" (Cermak, 1986, p. 70).

After accepting the label, other expected accomplishments in treatment involve: taking responsibility for the perpetuation of one's own problems and dysfunctional behavior; accepting one's limitations; recognizing that one's life has become unmanageable as a result of trying to control the uncontrollable; giving up the illusion of power and grieving its loss; exploring compulsivity; developing independence and autonomy; and finally, integrating a sense of personal power and self-worth.

This model of treatment has been adapted from the traditional approach to alcoholism, a crucial element being the acceptance of alcohol abuse as a disease over which one is powerless. The use of Al-Anon and CODA meetings, along with the twelve steps and sponsorship, is part of treatment.

Cermak's stages and treatment recommendations can neatly fit Betty's dilemma. Some of the treatment goals are ones which most therapists would choose even without this framework. Stage one requires forming an empathic connection with one's client, obviously essential to any successful treatment approach. Phase two focuses on looking at one's limitations, i.e., what one is able, realistically, to effect, and what one cannot effect. This is a usual part of goal setting in most treatment frameworks. Working on communication processes and skill development in this area are integral to most treatment models. Working with a client to help them identify and feel their feelings and to begin to grieve losses is again, generally accepted treatment. One may or may not look at how one avoids grief by labeling behaviors "compulsive." One normally will explore patterns of behavior that have been tried and have not worked to bring about change.

One of the initial and important solutions for codependency involves "detachment," trying to separate ourselves emotionally from problems that cannot be controlled. Operating from a codependency model of treatment would involve referring Betty to Al-Anon to try to help her detach from her focus on changing George. The Al-Anon daily book, "One Day At A Time," speaks to this issue eloquently.

> When we hear an Al-Anon member say, 'detach from the problem,' we may think rebelliously: 'How can I detach from my own wife or husband? Our lives are bound together and I am involved whether I want to be or not.' That is true, but there are kinds of involvement that can only make our difficulties worse. We make trouble for ourselves when we interfere with the alcoholic's activities, trying to find out where he is, what he's been doing,where the money went. Suspicious searching and prying will only keep us in a state of turmoil, make the situation worse instead of improving it. (1985, p. 131)

The choice of a referral of Betty to Al-Anon would involve substituting George's name for alcohol, so that she could remain aware that she is powerless over *his* choices and behavior. Although George was not drinking, Betty's feelings and behaviors could be seen as organized around *his* behavior. A support system composed of others in similar difficult situations is central to Twelve-Step programs such as AA, Al-Anon and CODA (Codependents Anonymous).

Treated from a codependency model, Betty would be expected to explore the ways in which she had exacerbated her problems, such as looking in George's pockets, checking to see if his car was at the office when he said he was working late, pursuing him to talk when he said that he didn't want to. Betty would evaluate these behaviors in light of her own compulsivity. She would begin to understand what factors in her own behavior create and maintain this obsession, and she would learn how to stop these behaviors. Betty would be encouraged to call people in the program when she felt the compulsion to pursue George. She would be encouraged to rely on her "higher power" and to "let go and let God." She would have inspirational literature available to read at such times, along with a variety of meetings where she could speak of her difficulties to a supportive audience.

In therapy sessions, she would focus on her feelings, and therapy could incorporate cognitive, behavioral and family systems techniques. Betty would explore her family of origin, looking at the dysfunctional family rules, and the ways in which other family members may have engaged in compulsive behaviors to avoid feelings. Betty might be seen in group, with other women who define themselves as codependents. Group therapy would provide support for expressing feelings, for growth and for change.

There is tremendous support within this context for women undergoing change. Self-help groups provide free support meetings, available day or night, weekday or weekend, lots of literature, many other people available to accept one unconditionally. These aspects of support-group involvement can be immensely healing. Combined with therapy, it is a powerful treatment. Its wildfire-like spread among the population attests to its magnetism and easy applicability.

What this model requires, however, is that Betty define herself as a person who has a disease, "codependency" and is now in recovery. She becomes not just a woman who has suffered a loss of faith and trust in her life partner, but the framework requires that she define her responses for the past year as emanating from a disease process that has affected her for years and which stems from a dysfunctional family of origin. She must develop a sense of acceptance about her limitations and accept responsibility for *creating* unmanageability in her life.

Working in the codependency framework requires that Betty accept that these problems emanated from her denial of limitations, her exercise of willpower and her need for control. The framework requires that the focus be on Betty and her compulsivity. The model minimizes the centrality, power and importance of a shift or loss in Betty's most primary relationship—her marriage. It minimizes the interactional patterns that contribute to Betty's feelings of self-worth and her desire to *know* what she can expect. It places the locus of the problem in Betty. This model negates the impact of relationship and context on feelings and behavior. It is normal to be affected by those we relate to. This isn't just Betty's problem, it's also George's and the marriage's problem. Betty cannot resolve the problem by simply detaching.

Betty's experience is also affected by the real difficulties she would face if she chose to leave George. Betty's income is half of George's income. For her to leave him and start life over as a single woman in her mid-sixties with one-third of their combined income puts her at a serious economic disadvantage. Her religious beliefs do not permit divorce. She would also face the last years of life suddenly without her life's partner, socially, economically and physically vulnerable to the consequences of aging. The changes in lifestyle would be difficult and would involve further loss and pain. George also has a higher chance of remarrying, and those social consequences cannot be ignored.

Inherent in the codependency model is an over-simplification of the existential issues which we all confront. The fact that "much of the universe lies outside our ability to influence it by force of will" creates a sense of fear and inadequacy in anyone who chooses to honestly confront the nature of human existence. A sense of loss and a fear of personal inadequacy are certainly not pathological ways of responding to such realities. Turning such responses into a simplistic formulation of individual pathology denies the social and universal forces which affect all of us as human beings in a complex world. We are powerless to affect much of what impacts on us daily, and much of what is crucial to our well-being: the quality of our air, water, food, the influence of corporate, military and political forces on our lives, the security of our banking institutions, the safety of our streets in inner cities. There is a reality to the experience of powerlessness in these arenas and it is often an adaptive response to take control of people and issues we have a better chance of influencing. Looking at the latter without the former distorts the nature of reality.

SELF IN RELATION THEORY

A theory which clearly incorporates culture, gender, social, economic and political factors into psychological development has emerged from the Stone Center at Wellesley College. Essentially, recent research has differentiated development of the "self" for women from development of the "self" for men. Traditional theory on self development now appears to be gender specific to men. Surrey distinguished self in relation from traditional theory in an early (1985) working paper. She has said that current theory places great emphasis on separation as an important aspect of individual development; separation from mother in early childhood, separation from family in adolescence and separation from mentors in adulthood (Surrey, 1985).

These staged periods of separation have been conceptualized as crucial in order for individuals to develop a sense of autonomy, independence and a clearly defined sense of self. While these stages may accurately reflect male development in this culture, a self in relation model suggests that women's development takes place differently, for women the self is "organized and developed in the context of important relationships" (Surrey, 1985). Relationships, not stages of separation, become the primary goal of development and other aspects of self are seen as developing in this context. Interpretations which make separation central to psychological health incorrectly interpret women's development. If separation is seen as the "hallmark of maturity," women's focus on connection and relationship will inevitably be defined as "other" and pathologized (Stiver, 1985).

The Stone Center Papers chart an evolving theory of women's psychological development. Basic themes include the importance of empathy, explorations of the ways empathy develops and a focus on the connections between people in the process of psychological growth (Surrey, Kaplan, & Jordan, 1990). Empathy has been described as a "cognitive and emotional activity in which one person is able to experience the feelings and thoughts of another person and simultaneously is able to know his/her own different feelings and thoughts" (Jordan, 1984). This capacity has not been a focus of psychological theory nor until now has it been valued for the high levels of "cognitive and emotional integration" needed to develop it (Miller, 1986). Jordan has stated that for women, empowerment and self-knowledge flow from the experience of mutual empathy.

Treatment choices in a self in relation model are myriad. One can utilize individual, group, couple or family therapy styles, as long as treatment is focused on issues of mutual relatedness and empathic connection. In this model development of autonomy and separation would not be the hallmarks of health; rather, the capacity to experience empathy and the development of skills to enlarge this capacity would be central to treatment. The relationship developed with the therapist would encourage empathic connectedness and would model relationship capacity as an indication of healthy development.

From a self in relation perspective, Betty's problem would be viewed as a failure in empathic relatedness. Because empathy is an interactional experience, the problem is defined as an interactional failure, not an individual one. Betty may contribute to a breakdown of empathy because of her anxious, overresponsible behavior. However, she cannot empathize with George's thoughts and feelings because he is unable or unwilling to express them. He seems equally unable to experience her thoughts and feelings.

From the perspective of male socialization, there are several factors that contribute to George's failure of empathy. Men's development does not focus on relationship skills but on separation, autonomy and independence. Skills for nurturance and empathy are not highly valued aspects of male development in this culture. When George is asked to utilize those skills of connectedness, his developmental deficits are obvious.

There are numerous consequences to empathic failure. When one feels distress and attempts to communicate it, then experiences an absence of empathy, the distress deepens. Feelings of fear, startle, and anger arise from the lack of responsiveness. This mix of feelings creates confusion. If the interaction can be corrected and one's feelings are ultimately accepted, one becomes less frightened and less isolated. The capacity to redo the interaction creates a sense of competence. The failure to make connections on a continuing basis with another person creates a very profound sense of loss and inadequacy. Feelings are experienced as unacceptable and the self as inadequate.

Other consequences can include: feeling immobilized, feeling that taking action will get one into trouble, loss of self-esteem, and fear that one's feelings and behavior might result in further cut-off and isolation. If disconnection continues, the person seeking contact may try to change herself. The inability to affect the relationship is extremely damaging, the ability to affect the relationship by reconnecting is extremely empowering (Miller, 1988).

Betty and George recognized that they had experienced a profound disconnection when George asked for a divorce. The relationship had obviously already suffered from multiple lapses of contact, which laid the groundwork for George to seek intimacy elsewhere. George's request for a divorce, however, made the depth of this estrangement overt. At this point Betty reacted with shock, fear and anger. When she tried to communicate these feelings to George, he was closed to discussion. Betty felt confused, increasingly frightened by her feelings and incompetent emotionally. The more Betty tried to engage George and failed, the more incompetent and frustrated she felt. She experienced a profound sense of loss and personal inadequacy. She feared that further attempts to pursue would cause George to leave her, yet she felt a growing sense of isolation from him.

The fears one experiences as a consequence of empathic failure when a longstanding relationship becomes threatened are a normal and realistic response to loss. The process of trying to reconnect in any way possible is understandable. Betty recognized that at 65 she cannot become a younger woman (Hazel is 35), but Betty has struggled with finding a way to become more "acceptable" to George.

Alexandra Kaplan has talked about women's tendency to take responsibility for any relational failure. She feels that this tendency often leads to depression in women and that this accounts for the significant ratio differential for depression in women and men. "As women in general experience failure or frustration in their attempts at effective connection with others, they, themselves, take responsibility for the relational failure assuming that if they were "better" they would not have such problems" (Kaplan, 1984, p. 3).

Other issues have arisen for Betty as she has contemplated her choices. Betty has thought of leaving George, but she has concerns about the impact on the extended family. She fears the consequences of emotional upheaval for her daughters, their marriages and her grandchildren.

When women contemplate the use of power on their own behalf and for their own interests, many of them equate the prospect with destructiveness and selfishness — characteristics that they cannot reconcile with a sense of feminine identity. Moreover, they feel that the use of power may lead to abandonment which threatens a central part of women's identity that affirms the need for relationships with other people" (Miller, 1982, p. 1).

The importance of relatedness to Betty, the value she places on connections, presents a major conflict. If she leaves George, in order to focus on herself, she may be seen as selfish and destructive. She may see herself as selfish, which will be intolerable, and she clearly is concerned about the damage to her daughters and their families.

The Treatment Implications of a Self in Relation Approach

If the lens of "self in relation" were chosen for Betty's treatment, couples therapy would be recommended. This is an interpersonal issue, as well as an individual issue for both Betty and George, and it has implications for the extended family. Obtaining George's agreement to participate in conjoint counseling is crucial in order to give Betty and George assistance in making and maintaining relational connection. George's relational skills are very likely limited. Betty would be asked to deal with the reality of George's skills and limitations as well as with her own limited ability to change him. Therapeutic intervention must assist George to develop a greater capacity for empathy and connection while supporting and affirming Betty's desire and capacity to create the same. Her skills at relatedness and her capacity for empathy would be identified, validated and supported. Their relationship would be explored, with particular emphasis on failures in empathy or mutual relatedness. Both of their histories in other relationships would be explored. If they are unable to redefine the relationship, the context will exist to bring in extended family members to help grieve the end of the marriage. If George will not enter treatment, individual work could proceed with Betty, with an exploration of the relationship disconnection and realistic options for future choices. This lens values and validates Betty.

The self in relation model would focus upon relatedness and movement in relationship as opposed to control or self-sufficiency. The focus is on looking to the meanings people have attached to their pain and how those meanings have affected their understanding of life experience (Jordan, 1989). Utilizing both Betty and George's histories of relational failures, exploring and grieving past losses, and connecting those with their present reactions to each other would be part of the therapy process.

The Effects of the Choice of Lens

The choice of a codependency lens versus a self in relation lens would have a marked impact on Betty's treatment and on her view of herself. Goals of therapy in a self in relation model are not the "attainment of a state of harmony and happiness" but rather the development of openness to learning and growth as well as the capacity to tolerate tension and conflict so that connections can be retained (Jordan, 1989). Sometimes, however, a fact of relational life is that mutuality and empathic connections fail. People change and those with whom we have been intimate close up to us. Fear, sadness, denial and attempts to reconnect are not pathological. A self in relation model would say "suffering becomes a cause for joining others in alleviating pain and developing compassion. This is very different from experiencing suffering as a personal injury which reveals personal insufficiency" (Jordan, 1989, p. 4).

The danger of using a codependency model lies in the facile equation of focus on relationship with symptoms of illness—"defects of character." This attribution feels to many women like "personal insufficiency." The focus on attaining a state of serenity may short circuit not only the development of skills in tolerating tension and conflict, but the realistic and adult expectation that life at times involves tolerating pain. It is crucial for women to learn to accept limits without pathologizing them.

In a self in relation model of therapy, Betty could experience her feelings in the context of a mutually responsive relationship and any failures of empathic connection could be examined. As an adjunct to therapy, work in a twelve-step program could be helpful to Betty if she could disregard the concept of disease. Betty could use the program to explore what behaviors of George were beyond her control as well as to develop other mutually enhancing relationships. Therapy would validate her desire and capacity for connection. These interventions differ from use of a codependency model in one very crucial aspect: a codependency model could too easily view relational needs and skills as pathology and tell Betty she has to recover from her compulsive need to connect. This distinction results in a profoundly different perspective in Betty's view of herself.

In either framework, Betty can learn to change what can be changed, accept what cannot be changed, and move on. The crucial difference is whether she will see herself as recovering from an illness or as a woman who appropriately places value on connecting empathically, yet may need to let go of trying to have contact with someone who has become unavailable. If the relational connection with George cannot be restored, then Betty needs help to grieve the loss.

THE IMPLICATIONS FOR FEMINIST FAMILY THERAPY PRACTICE

Feminists have pointed out that male values permeate the use of concepts such as fusion, enmeshment, individuation, differentiation and boundaries (Goodrich, Rampage, Ellman and Halstead, 1988, p. 19).

Feminist family theory emphasizes that "the family" exists in a culture that is patriarchal. The ways in which our society defines male and female roles support and encourage power differentials rooted in gender. Feminist family therapy explores and exposes these characteristics; it asks therapists to increase their own awareness and to explore such issues in therapy with clients. It presupposes that we critically examine the ways in which our treatment supports inequitable hierarchies and power imbalances. It asks us to address economic dependence, independence or parity. Feminist family therapy looks at stereotypes in gender, relationships in families, relationships in society and in treatment. It asks us to look at our expectations, suppositions and our language. Traditional interpretations of mental health and development are explored for value biases. The use of language is crucial to our awareness of gender bias. Sex differences often become exaggerated through the use of pejorative labels which focus on individuals and ignore the social structures that contribute to the widespread unhappiness of women in relationships (Hare-Mustin, 1978). This is a crucial factor in choosing a lens for treatment.

With these issues taken into account, codependency theory seems based in traditional gender-biased values, stressing the importance of individuation, self-orientation and boundaries. Context appears limited to family, ignoring important culture-based factors. Women's development of other-focus and desire for connection are associated with poor boundaries and pathologized. A client treated via a codependency model will be labeled as "diseased" for her culturally predetermined gender-associated traits.

Self in relation theory is more closely consistent with feminist family therapy values and goals. Women's development of a sense of self within the context of relationship can be valued as well as being seen in context as influenced by economic, social and political factors. The importance of women's skills in seeking and maintaining empathic connectedness are validated as important means for sustaining human life, relationships, families and the changing fabric of society.

REFERENCES

Al-Anon. (1983). *One day at a time.* NY: Al-Anon Family Group Headquarters, Inc.

Beattie M., (1987). *Co-dependent no more.* Center City, MN: Hazelden Foundation.

Cermak, T.L., (1986). *Diagnosing and treating co-dependence.* Minnesota: The Johnson Institute.

Goodrich, T.J., Rampage, C., Ellman, B., Halstend, K., (1988). *Feminist family therapy: A Casebook.* NY: W.W. Norton and Company.

Hare-Mustin, R.T., (1978). *Family Process.* A Feminist approach to family therapy 17: 181-194.

Jordan, J., (1984). *Empathy and self-boundaries.* Work in Progress, No 16. Wellesley, MA: Stone Center Working Paper Series.

Jordan, J., (1989). *Relational development: Therapeutic implications of empathy and shame.* Work in Progress, No. 39. Wellesley, MA: Stone Center Working Paper Series.

Kaplan, A.G., (1984). *The "self-in-relation": Implications for depression in Women.* Work in Progress, No. 14. Wellesley, MA: Stone Center Working Paper Series.

Mellody, P., Miller, A.W., Miller, J.K., (1989). *Facing codependence.* New York: Harper and Row.

Miller, J.B., (1982). *Women and power.* Work in Progress, No. 82-01. Wellesley, MA: Stone Center Working Paper Series.

Miller, J.B., (1986). *What do we mean by relationships?* Work in Progress, No. 22. Wellesley, MA: Stone Center Working Paper Series.

Miller, J.B., (1988). *Connections, disconnections and violations.* Work in Progress, No. 33. Wellesley, MA: Stone Center Working Paper Series.

Schaef, A.W., (1986). *Co-dependence: Misunderstood — mistreated.* Minneapolis: Winston Press, Inc.

Stiver, I.P., (1985). *The meaning of care: Reframing treatment models.* Work in Progress, No. 20. Wellesley, MA: Stone Center Working Paper Series.

Surrey, J.L., (1985). *Self-in-relation: A theory of women's development.* Work in Progress, No. 13. Wellesley, MA: Stone Center Working Paper Series.

Surrey, J.L., Kaplan, A.G., Jordan, J.V., (1990). *Empathy revisited.* Work in Progress, No. 40. Wellesley, MA: Stone Center Working Paper Series.

Wegsheider-Cruse, S., (1985). *Choicemaking.* Florida: Heath Communications, Inc.

Chapter Twelve

Reflections on Male Codependency

Jeffrey McIntyre

SUMMARY. While the concept of codependency is said to apply equally to the behavior of men and women, little has been written that discusses the meaning of the concept within the context of male behavior and psychology. This paper explores some of the critical issues faced in the treatment of men affected by the addiction of a parent or a partner. Based on the author's personal reflection and clinical observation, it describes the differing approaches to issues of power that distinguish codependent experience from more traditional male norms of behavior.

I am walking around the Fresh Pond Reservoir. I am alone, the way men often are when they think things through. That is what I am here to do; walk the dog and think through a discussion of male codependency. I am organizing myself to fulfill an agreement, something that began as a simple request. Rapidly I escalate this simple agreement to an obligation. Soon it will become a Duty. Something that began as a request is transformed into this more heavy and onerous thing, *an obligation.* This is just one of the ways that codependent men work.

As I walk I wonder about the many connections between men's psy-

---

Jeffrey McIntyre practices family and marital therapy with Cogswell Associates and is on the adjunct faculty of the Graduate School in Counseling Psychology, Lesley College, Cambridge, MA. Correspondence may be addressed to him at 25 Cogswell Avenue, Cambridge MA 02140.

The author wants to convey his gratitude to Claudia Bepko for her encouragement and support in editing this paper. Her extensive efforts have been much appreciated and vital to its completion. She helped shape a wide-open and complicated gathering of ideas and clinical material into a communicable form.

chology and codependency. I think about my own changes and developments over the last twenty-one years, as a man and as a recovering codependent ACOA.

I grew up in a working class home. My parents were good people who had each had the misfortune to be raised in a household where one parent developed an addiction to alcohol. Both my grandfathers did nothing about their addictive drinking and the consequent behavior. My dad was smart enough to stop his own drinking when I was nine. My brother and I were fortunate that our parents made the effort to care for us in much more loving and effective ways than their parents did. But many of the issues and complex covert communicational processes that make up the interactional system of chemically dependent families continued. The whole family was often caught up in webs of complicated emotional triangles and managed disappointments that no one was even aware that they were creating. They did everything they could to be good and to look good, to use Ann Smith's phrase (1988), and to fulfill the American ideal of putting the past behind them. They hoped, like so many people, that being different from their parents would make the emotional experiences of their childhoods magically go away. But even though my father stopped drinking, the fundamental, underlying system of rules and expectations, the dis-eases of the chemically dependent family system, were passed along because they were not talked about in any overt way.

As loving as they could be, my parents were completely unaware of the fact that many of their struggles were connected to their parents' addictions and codependencies. This is the way that fear, disappointment, exaggerated pride, poor self-esteem, shame, denial, codependency, and other complex unresolved developmental issues are transmitted through the generations (Bepko and Krestan, 1985; Black, 1981; Elkin, 1984; Steinglass et al., 1987; Subby & Friel, 1982; Treadway, 1989; Wegscheider-Cruse, 1989). Wounds are felt and communicated, in this case in a context of love and good care, but they are not healed. The next generation (in this case my brother and me) feels a vague sense of responsibility for something they don't understand. One generation's denied fear and disappointment seem to lurk in the Dark Places of the family. The process affects everyone. It shapes and holds beliefs and behaviors, usually in covert, less than conscious ways. When there are long-standing addictions that do not remit, the sources of the pain become more profound. This is the ground in which the seeds of codependency are transmitted and planted.

CODEPENDENCY AS CONTROL

In 1982 Robert Subby and John Friel, two family therapists from the Minneapolis area, may have given the first public naming to the issue of codependency in a pamphlet published by the Health Communications group, "Co-Dependency and the Family." A book of edited articles followed in 1984, by Michael Miller, *Co-Dependency: an Emerging Issue.* Then, in rapid succession, there followed Sharon Wegscheider-Cruse's *Choicemaking* (1985), Ann Wilson Schaef's *Co-Dependence* (1986), Subby's *Lost in the Shuffle* (1987), Melody Beattie's *Co-Dependent No More* (1987), John Bradshaw's *The Family* (1988), Pia Mellody's *Facing Codependence* (1989), and Beattie's *Beyond Codependency* (1989). The ideas of these authors seemed to grab the consciousness of a country starving for an effective way to explain a compulsive drive to control others, a way to explain the emptiness, poor self-esteem, loss of self, pain, shame, and fear that is pervasive in many people's lives.

What all the codependency theorists have described quite accurately are issues that have to do with the management of self. The concept of codependency speaks to a certain pain many people seem to feel as they live with their desires for control, predictability, and safety in a world that cannot guarantee those in any constant way. The codependent person seeks to control the Self by controlling the Other. The illusion of control over the other seems to grow out of misunderstanding that one can protect oneself from internal fears and anxieties, anticipations of embarrassment, humiliation and shame, confusions and binds, emotional triangles, losses of self-worth/esteem, and/or physical/sexual abuse by keeping accurate, vigilant control over the world outside of one's self.

There is no doubt that this defensive process can wreck havoc. Paradoxically and invariably, like so many things in life, behavior produces its opposite, less control. Contrary to the thrust of the literature defining it however, codependency does not, in and of itself, constitute a disease. Even though it can leave people in a complex state of dis-ease that requires psychological and possibly even physical attention and intervention, it stands only as a concept that is useful to describe a range of beliefs and behaviors. It is these beliefs and behaviors that men and women need help with in therapy. To say they have a disease often adds an extra and unnecessary layer of shame or confusion to the negotiation of a therapeutic contract. Utilizing the word as a descriptive concept is sometimes helpful to some people. Other times, with other people, it only hinders the successful treatment of the presenting issues.

One of the dilemmas of discussing male codependency is that the definitions of this concept are based on descriptions of female behavior and identity that are often antithetical to the ways men are raised to think about their experience. This is not to say that the concept is completely misapplied. But codependency is a relational term and men, for the most part, are raised to think of themselves, to define themselves as separate from, distant from, independent of the forces of relationship. Or, in fact, they think of themselves as being in charge of relationships. While women are raised to define themselves inside of relationship, in many instances too much so, they think about and understand issues of power and control in a fundamentally different way from men. They are often more easy with transactional equality. They do not seem driven to organize their emotional lives around the dynamics of power and control in the same ways as men. This is why many men of the early, progressive men's movement felt they had much to learn from women! And this is why discussing male codependency is a complex issue that must be grounded in an understanding of basic male psychology.

MALENESS AS CONTROL

The psychological experience of maleness rests on the acquisition of power and the hope of control. A man feels good if he thinks he's got power and control, interpersonally and/or financially, or if he feels he is acquiring it. He feels some degree of inadequacy if he thinks he isn't. In their quest to maintain hierarchy and control, men have a long history of directing violent behavior that is sexually, racially, ethnically, religiously, and tribally/nationally motivated towards themselves as a gender group and towards women. This process of "affirming" self by asserting territorial, ideological, economic, or personal control over others leads men to participate in an array of destructive behaviors. Competition, being "better than . . . ," is a significant aspect of maintaining this hierarchy. Even men who don't want to behave in certain ways and who want to relate in new or different ways are usually still being "better than" all those other men.

Although women have their own unique problems with relating, they don't seem to play out these complex dynamics of hierarchy, power, competition, and aggression at every turn of relationship. A strange feature of this aggression is that many men don't value it either. But if certain forces are set in motion by the predominantly male leadership of a given group, then some compulsive process of duty, loyalty, and/or obligation seems to take over. In groups men often lock into some well-socialized, almost somnambulant, hypnotic process about being "man enough." When these dynamics are intimately focused in the family, the reactions can intensify in ways that are painful for everyone.

* * *

(In the neighborhood where I grew up there was a phrase spoken among the boys, like insidious phrases that are said among boys, in one way or another, everywhere. These phrases invariably made one feel much pain, fear, doubt, ambiguity about being vulnerable. One would say "Maybe I can, maybe I can't" when challenged or taunted about the possibilities of one's powers. The tone always had to be defensive, disparaging of other, disinterested, and competitive to the challenger when feeling challenged. This either implied "I don't know what I'm doing but I won't let you know that" or it implied that you had to, worse yet, get your parents' permission. Either way, one felt on edge, on guard, about to lose. Friends would retort in equally undermining and demeaning tones, "Maybe, maybe, such a little baby.")

These interactions have gone on in a thousand different ways between men as boys. Being a man usually means there is little space for anxiety, hesitation, fear, vulnerability, ambiguity, or any open-ended emotional process. The digression, deliberately set in parentheses, is important to the understanding of the psychology of men. Men are often filled with hundreds of parentheses of memories of not being adequate enough, memories of possible humiliations where they did not feel competent, in control. This is true for men in general and it is usually more so for those men raised in chemically dependent/addicted, out-of-control homes. An awareness of the presence of these parentheses is important to remember in discussing codependency with men. There are the external "parentheses" that happened outside of the house, and then there are the other ones that happened inside the house. In a chemically dependent family, the latter memories will be shaping the way men listen. Seemingly inconsequential words can mix with the memories, the parentheses, and rip asunder whole experiences, creating "the reasons" for keeping distance in relationships, for wanting certain illusions of control.

Parentheses reinforce and shape larger forces of competition, hierarchy, and distance. Men jockey for power, for control. They want to establish who's up, who's down, who's right, who's wrong, usually without revealing too much personally. Men are usually not mutual or equal unless they work at it diligently. This hierarchal gamesmanship pervades the professions, the job site, the home, the barroom, the lunch meeting, the sporting event, the social organization.

As a man and as a therapist, I want something "To Do" about these issues. And there it is. The almost invariable word, the possible center-piece of most men's psychology and experience: To Do! I shall generate a solution to the problem and act with authority. Then I will be believable. Most men listen to their partner, their colleagues, their children, their friends, and fairly immediately begin to feel a compelling drive to do something about the issues being discussed. There seems to be a primary, almost genetic drive to give advice, to have an opinion, come up with a solution to the problem. This may be the singular difference between the psychology of women and men. Men experience a seemingly strong drive to act, to establish hierarchy, authority, control, by solving a problem. Often if a man doesn't know something almost immediately, if not in fact then in opinion, he feels that there is something wrong with him. As Deborah Tannen, author of *You Just Don't Understand: Women and Men in Conversation,* says in an interview:

> A central area of confusion for couples, (I would add, almost all male/female conversation) involves what I call 'trouble talk.' For women talking about troubles is the essence of connection. I tell you my troubles, you tell me your troubles, and we're close. Men, how-ever, hear troubles talk as a request for advice, so they respond with a solution. (Taylor, 1990, pp. 33, 60)

If a solution I suggest is utilized then I am both validated as competent and I am allegedly in charge of the interaction. Tannen goes on to discuss many aspects of the way she observed men establishing hierarchy as a primary attribute of their interactional activity. Men expect to be in charge in some way or another. Equality, genuine equality, seems to be difficult for men because it does not reinforce the drive to hierarchy or meet needs for competitive placement of self in relationship to others.

UNDERSTANDING THE CODEPENDENT MAN

Within the context of this concept of relatedness as a mandate to have power and control over others, the codependent man may manifest *covert* forms of control. It is useful to understand that men experience two kinds of codependency. One derives from relating to a partner, lover, spouse who is chemically dependent/addicted. The other involves being the son of compulsive, chemically addicted parents. When they overlap in a person's life, as they often do, the psychological forces at work that are guiding a man's behavior can be quite complicated. In both situations behavior is progressively organized by the attempt of someone to gain control over his internal emotional experience by controlling his partner and her use of chemicals or by controlling others in the family. When one feels powerless, as a child, to control others then they will often set in motion compulsive behaviors, like the abuse of food or masturbation, to provide themselves with a sense of control and security. These patterns often continue into the adult years. The codependent's efforts at control can manifest as lectures, criticisms, directives to others to behave differently. Or he may exert control more indirectly by being very good and pleasing. The effort is to get the other person to meet needs by indirectly shaming them into meeting them with friendliness and goodness, without direct, responsible negotiation for those needs. Codependent men, when confronted with a spouse/partner's addictions, tend to work hard, to keep their distance, and to focus on being "good" providers. They create an area of control and distance (boundary) with their work.

Codependent men who were raised in chemically dependent families were often expected to be the ally of one particular parent, usually the mother. They were "trained" in that context to make an effort at relationship, to take a woman's emotional experience seriously, sometimes too seriously. This type of codependent male wants to be good to his spouse, and seeks closeness. This capacity for close relationship with women may be what distinguishes codependent males from men in the population at large. It can be, ironically, one of the potentially positive outcomes of addictions. If this man was/is the son of a codependent father who stayed in relationship, he can also be following a positive role model. In either case a man may have learned something about relatedness outside the context of hierarchy and control. He may feel certain stressful conflicts between what he knows how to do inside a house, that is, be good, and other social role expectations that would define him "as a man." If the codependent mother was demeaning, abandoning, displacing her rage at her husband onto her son, chemically dependent herself, or physically/sexually abusive to her son, the emotional results can be profoundly debilitating. The son, just like a daughter, usually becomes a container of despair about relationships, even if he is successful in other social relationships. He will feel internally devastated and alone, with complex experiences of rage, fear, and extreme shame. He may feel abandoned by both parents.

It is the unpredictability of emotional experience within relationship that sets the stage for codependency in a man. His desire is to have rational understanding of the incoherent, rapid alterations in the interpersonal field. Men often respond to this unpredictability by feeling like they have failed. They have a problem they can't solve. They will rely on their male socialization to solve the problem, seeking control in task accomplishment and in getting something "done" about the problem. Just as codependent women attempt to overfunction emotionally and behaviorally in the house when the man is the addict, men will move into the overperformance mode at home *and* at work. They will double efforts to handle their anxiety that there is a problem at home that they can't control. While internal feelings of inadequacy may abound, work performance reviews may soar.

Men will follow the rules of chemically dependent families. They will rationalize the problem and feel compelled not to talk about it to other family, friends, and colleagues. If they learned to keep their parent's drinking a secret, they will feel compelled to do the same with their spouse's. They will feel bound by shame and inadequacy, blame other factors and forces in their partner's lives, and deny that their partner has a developing addiction that is the source of the problem. The codependent man's compulsive feeling of gaining control of the emotional experience through better performance becomes an obsession, an abstraction pursued for it's own ends. Paradoxically, this distancing is often what the chemically dependent wife was reacting to all along. It reinforces her desire to drink or use drugs to escape her loneliness. The boundaries and rules of the relationship become organized by more severely escalating reactions against one another. The man will then focus even more on the accomplishment of tasks, something "to do," often moving further emotionally out of the house. If he has a desire to be a good father he will often take the children with him, organizing events, weekends, and other ways to distance himself from the addiction.

While men in general may have a greater tendency to create emotional distance in intimate relationships, codependent men may make the special effort at seeming "as if" they want very much to work out issues in the relationship while keeping their fears and desires for distance "a secret." They may act these desires out in a variety of covert ways. They may experience a compulsive drive to be different from dad and hence become threatened by their own anger with their partner's addiction. They may work even more compulsively than described previously. They may make efforts at closeness then disappear, unpredictably, with no effort at responsible negotiation or communication. They may intensify, rekindle, or develop new secret compulsive behavior patterns of food abuse or sexual behavior including excessive masturbation and use of pornography. They may gamble compulsively. They may utilize an allegedly non-addictive chemical like marijuana, where they can quietly "disappear" into themselves while seemingly being "present" in the house. They may disappear into some sort of hobby, sport, talent, spiritual practice, protesting, especially in this day and age, that they are doing it to take care of themselves. The important aspect of these behaviors is that the codependent man considers them all to be safe, which, for the most part, they are. He seeks control and security as his despair about his partner's addiction deepens. What is sacrificed is access to his own complete range of needs and feelings, and access to any intimacy in the relationship. The man may have negotiated differences with his spouse/partner, but fundamentally he has given up and has assumed power without responsibility (Elkin, 1984). He draws into a closed, narrow range of "controllable" behaviors.

THERAPEUTIC ISSUES
WITH CODEPENDENT MEN

From my experience as a man in recovery, from my own experience of organizing and starting men's groups, and from my experience of working with men in all variety of relationships, I know that men walk into every therapist's office with a complex interplay of hope, fear, anticipation, anxiety, and denial flowing through their systems. In this day and age, there is an especially high level of anticipation about men's gender-related behaviors and beliefs (Passick, Gordon, Meth, 1990). Men's actual emotional experience is often hidden behind the rigid forms they have evolved to express those experiences. Therapy offers a hope and a threat. The work is often challenging for the client(s) and the therapist.

To work with codependent men, the therapist has to pay close attention to the covert, underlying, "secret" feelings. When men enter the therapy office, they enter to win in what they may experience as a losing situation relative to their usual ways of conducting a male life. Or they enter feeling like losers already, particularly when they are confronted by their own or another person's addiction. For men to admit that they have lost control of an area of their life, or to open themselves to help from somebody else may be humiliating at best. To accept the fact that a partner, and by implication oneself, has lost control over alcohol or drugs when the entire ideological/theological assumption of Judeo-Christian culture is that Man has dominion over nature is often an unconscious, implicit insult of the highest order. When men come in for therapy they may feel stumped or lost anyway, since the process of interactive therapy is constructed more around women's ways of knowing and behaving, women's styles of interacting and talking about emotional experiences, than it is around men's ideas about hierarchy and control.

To be effective with codependent men, it is important to appreciate this sense of failure, this sense of a loss of self. It is useful to find a way to be emphatic without ever necessarily discussing feelings of failure. Usually the therapist is most effective if he or she finds a positive aspect of competency to highlight directly. Or one might tell a story about the fact that different men feel differently at the beginning of therapy, covering many possible alternative experiences (Gilligan, 1987), while observing which alternative may receive acknowledgement verbally or non-verbally. If the man starts out being very much in charge/in control, with a strong, positive description of how well everything is proceeding in his life, the therapist may have to join with that in a friendly manner and wonder at the same time, in the questioning, where the pain is, what the issues are, since everything seems to be fine. Therapy proceeds when the codependent man can articulate his ideas about what he wants to develop or change and can indicate his willingness to be involved in developing new beliefs and behaviors in his life and his relationships. Establishing an effective conscious/unconscious contract (Lankton, Lankton, & Matthews, 1991) regarding the issues to be worked on is one of the first steps in the therapy.

The fear and anticipations mentioned above are often held deeply in men's souls. They are not easily acknowledged. This does not mean that men must be treated as special or with kid gloves; it just means that it is important to be thoughtful, affirmative, and creative in some of the initial joining steps. It is important not to repeat the mistakes of the early male and female family therapists and treat men as though something out of the ordinary had to happen to keep them in therapy, usually at the expense of the women. These errors in judgment and behavior, usually implicitly if not grossly sexist in nature, have been well described in Luepenitz (1988) and McGoldrick, Anderson, and Walsh (1989).

One other issue to consider in establishing the therapy, particularly in a relationship where alcohol or drug use has functioned to maintain a symmetry in conflict, is the issue of competition. Competition may organize many interactions and transactions between a couple as well as with the therapist. There are many codependent men who don't want to acknowledge their competitiveness openly. They relate well on the surface, but with a covert competitiveness with the women in their lives. They want to win, be in charge, not cooperate, but they can't openly acknowledge these desires. The women pick up on this, feel bad about themselves and drink or drug to make the feelings go away. Men may also keep their distance from the support of other men to avoid feelings of competitiveness. This only reinforces a sense of isolation and aloneness and heightens a man's sense of dependency on the woman, which he also has to deny. This reinforces the woman's experience of failure. Both members of the couple feel lonely, like they are failing in any direction they turn. The situation is painful for everyone.

Codependent men are often the sons of very aggressive, competitive, intoxicated fathers. To be different from dad, they deny their aggressiveness and competitiveness and thus constrict themselves. When they work on this in the therapeutic dialogue and learn the differences between useful and successful assertiveness and the old, hidden aggressiveness, many dimensions of aliveness may open for the man and unbalance the system as much as the partner's sobriety. The therapist has to be prepared for these unbalancings of the system, and help the couple prepare for these changes. Rules and expectations will shift as well as all the structures of over and under functioning that have been established in the previous years of the relationship (Bepko and Krestan, 1985; Treadway, 1989). This is where recommendations of effective twelve-step and gender-related support groups will be helpful in overcoming isolation and in supporting the work of the therapy.

There can be quite a paradox at work in the initial sessions of therapy. Over and over I have experienced myself and have observed colleagues make the mistake of going right in after men's emotions. What transpires often is denial of the emotions. The client becomes reactive, ready to leave the therapy. The therapy becomes stonewalled with defensive maneuvers, anger, confusion, anxiety. What we are often given, in what Michelle Ritterman (1983) refers to as the "gift exchange" of the initial, contracting steps of therapy, is the person's pain and fear. It is the trance state Perls (1969) referred to as "the death layer" (p. 55). At the same time there is a yearning for someone to understand, for someone to help make sense of the fear, the angers, the anxieties. The gift the therapist returns to the client is to reframe defensiveness and anger in a positive manner that helps the person feel safe and open to the therapy.

The first stages of work often involve helping men to learn new ways to structure boundaries, to define what they are and how they work. As men change their internalization of the family structure they grew up in, they engage in a process of developing new and different attitudes and beliefs about relationships and about themselves in relationship. They work on self-image, social role expectations, and identity beliefs (Lankton & Lankton, 1986). In the midst of developing these new ways of believing and behaving men may develop a capacity for handling affect differently. They will usually have to learn how to identify when an emotion besides anger is being experienced and to understand that one can actually utilize the energy, the experience of the emotion, in some positive way. They will have to learn how to speak about their emotions in "I" terms. For a codependent man this will mean learning to make new choices about the following patterns of behavior: meeting one's needs indirectly by taking care of others; having a defensive pride about being "so good"; denying his disappointment and anger; projecting and displacing his feelings onto his partner; defending his hurt and fear by being judgmental, self-righteous, and perfectionistic.

In the early stages of therapy men have to learn about the effective management of sadness. They learn to understand that there is a core of wisdom in sad feelings that is connected to their needs. They have to learn how to grieve, be gentle, and still negotiate for what they need and want directly. They learn about the development and management of tenderness, affectionate touch, humor, letting go, and being flexible. Most of these steps or aspects of the therapy are variations of the theme of reparenting self. There are many decisions about the conduct of self that have to be integrated and much about the past that has to be grieved as one heals painful wounds from childhood and the present relationship. This is another place where effective support groups can be helpful. Groups help to normalize these emotional experiences for men because men learn to be with other people they can identify with.

It is an important challenge for all men, not just codependent men, to learn how to define self-in-relationship in mutual, interactive, non-hierarchical ways. These changes do not come easily. There are constant invitations to head in old directions. The most complicated irony of all is that it is probably better for men to start out more codependent, that is, more focused on relationship, than not. We almost ought not be discussing male codependency as a potential problem. Where women may need to learn how to be less relationship-focused in such all-consuming ways, men need to learn how, in the positive sense, to be more genuinely co- or interdependent. Often they need to learn how to hold others steadily in their attention.

The work is to develop strategies to help codependent men experience positive emotions about themselves as men, and responsibility for self in terms of language, beliefs and behaviors. It is important to encourage connections with other men that do not involve having to be aggressive, violent, controlling or distracting in the old male ways as the bonding experience. Finally, like all men, codependent men have to learn to develop relationships with their partners based more in mutuality, and based less in either overt or covert attempts at power and control.

Many men want to learn to touch, hug, laugh, dance, weep, play with children, fly about in ecstacy, be connected to good relationships powerfully and equally, and walk steadily on the earth with a sense of purpose and esteem. As men recover from the damaging effects of addictions in their lives, as well as the impact of thousands of years of being taught that we must have power over others, we may learn to do exactly that.

REFERENCES

Beattie, M. (1987). *Codependent no more.* San Francisco: Harper & Row.
Beattie, M. (1989). *Beyond codependency.* San Francisco: Harper & Row.
Bepko, C. & Krestan, J. (1985). *The responsibility trap.* New York: The Free Press.
Black, C. (1981). *It will never happen to me.* Denver: M.A.C. Printing & Publications.
Bradshaw, J. (1988). *Bradshaw on: The family.* Deerfield Beach, FL: Health Communications.
Elkin, M. (1984). *Families under the influence.* New York: Norton
Gilligan, S. (1987). *Therapeutic trances: The cooperation principal in ericksonian hypnotherapy.* New York: Brunner/Mazel.
Lankton, S.R. & Lankton, C.H. (1986). *Enchantment and intervention in family therapy.* New York: Brunner/Mazel.
Lankton, S.R., Lankton, C.H., & Matthews, W. (1991). *Ericksonian family therapy.* In Gurman, A. & Kniskern, D. (Eds.), *The handbook of family therapy.* (2nd ed.) New York: Brunner/Mazel.
Luepnitz, D.A. (1988). *The family interpreted.* New York: Basic Books
McGoldrick, M., Anderson, C.M., & Walsh, F. (Eds.) (1989). *Women in families.* New York: Norton.
Mellody, P., Miller, A.W., and Miller, J.K. (1989). *Facing codependence.* San Francisco: Harper & Row.
Miller, M., (Ed.) (1984). *Co-Dependency: an emerging issue.* Deerfield Beach, FL: Health Communications.
Pasick, R.S., Gordon, S., Meth, R.I. (1990). *Helping men understand themselves.* In Meth, R.L. & Pasick, R.S. (Eds.). *Men in therapy: The challenge of change.* New York: Guilford Press.
Perls, F.S. (1969). *Gestalt therapy verbatim.* Lafayette, CA: Real People Press.
Ritterman, M. (1983). *Using hypnosis in family therapy.* San Francisco: Jossey-Bass.

Schaef, A.W. (1986). *Co-dependence: Misunderstood, mistreated.* San Francisco: Harper & Row.

Smith, A. (1988). *Grandchildren of alcoholics.* Deerfield Beach, FL: Health Communications.

Steinglass, P. et al. (1987). *The alcoholic family.* New York: Basic Books.

Subby, R. (1987). *Lost in the shuffle.* Deerfield Beach, FL: Health Communications.

Subby, R. & Friel, J. (1982). *Co-dependency and the family.* Deerfield Beach, FL: Health Communications.

Taylor, P. (1990). Can we talk? An interview with Deborah Tannen. *New Age Journal,* December, 1990, pp. 31 ff.

Tannen, D. (1990). *You just don't understand: Women and men in conversation.* New York: Ballantine Books.

Treadway, D. (1989). *Before it's too late.* New York: W.W. Norton.

Wegscheider-Cruse, S. (1985). *Choicemaking.* Florida: Health Communications, Inc.

Wegscheider-Cruse, S. (1989 rev.ed.). *Another Chance.* Palo Alto: Science & Behavior Books.